C000297783

HavanaDays

Elizabeth Brown

January 2023

Elizabeth Brown

The diary of events in
This Story is True

Fleet Publishing

ALSO BY ELIZABETH BROWN

CaymanStar – *The True Story of a Horse's Life*
Published in 2011 by Fleet Publishing Ltd
ISBN 978-0-9570014-1-1

CaymanHavana – *The True Story of a Horse's Return*
Published in 2012 by Fleet Publishing Ltd
ISBN 978-0-9570014-3-5

for my lovely niece Alex
with love,
Liz x

HavanaDays

The True Story of a Foal Growing Up

(See page 114)

First published in The United Kingdom in 2023 by Fleet Publishing Ltd

1 Knights Court, Archers Way, Battlefield Enterprise Park,
Shrewsbury SY1 3GA

Fleet Publishing Ltd is registered in England and Wales with company
number 7482057
email: info@fleetpublishing.com
www.fleetpublishing.com

Nothing in this book is intended as a substitute for veterinary, or other
appropriate professional advice. Unless otherwise stated, all opinions
expressed in this book are those of the author.

"HavanaDays" is a true story about real people, and animals. Save where
information is already in the public domain, each living person and
organisation specifically identified in this book has approved publication of
their name and references to them. Names have been changed only where it
has been impractical to trace individuals to obtain permission to use their
actual names.

ISBN: 978-0-9570014-4-2

A CIP catalogue record for this title is available from the British Library.

Typeset by Troubador Publishing, Leicester
Printed and bound by TJ Books Limited, Padstow, Cornwall

Drawings Copyright© 2023 Roxanne Gooderham

Photographic editing and cover design by Depinder Juttla

All photographs reproduced courtesy of the author.

ACKNOWLEDGEMENTS

So many friends have helped on our journey and I should like to thank them all for their kindness, particularly:

Pat and Ted Brown, Terry Jones, Jennifer Blenkiron, Jan and Den Parker, Gillian Parton, Edward Evans, Alison Goodwin, Judy Heywood, Sarah Dakin, Alison Whitehurst, Lisa Smith, Claire Bullock, Stuart Deane, Sue Taylor, Geraint Hughes, Laraine Beranic, Depinder Juttla, Elaine Auliffe, Caroline Morgan, Roxanne Gooderham, Ricky (the hearing horseman)

… and CaymanHavana, for being patient enough to teach me so much.

CONTENTS

Two-Year-Old

Three-Year-Old

Postscript

"Thou must learn the thoughts of the noble horse
whom thou wouldst ride.
The horse is a wise animal. Let him show you
the best and most natural way to accomplish
a desired end."
Johann Wolfgang von Goethe
(1749-1832)

Dedicated to

Mr B.

My father
and CaymanHavana's big friend.

ILLUSTRATIONS

Photographs

Drawings

AUTHOR'S NOTE

Please excuse my misuse of the term 'half-brother'.

I am aware that, technically, this term refers to colts out of the same mare. However, Havana's genetic link with my horse Cayman (both were by the same stallion – Falconwood) is so crucial, that I needed a succinct term by which to describe it.

HavanaDays

The True Story of a Foal Growing Up

GOING HOME
Wednesday, 12 September 2007

"*O*ch – he'll be big enough! Just look at those long back legs." Jennifer's soft Scottish Borders accent added comfort to her already comforting words. Her endorsement was a relief, having bred horses for many years, she knew what she was talking about.

When I had first met Havana, aged fourteen weeks, he had seemed scarcely taller than the tallest dog. My decision to buy him was complicated by my fear that he would not grow big enough for me to ride. I am neither unusually tall, nor unusually heavy, but I had become used to his 17hh giant half-brother, Cayman – who had died so tragically.

The impact Havana made on me at our first meeting meant that our fates were sealed. Even if he had been the tiniest miniature pony, he had so successfully catapulted himself deep into my heart that I had no choice, he was to be *my horse*. I had decided then that if he grew tall enough for me to ride, that would be a bonus.

On the question of Havana's eventual height, his breeder Terry's answer was superb:

"He'll be 15hh; 15.2hh – he'll be whatever you want him to be."

So, a magic horse; I wished … and he grew! There was nothing else for it, I'd just have to wait – and trust.

Jennifer and I walked over the neat lawn, dotted with shrubs, and around the corner of Terry's white farmhouse to the paddocks. The composure of the bright bay baby horse, grazing calmly in his own enclosure, was

1

striking. Why had I expected that Havana, now aged seven months and recently weaned, would be in a stable? Probably because I imagined the exuberant little firecracker who, in the field with his herd, had been so full of mischievous games and biting, might have needed restraining once no longer under the concerned eye of his tenderly long-suffering mother.

Terry had thought out the grazing arrangements carefully. There was a mature riding horse grazing quietly in a paddock adjacent to the lawn, and a field of half-a-dozen two and three-year-olds bordering Havana's paddock. In the distance, in the large field sweeping away up the hill, I recognised the solitary dark figure of Falconwood, the beautiful Thoroughbred stallion, who is Havana's father. From his elevated vantage point, he was able to observe the goings-on around the farmhouse below him.

Havana wasn't really alone; in fact he was surrounded by other horses, but his determined focus on the task in hand – eating – meant that he did not feel it necessary to interact with any of them. A long-experienced horseman, Terry knew the other horses were a comfort to Havana; they were there, which was all Havana needed.

Havana's weaning had been delayed by a couple of weeks as his clever and sure-footed mother, still only six herself, had successfully evaded capture by Terry and a team of several athletic lads. On her home territory of many acres of undulating meadow chequered with mature trees, well-established hedges, a meandering stream and areas of reedy bog, a Welsh Cob mare can easily outwit her clumsy, exhaustible human would-be captors, and her cheeky foal will stick close by her side, mirroring each wily move and enjoying the game.

Eventually Bonnie was caught and led, with Havana invisibly bonded to her side, the quarter-mile or so to the farmyard.

"Were they upset when they were separated?" I asked Terry. He replied reassuringly:

"No, she just called a couple of times as she was being walked back to the field; he wasn't bothered." My heart went out to Havana's mother, it must have felt so strange no longer to have her boisterous little shadow cavorting by her side. But I was sure that by the next morning, she would have acquired a new sense of peace at being rid of her demanding, increasingly rough offspring. I was certain that Bonnie would enjoy the respite and the ability to graze in peace and rest, in readiness for the birth of her next foal whom she was already carrying.

At the bottom of the ramp of Jennifer's trailer, Havana stood, absorbing the sight of what would have appeared to be a stable, but one unfamiliar to him. Standing by his shoulder, I urged him forward. Nothing happened. Without words, Jennifer and Terry, who were standing directly behind Havana, quietly linked arms, like people who both know the movements of a dance. With hundreds of 'loadings' between them, they confidently braced their interlocked arms under Havana's tail, so his weight was taken off his stalled back end, which was now being pushed forwards; he just had to move his front feet, or fall on his nose. At the same time as Havana's equilibrium was being rearranged by Jennifer and Terry, I walked up the ramp in front of him, keeping the lead rope taut.

"Come on boy – let's go home." Without a second's hesitation, the trusting little creature was in the trailer. As I rubbed his forehead and praised his bravery, the ramp was raised and secured. I slipped off Havana's head collar and he started exploring his new environment. A cushioned playpen could not have been safer for this infant. Jennifer had prepared the ideal transport for a young horse; there was absolutely nothing in the trailer except Havana and thick straw, banked up on every side to form a dense buffer keeping him away from the hard, metallic walls. I would have transported the Crown Jewels less carefully than my baby horse; he was very, very safe.

Terry briefly vanished, before returning with a half-sack of Havana's feed, which he generously donated to provide some continuity, at least for Havana's insides, at their destination. Jennifer and I declined the offer of a cup of tea before we set off on the hundred-mile journey home; we all agreed it would be best for Havana if we got going. I promised faithfully, through the Jeep window, to let Terry know how

Havana was getting on, and we rumbled into motion. Jennifer pulled away from Terry's yard and up the steep hill, as if she *were* transporting the Crown Jewels.

"Be prepared Liz, he won't look the same horse when he comes out, he'll probably be wringing wet with sweat. We'll stop about every fifteen minutes to start with, so you can check him and see whether he wants a drink."

Somehow, I was unconcerned about Jennifer's sound advice that Havana might not travel well. The steady chug of the Jeep engine and the consistent weight of the trailer behind it reassured me; Havana would be fine. At last, we were going home … and everything would be alright.

HOME
Thursday, 13 September 2007

*M*y email to Terry – Havana's breeder.

"Hi Terry,

Just in case you didn't get my telephone message, I thought I'd let you know that Havana travelled *brilliantly*; we got home at 5.30 p.m.

We checked him regularly on the journey.

At the first check he was sweaty, but by the second he'd dried off.

By the final check he looked as if he couldn't understand why we kept stopping and coming into the trailer – or what we were faffing about at!

He's in a really nice stable just ten yards from the farmhouse, there are people about and he can see the other horses who are close by.

The farm's owners are going on holiday for a week from Sunday, so Havana won't be turned out until they're back to keep an eye on him.

As well as having his feed and haylage, he has been walked out into a field to graze for an hour this morning (he's good at walking in-hand) – his appetite is huge!

I've left him in for the afternoon to settle down quietly; he'll get more feed, haylage and in-hand grazing later.

He does seem to be a very happy lad.

With best wishes,
    Liz."

"...a really nice stable. *I'm not Freddy!*"

ESCAPE
Monday, 24 September 2007

*T*he scene was enchanting.

In the golden evening sunlight, the stubble field in the distance rolled up the hill to the ancient village church.

White Charollais cattle grazed peacefully in the marshy field with their suckling calves.

In the lush pasture close to the farmhouse Havana gleamed … as he *soared over the electric fence* like a gazelle.

It was the first time he'd been turned out at his new home and Havana had escaped: he was trying to get back to North Wales!

The *un*welcoming reception he had received from the herd of six adult horses he'd seen across the field, and with whom he now found himself, told him they were not his family and the far side of the field was not North Wales.

Panicked, Havana fled to the bottom of the field – as far away from the other horses as possible – and, disorientated, started grazing.

He looked so relieved when I walked down the field to rescue him.

Breaking my own 'no feeding from hands' rule, I pulled up a big tuft of grass with which to tempt Havana – although it was, of course, the same as the grass he was already eating!

Being the only 'friendly face', I easily lured him back up the field.

As we walked, Havana made a great effort to ensure that I was in between the unfriendly horses and him.

I put him back into the small paddock; moving and then replacing an electric fence post, to make a gap for us to pass through.

Havana wasn't alone in the paddock. It's the 'nursery' and already home to two other youngsters: Ben – a fifteen-month-old Shire gelding, and Flower – a three-month-old filly. Flower's mother – Faith – an aged black Hackney, keeps a watchful eye on the foals.

This time, Havana did settle down to graze with his new herd.

Terry had certainly been right when he counselled me about feeding Havana in his stable:

"When he's in, *you* feed him – *just you*."

It is obvious that Havana now views me as an ally, who not only feeds him but also rescues him from difficult situations.

"… the nursery." (Faith, Havana, Flower, Ben)

VET
Wednesday, 26 September 2007

*P*oor little Havana!

Today he had a microchip inserted into his neck – via an enormous needle – then blood taken, followed by his flu and tetanus injection.

He just stood there and took it all.

Sue, the vet, said that she had known horses try to leap over their doors, especially with the pain of the microchip needle.

He was a complete star.

Sue was Cayman's vet.

She is very impressed by Havana's lovely nature, acknowledging that this must be mostly down to their Thoroughbred sire – Falconwood – as they have different mothers.

"I can hardly believe you've only had him for *two weeks!*" was Sue's affirmation of Havana's good manners.

I am so proud of him.

SHELTER
Thursday, 27 September 2007

*I*n the evening it started to rain, so I went under the barn to shelter.

The mare, Faith, and her foal, Flower, came in along with the enormous Shire foal, Ben, who stood across the doorway, blocking most of it.

Havana was left outside in the rain.

He looked upset as he milled about, uncertainly – but he was too subordinate and too nervous of the others to barge in where he might not be wanted.

I called him, encouragingly:

"Havana! – Come on boy!"

This was just the reassurance he needed. Mustering all of his juvenile courage, he *darted* through the two-foot gap, between Ben's rump and the wall, to where I was standing.

Having arrived so spectacularly, Havana then stood facing the barn wall, his head low in complete submission – as if he was trying to make himself invisible – so as not to further disturb, or antagonise, either Faith or Ben; fearful of an instant physical rebuke in the form of a bite or a kick.

Filled with compassion for this tiny, vulnerable horse – who had been brave enough to trust me and overcome his fear so he could stand with me in the barn – I coaxed Havana to turn ninety degrees, to face me.

I comforted him with a hug, putting my arms around each side of his chest and neck.

I sensed Havana's relief as he allowed his forehead to sink gently into my chest. The top of his head made a convenient pillow where I rested my cheek.

We both closed our eyes.

After about five minutes, Ben woke us up by nipping Havana's belly.

Ben's mean reaction seemed to be caused by jealousy – that Havana was being comforted by his person – rather than annoyance that he was under the barn.

GRAZING TIME
Friday, 28 September 2007

In the middle of the morning, Havana was grazing peacefully with Flower, Ben and Faith.

I had decided it was time for some discipline, so I went to him with his head collar. He let me put on the head collar – although his bemused look suggested he could not understand why.

When I asked him to walk up the field with me, his lack of enthusiasm seemed to confirm this, but he came with me anyway, because it was what *I* wanted.

After only a short distance, he obviously felt the need to protest. He stopped; his earnest, wide eyes asking for a logical explanation.

It was grazing time – 'why was I taking him away'?

When I asked him to walk on again, he did so – now with a quizzical, slightly grudging expression – he knew it was *not* the right thing to do.

Flower knew too.

She stood with her head up, watching intently and looking concerned. Her shrill whinny quite clearly said:

"Come back Havana – it's grazing time!"

Havana whinnied back, helplessly:

"I *know* it's grazing time – but my person wants me to walk with her!"

The further from Havana's herd we went, the more *wrong* it felt to him.

When we reached our destination – the barn – he really didn't want to stand in it for a while, 'for discipline', but reluctantly did so because it was what I asked him to do.

Havana's eager steps proved that he was very relieved when I regained my senses and led him back down the field again to Flower, Ben and Faith – and the urgent task of grazing.

As I took off his head collar, I sensed Havana was wondering:

"What was the point of that?"

HUGS
Tuesday, 2 October 2007

*A*ll of the horses were in the barn; Havana was nearest the outside, with Ben.

I walked quietly round the mud at the entrance and stood leaning against the gate at the front of the barn.

A minute later, Havana left Ben – came out of the barn, round the mud – and snuggled up to my left side.

I put my arm over his neck and rested my cheek above his eye.

After a while, Havana started some very intense exploratory sniffing: first of my face, then in front of my ear and finally of my head.

Ben came up to join us, so I was sandwiched between the two horses; *he* wanted to be included too.

Havana didn't seem to mind Ben standing close to my right side … but it was *Havana* whom I continued to hug.

HAY BALES IN THE SKY
Thursday, 4 October 2007

*A*s I approached the paddock, I saw that the tractor was being manoeuvred laboriously into place to drop an enormous, heavy, bale of hay over the fence.

All of the other, more sensible, horses had moved back and were waiting in a fairly orderly – although excited – row.

With horror, I also saw that Havana was standing *directly below the hay bale* …! Oblivious to the danger he was in, and entirely governed by greed, he was eagerly pulling at the loose bits of hay above him.

Like a frenzied harpy I shot into the paddock, shrieking and flailing my arms to scare Havana away from the bale – which was about to be tipped off the prongs of the loader.

He instinctively fled away down the paddock, believing all the wrath of hell was after him.

Seeing that Havana was now out of the way, the tractor-driver slid the bale, harmlessly, into place on the ground and the other horses' patience was rewarded as they settled around their new fodder.

Not surprisingly after the fright I had just given him, when Havana came back up to the top of the paddock he was a little reluctant to step forward and join the others at the bale. However, as this experience has now obviously made him cautious of hay bales in the sky, he should be safer in future.

"… hay bales in the sky …"

TICKLY-TAIL
Sunday, 7 October 2007

*T*he top of Havana's tail was so scurfy that Ricky generously suggested that I should wash it in some of *his*, particularly effective, antiseptic shampoo.

I did this in the field, hoping that the familiar environment – with plenty of space – would be less frightening for Havana than the stable, where he may feel trapped.

I used a bucket of warm water and a sponge – and Ricky helped.

Havana was very good; he enjoyed having the top of his tail massaged with the shampoo, but he was *not* so keen on the irritating streams of water that ran down his back legs when I rinsed his tail with a saturated sponge.

I held him with the lead rope and let him circle me whilst I sponged. He looked very unsettled but, as we went round and round, there was not a kick in him.

Then … to add insult to injury … I needed to apply some fly repellent, from an aerosol can, all over Havana's body.

Coming straight after the trauma of the wet sponge, Havana seemed to find the aerosol quite insignificant. In fact, he was so unconcerned by it, that I could have sprayed graffiti on every bit of him!

(P.S. Ricky's shampoo worked. Havana's tail was far less itchy for a week afterwards, which I'm sure was a great relief to him.)

I'M A RACEHORSE
Tuesday, 9 October 2007

*I*t was 11 a.m., and wet.

Ben, who must weigh about a ton, seemed a bit bored. To liven things up, he jumped up and down – very nearly on the spot – with all four feet off the ground at once.

Flower, being influenced by Ben, did some 'ballet'; delicately springing in all directions, like a darting firefly, whilst flinging out elegant long legs – and always managing to stay close to her unconcerned mother, Faith.

Havana *had to* join in.

His game was the best of all, it could have been called 'I'm a racehorse like my father'. It consisted of cantering very big circles in one direction, stopping abruptly – with a lot of springing and bucking because this is so exciting! – then cantering enormous circles in the opposite direction; before doing it all again.

Once, Havana stopped and reared high – so he stood vertically on his hind legs and pawed the air.

His canter is smooth and effortless.

Although he's only about 13hh, in the distance he *does* look like a racehorse.

Yesterday, I walked behind him as he trotted excitedly up to the gate to be fed. In trot, he is perfectly straight … and he *floats*.

I have only just realised what lovely paces he has and how beautiful, and refined, he looks in action.

BELLY ACHE
Friday, 12 October 2007

*A*s I approached, Havana lay completely flat, and still, on the field.

I have only had him for four-and-a-half weeks, but I have never seen him lie down like this before; I was very worried.

Ben was sitting by him. I was relieved to see Havana's tail move, so

I knew he was alive.

Ben got up; but as I reached Havana he remained lying down, neck outstretched, eyes closed and his breathing laboured.

I called his name; his eyelid lifted very slightly – his eye was glazed.

I stroked his neck and talked reassuringly to him. Then I called the vet; fearing colic, I was taking *no* chances.

I needed to know how ill he was, so I lifted Havana's hind leg vertically.

He sat up, then stood up – and walked off to graze with the others.

They soon all cantered to the gate, where the hay was, and he cantered with them.

Having already telephoned my mother, Mrs B., for moral support, I put Havana in a stable.

After half-an-hour the vet arrived.

She established that Havana's temperature, pulse and heart rate were normal – and gave him some pain relief.

As we chatted, I would have said that Havana was not in pain, but I would have been wrong. After about twenty minutes he sighed, then visibly relaxed and dozed as the pain relief took effect.

The vet suggested 'giving his belly a rest'. I was afraid that he would eat the straw bedding if he stayed in the stable, so it was agreed that he would go out onto the short-grass 'starvation paddock' over the weekend – with the two ponies Toffee and Freddy.

Havana was frightened of the ponies and tore round the paddock at a canter – at one point slipping over.

He hurtled for the gate into the next field, where his friends were eating hay. Fortunately, Ben was standing in the gateway – just about filling it – which stopped Havana trying to leap over the steel gate and possibly injuring himself in the process.

Eventually, Havana settled to just pacing along the high hawthorn hedge, looking for an escape route.

Before putting him out, I had already satisfied myself that there were no gaps – either in the post-and-rails fencing or in the hedge – through which Havana could jump, or squeeze, into the next field.

It was now 4.30 p.m., and *my* belly was complaining, as I had not eaten since breakfast. The vet had said that if I were to leave Havana, it should be before 6 p.m. when the pain relief wore off, so I took the opportunity to go home for some food.

At 6 p.m. I was back at the farm.

I could not believe my eyes; there was Havana standing with his friends in his *original field*, hay cascading from his mouth. He looked at me very sweetly as he munched, as if to say:

"I feel better now!"

No one had moved him; he had jumped the four-foot-high gate. He must have springs in his feet!

For his own good, Havana spent the weekend in his stable, on a restricted diet.

A DEN
Thursday, 18 October 2007

*H*avana and Flower have got a den.

It's at the back of the barn; just a cool, narrow passage leading towards the yard, overhung by elder trees and bordered by the wood. Nevertheless, for them it's special because it's a *secret* place, out of sight of the older horses.

They were standing there side-by-side, not doing anything (except stamping because of midges) and enjoying the camaraderie of hiding away from the others, like conspirators.

Flower is adorable!

She has a pretty, bright face and enormous dark eyes, with eyelashes so long that they sweep downward, shading her eyes at forty-five degrees like a giraffe's.

She is obviously very fond of Havana, her new 'big brother'.

They look so sweet together.

"Flower is adorable!"

TWO-THIRDS
Friday, 19 October 2007

*O*n Wednesday Havana was '*two-thirds*' (i.e. eight months old)!

I decided to measure him as, standing in the stable, he seemed to have grown.

I showed him the retractable steel ruler and let him listen to the metallic, sliding noise it made as it extended.

When I carefully pulled it out, to about the length I thought would correspond with his height, then held it vertically, he was obviously a bit unsure about it.

He went and stood in the safety of the back of the stable … *for all of thirty seconds,* before coming back to stand with me in the doorway and be measured, with the ruler down his shoulder.

He didn't mind when I also held a riding crop horizontally across his withers to get a more accurate reading.

He seems to be about 13.2hh.

That means he has grown one hand since I first met him, when he was three-and-a-half months old.

I think he'll be a big boy – and a perfect size for me.

He will be beautiful.

AT EASE
Saturday, 20 October 2007

*H*avana's second worming.

He can't go into the field until tomorrow, so I took him out to graze by the stile.

When the big red post van came tearing down the lane – windows down, radio blaring – Havana didn't even look up from the grass!

Whenever he put a front hoof on the lead rope, preventing himself from lifting his head, he just continued grazing – with his muzzle restricted to the area within a ten-inch radius of his hoof.

He evidently doesn't panic.

We are at ease with each other. I feel more confident in Havana – there is trust between us.

Whilst he was grazing, the hens had got into Havana's stable and made a perfect nest, right in the middle of his straw bed.

As they wouldn't come out voluntarily, we both went in to 'shoo them out'.

Even though – when added to the four preoccupied hens and a rather self-important cockerel – Havana and I increased the population of his stable to *seven*, he didn't have a second thought about going into such a confined space with me.

In the evening there was just *one* two-inch roundworm.

This was far better than his first worming, which produced enough roundworms to put me off my favourite dinner … *spaghetti*.

RACEHORSE AGAIN
Sunday, 21 October 2007

*W*hen Havana went out after being in for worming, the shape of his field had changed! It was shorter but much wider, because the electric fence had been moved.
This miraculous overnight transformation of his world made Havana so excited that he had to play 'I'm a racehorse like my father' … again.

Flower joined in, looking ever so sweet and trying her best to catch up with Havana, although her father was a hefty Cob, not a racehorse.

As I stood in the middle of the field, Havana galloped by *very* close to me; probably his way of making his game even more exciting – and trying to get me to join in too!

COLD WATER
Monday, 22 October 2007

*T*o get Havana used to the idea of being tied up, I've made some big knots in the end of the lead rope, to give it some weight, and started hanging the rope over the stable door whilst Havana is inside.

When he moves his head or takes a step back, there is slight resistance due to the weight of the rope.

He is very unconcerned about the whole thing.

In the evening, it was time to wash the top of his tail again, with antiseptic shampoo.

Ricky came to help and, rather than tying Havana up in the stable, I asked Ricky to hold the lead rope, from the safety of the other side of the door. I also gave him instructions not to start a 'tug-of-war' if Havana obviously needed to retreat.

The shampooing part was fine, but Havana was very upset by the saturated sponge of cold water I used to rinse off the shampoo. He really didn't like the feeling of chilly water trickling down his back legs.

He was so adamant that he was not going to have any more nasty cold water on his tail that he managed to pull back and wedge his rear end into the opposite corner of the stable. Sensitively, realising that Havana was genuinely distressed, Ricky did not resist and let go of the lead rope.

Havana's tail was now well and truly 'hidden' – and certainly protected from further assault by the sponge.

My strategy of taking the pressure off Havana, by turning my back to him and talking quietly and calmly to Ricky over the stable door, worked.

Being a sociable and inquisitive horse, it wasn't long before he walked forward again to see what Ricky and I were doing.
I decided that enough was enough; most of the shampoo had been rinsed out and I didn't want to upset Havana any more.

To reassure him that the cold sponge really had gone, and to re-establish his trust in me, I rubbed his rump and tail with my hand which, thankfully, he didn't object to.

I then gave him his hay, as I know that eating takes his mind off most things! As he ate, I continued, gently, to massage his rump and tail, which relaxes him.

By the time Ricky and I left, Havana was completely settled.

I was sorry I had upset him; it's obvious that he dislikes having water running down his back legs – and who can blame him?

It would have been more considerate of me to at least use warm water as I did before – rather than cold.

BOW
Tuesday, 23 October 2007

*F*or the first time, Havana managed to stand on three legs whilst I picked-out all of his hooves.

After that, I thought we should practise in readiness for what would become the routine task of 'putting feet on a farrier's tripod'.

When I extended Havana's first front leg – as if to place it on an imaginary steel tripod, at about knee height in front of him – he knelt into a beautiful deep 'circus horse bow', which he then turned into a luxurious stretch.

Although Havana's display was very impressive, it was not what is required of a horse having his hooves trimmed.

However, when asked, Havana did manage to extend his other three legs – far less theatrically – which was good practise for simply resting the tip of his hoof on a tripod.

WORMY AND LOUSY
Wednesday, 24 October 2007

*T*he vet, Andrew, came to give Havana his flu and tetanus booster. Havana was brilliant, as usual, about having the injection into his chest muscle.

He had not wanted to leave the field – where he'd been down at the bottom with the others. Flower came up the field with us, which helped, but by halfway he was starting to question why we were leaving the grazing.

Havana was not far off a serious protest, when he noticed Mrs B., my nieces Alex and Hattie, and the vet, in the yard – which evidently caused him to change his mind.

Havana is always interested in visitors and was keen to get to them, so he continued the walk to the gate perfectly happily and got a bit of food for being so good.

I'd been concerned about the disproportionate size of Havana's belly and took the opportunity to ask Andrew about it. He informed me that Havana would "grow into his belly" – showing me that, actually, his size is due to his ribcage.

I was reminded that horses have a lot of ribs (eighteen pairs), which go back a long way; there are also several layers of muscle where their ribs end.

Andrew agreed that Havana has a big ribcage and therefore a big belly. His logical explanation reassured me.

We will have some liquid to treat Havana's scaly tail and the new scales in his mane which, Andrew said, "may be caused by lice".

I see: Havana is not only wormy, but *lousy* too!

Havana's protection from tetanus will last for two years, but he'll need a flu booster in six months – and then annually. I'm glad that the surgery will send me reminders about this.

What I *do* have to remember is to ask the surgery to complete the flu and tetanus record in Havana's passport, as soon as I receive this from 'Weatherbys' (the racehorse stud book).

HELP
Saturday, 27 October 2007

*W*hen I arrived this morning, Havana and Ben were eating hay by the gate and Faith was standing at the side of the paddock.

I noticed that Flower was lying down – flat.

As soon as I had greeted Havana, he walked purposefully to where Flower lay and then – almost immediately – walked straight back to the hay and resumed eating.

I knew that he wanted me to go and look at Flower.

As I approached, gently, Flower did not lift her head; that's unusual. She looked miserable and her breathing sounded 'rattly' and wet.

Then she did lift her head and laboriously got to her feet – coughing twice as she did so. Her cough sounded wet and she looked lethargic.

Fortunately, Flower's owner was in the house so I was able to alert her.

I was very proud – although not really surprised – that *Havana had let me know* Flower needed help.

I am glad he sees me as 'a helpful person'.

REARING
Monday, 29 October 2007

*H*avana did not want to leave the grass this morning.

However, when I picked up an empty feed bowl and started to walk out of the field with it, followed by Faith, Havana could not follow me quickly enough.

Once in the stable, he had a tiny amount of feed in the bowl, as a reward for coming out through the gate and into his stable – in record time!

As Stuart, the farrier, is coming tomorrow, I thought we should practise 'feet' again.

After I had groomed Havana, I picked-out all four feet with no problem, put each foot on my knee and stroked his fetlock, then did 'front leg stretches'.

Last time I asked Havana to stretch his front legs individually, he thought it was a cue for him to 'bow'. This time, as I encouraged him to stretch out one leg, I felt him begin to take his weight off *both* front legs at the same time – the start of a rear.

Immediately, I put down the leg I was holding, stood up straight and told him very firmly:

"You *never* rear with humans. Rearing is *only* for playing in the field!"

He didn't try to rear again.

When I put him back out in the field, Flower emerged from the barn; she had been waiting for him.

FIRST FOOT TRIM
Tuesday, 30 October 2007

A complete non-event!

I had been quite nervous about Havana having his feet trimmed for the first time. I needn't have been – he was a complete little star, as usual.

I was glad that we had practised; I could see that Havana knew what he was doing when Stuart put his hoof on his knee, to trim it.

Stuart is very gentle and quiet.

He is also agile; once he had picked up a foot he did not put it down again until he had finished trimming – no matter how much Havana needed to hop about on three legs to keep his balance.

It helped too that we were in Havana's stable, so he couldn't escape. However, as he feels safe in his stable and Stuart was so kind to him, I saw no signs that Havana felt this new situation was one from which he needed to escape; he seemed to find it far more intriguing than frightening.

FIRST FIREWORKS
Friday, 2 November 2007

I wanted to be in the field, with Havana, for 6.00 p.m. because there was a fireworks display at one of the local schools; I hoped he would be less frightened by it if I were there with him.

At 6.00 p.m. nothing happened – *no fireworks* – nor at 6.30 p.m.

The horses were all standing quietly in the dark field – dozing. Flower was with her mother and Ben was by himself.

I stood in the darkness with my left arm over Havana's neck, and scratched his tail with my right hand (he's still little enough for me to reach both ends at once).

It was very peaceful; Havana liked me being there – what a privilege to be so accepted by him.

This was a time for relaxation. It made me realise there is no point at all in expecting to have Havana's attention when he is grazing – I have to ask for it at the right time.

At 7.00 p.m. – concluding that I must have got the date of the fireworks display wrong – I went home.

At 7.15 p.m. the sky above my house (just a mile from Havana's field) looked, and sounded, like a battleground – the fireworks had started!

SUGAR BEET
Monday, 5 November 2007

*H*ave you ever come across a horse who does *not* like sugar beet? Havana doesn't.

I thought I should fatten him up; he's a bit 'ribby' and we're coming into winter.

I got sugar beet because it has a lot of calcium – barley rings don't, although they have a bit more protein.

I've decided to give Havana a midday feed, as well as morning and evening, and take him out of the field for his 'lunch'.

He did not find the soaked sugar beet at all appetising – probably because it's not 'molassed', so doesn't taste particularly sweet.

I had to take half of it out of the bowl and add some familiar 'Mare and Youngstock Mix' before he would eat it.

I put louse powder from the vet on the top of his tail. He was more interested in the smell of the louse powder pot than the sugar beet!

My good friend Judy's daughter, Rita, came to see Havana for the first time. He was not an impressive sight: all muddy, with a curly coat where he had been lying on the wet field. However, as Rita – who is not at all 'horsey' – gazed at him in wonder, I could see that the state Havana was in was irrelevant. Refreshingly unburdened by equine knowledge, Rita was spellbound by him, just as he was.

In the evening, Flower, Ben and Havana were all sitting down in the top corner of the field, near the footpath. Faith was standing, keeping guard and watching the fireworks.

I squatted down by Havana and stroked him; he was very contented.

Ben was snoring and passing wind – not the sort of friend with whom to share a stable!

None of them were bothered by the fireworks.

REFLEX
Wednesday, 7 November 2007

*W*hen I checked Havana in the field, in the dark, Ben and Flower came crowding round us, wanting some fuss too.

At the same time as I went round one side of Havana, Flower crashed into his other side. I was surprised when Havana quickly threw his head round to my side, with his mouth open.

I was surprised, because I thought he was going to bite me – but he had never done so before.

Then it dawned on me that – far from being aggressive – poor Havana had actually been 'mouthing' (snapping his mouth open and closed) *in submission* because he thought he was in danger, on two sides at once.

I felt sorry that he had thought *I* was dangerous (not Flower!), but I suppose it was a reflex action – and he is not really frightened of either of us.

STARS
Thursday, 8 November 2007

I went into the field at about 7.30 p.m. It was dark and starry.

Faith was on guard, Flower was suckling, Ben was lying flat out, snoring, and Havana was sitting down, asleep; he roused.

I squatted down in front of Havana. He let me put my forehead against his, closed his eyes and breathed very deeply.

For about five minutes, we were both peaceful together – with our eyes closed.

If I opened my eyes and looked up, all I could see was Havana's ears and the bright stars above us.

Then Ben woke up.

Curious about the attention I was giving Havana, he came lumbering up to us. Poor little Havana had to jump to his feet – for fear of being trampled – and I had to move pretty fast too, to avoid being jumped on by Havana and trampled by Ben!

LUNCH
Saturday, 10 November 2007

*W*e only started the 'lunch' routine six days ago, but now Havana has really got the hang of it. He led the charge up the field when he saw me.

Ben would like to come in for lunch too, but he doesn't need it, so I have to frighten him away from the gate by looking hard at his back end and making explosive noises.

Havana just stands there – all smug and confident – whilst I do this. He reminds me of the 'spoilt-boy' in the school playground; he knows that *he* is about to be fed.

After lunch, Havana wasn't keen to go back into the field.

He stood outside the gateway; first looking left, up to the wood, then – when I said we couldn't go that way – right, to the footpath by the stile.

I sensed that he wanted to go on an adventure.

There wasn't time today, so I promised him an adventure soon – and he went back into the field.

PROGRESS REPORT
Sunday, 11 November 2007

*P*rogress Report.

Manners:

Having his hooves picked-out, stretching front legs and putting front and back hooves on my knee – A*.

Well done Havana!

Physical Development:

Although he has only had sugar beet for one week, Havana has already put weight on his sides, rump and back.

He is beginning to look 'horse-shaped'.

Today we went on the adventure that Havana had asked to go on.

We walked up the drive to the telegraph pole (about twenty yards!). There were horses in the fields on both sides. Havana was intimidated by the ones on the right, but more interested in the ones farther away; he whinnied to them.

When Havana feels insecure, he becomes very light on his front end and spins round – checking behind and in front of himself. I put my arm over his neck to settle him. I then distracted him by asking him to walk back towards the gate by the stile, which is familiar territory.

For a while, Havana ate grass in the gateway, becoming calmer with each mouthful. It helped that whilst he was grazing he could see Ben, who was also grazing.

Next, we went exploring in the little bit of woodland: walking past the hen house … round the tree … to the swing … and on past the slide.

Havana walks very willingly.

I sensed that he had had enough excitement for one day, so I put him back in the field.

A milestone!

For the first time, I saw Havana defend himself.

Ben was marauding and generally harassing Havana, who retaliated by 'double-barrelling' him (kicking with both back hooves at the same time) in the chest and then, with great determination, sinking his teeth into Ben's neck.

I was surprised – and rather proud!

TRICK

Wednesday, 14 November 2007

*A*nother milestone!

For the first time, Havana came out of the field with me, without the whole herd coming up to the gate.

He was in the big field; I put on his head collar but, although I had a feed bucket with me, he did not want to walk up the field. In fact, he didn't want to walk anywhere.

I needed a plan, so I unclipped the rope from his head collar, put it in the empty bucket and walked off – shaking the bucket noisily.

Excitedly associating the substantial sound from the bucket with substantial contents, such as *a lot of food,* Havana eagerly followed me up the field and out of the gate.

Thankfully, the other horses didn't fall for my trick and stayed where they were.

THREE-QUARTERS
Saturday, 17 November 2007

*I*t's Havana's (sort of) birthday – he's three-quarters!
It was an honour to have been loaned Jennifer's precious, and very deceptive, wooden walking cane – inherited from her beloved father – with which to measure Havana.

This special stick is as ingenious as any 'James Bond' device.

When you lift the brass knob on the top, a hinged, brass ruler folds out vertically; this is calibrated in 'hands' especially for measuring horses. To ensure total accuracy, there is even a horizontal spirit level.

With this glorious example of craftsmanship, I established that Havana is 13.2hh (and his rump is 13.3hh).

FOLLOW ME
Monday, 19 November 2007

*T*his time, I got Havana in for his midday feed without the other horses – or a bucket.

He was in the big field, so I simply went to the top of the field, called him, looked hard at his back end for ten seconds, walked off towards the gate – and he followed me!

The gateway is so muddy that I had to open the gate very wide.

I trusted Havana to walk into the yard without even putting on his head collar. As he was walking through mud, it was only fair to let him keep going.

I guided him into the stable with just his nose in the head collar. There was no need to put it on, as I would soon be taking it off again so he could eat without any restraint.

What a good boy!

KICKING ETIQUETTE
Wednesday, 21 November 2007

*N*aughty Flower! She hasn't learned 'kicking etiquette'.

She and Havana both wanted to stick their heads through the gap – where the edge of the hanging tarpaulin doesn't quite meet the barn wall – to get at the hay on the other side. As there is only room for *one* horse at a time to do this, they needed to take turns.

Flower must have decided that Havana's turn had gone on for too long.

I was shocked to see her impulsively square-up her back end to the broad expanse of his side and to hear the heavy thud of unshod hooves on solid flesh and bone. She had kicked him in the ribs with both back feet at once.

Poor Havana! No wonder he looked shocked as he shot backwards, extricating himself from the gap between the wall and the tarpaulin. With his head and neck effectively screened off, he had had no warning of Flower's imminent attack, nor any opportunity to defend himself from it.

In retaliation for Flower's cowardly assault Havana very sweetly only threatened to kick, by bunching-up his back end and bucking at her, *without* extending his back legs – so she wasn't actually kicked at all.

In fact, Flower didn't even see this remarkably restrained threat of Havana's, because as soon as he had pulled his head out of the gap she had shoved her's in and was oblivious to anything but the tasty hay she could now reach.

Later Mrs B. came to visit, so we went for an 'adventure', up the lane to the telegraph pole. This was the third time we'd been that far.

Havana walked-out beautifully, with so much confidence (and no sign of bruised ribs). He was so good that we did the walk twice!

I'll wait until *he asks* before we go any further.

FORCE FIELD
Friday, 23 November 2007

*W*hat a trusting boy!

As going through the mud in the gateway upsets Havana so much, I decided to take him out of the front field by a different route.

Turning off the power supply to the electric tape fence, lifting out the final plastic fence post and pegging back a few feet of fence would allow us through – so we could leave the field by the other gate, at the end of the footpath, where it is much drier.

All of the horses are very wary of touching the electric fence – which '*bites*'.

It was dusk and, as Havana was in the corner by the electric fence anyway, it would be quite easy to get him through it into the rest of the field, without the others noticing and trying to follow.

I pegged back the electric fence and – without putting on his head collar – encouraged Havana to step through the gap.

It was as if there was an invisible force field where the length of electric tape used to be. Havana was reluctant to cross it.

However, as I encouraged him by speaking to him again, he gathered all his courage and walked through the gap to me.

What trust!

DEFENDER OF THE HAY
Monday, 26 November 2007

*T*offee and Freddy are two ponies prone to laminitis (a metabolic imbalance causing lameness, that is alleviated by restricting their access to grazing), so they live on the 'starvation paddock' in the field at the back of the house.

Now that the grass is less rich and they need the shelter of the barn, the gate between their paddock and the paddock with the barn is open and the electric fence enclosing their paddock has been taken down.

This means that Havana and his herd are now able to get into the back field, and Toffee and Freddy can get into the others' paddock and the field. They are hardly one herd though, as Toffee and Freddy always stick together.

Toffee is grumpy and kicks; he is very old. Freddy is his 'henchman' – he is aggressive because he is with Toffee. Together, they are not a very nice pair.

There is a big bale in the back field where the ground is drier. Two heaps of hay from the big bale have been separated out, a distance away, so the two herds need not mix.

Havana, Faith, and Flower were eating peacefully from one of the heaps. Toffee and Freddy monopolised the big bale and Ben was standing, snoozing.

I watched as Freddy came marching straight to Havana's heap of hay, looking aggressive, with his head low and ears back.

No one dominates Faith, but she turned away with an air of: 'Oh, I really can't be bothered!' – and Flower followed her.

That left Havana, who bravely made a stand by walking forward towards Freddy and standing right in the middle of the heap of hay – as if defending it.

Havana was defiant, standing his ground and nipping at Freddy.

The nipping quickly turned into a game, of which Havana was the instigator; Freddy could not have been in such a bad mood because he went along with the game.

Havana was trying to grab the noseband of Freddy's head collar in his teeth (which reminded me of Cayman's game of 'pony-dragging').

The game escalated with Havana nipping Freddy's neck, shoulders, belly, then back legs – and Freddy matching each action.

It got more and more serious until Havana was in a vertical rear – waving his front legs at Freddy.

Freddy is old and wise enough to know that when the ground is slippery, it is not sensible to rear that high.

Havana went ... Slam! Flat on to the ground.

When he got to his feet his first few strides were very strange, his front legs crossed each other as he walked. He was concussed.

What a pitiful sight! With his head down and mud plastered on the nearside of his neck and shoulder, Havana came straight to me.

I comforted him by putting my arm over his neck and speaking to him, softly. He stayed close to me for a while.

His bravado had evaporated; he is such a young horse after all – but very brave.

Eventually Havana went, quietly, to eat hay by himself from the big bale which Toffee and Freddy had now vacated.

TRAPPED

Sunday, 2 December 2007

I rescued Havana today.

I walked over the footpath from the church and thought it strange that, in the distance, I could not see Havana grazing in the field with the others.

As I got closer to the farm I heard a distant whinny. I walked through the field, where everyone but Havana was grazing, and into the muddy paddock with the barn in it.

There, in the barn, was Havana ... all by himself. He whinnied again.

As Havana does sometimes like to be apart from the herd, I did not think too much of his situation and decided to give him his midday feed in the barn, as the others were out of sight and would not interfere.

After he had eaten, I trudged through the mud to get Havana a bucket of water; I knew he would not go to the buckets in the muddy gateway.

I expected Havana to go off to join the others, but then it became clear why he was still in the barn, alone – he was trapped by the mud.

He really did not want to venture off the straw on the barn floor into the deep, sticky mud that he would have to cross to get into the grass field where the others were.

Havana kept going to the long, high feeder which, together with a gate tied to it with bale string, formed a barrier along part of the open side of the barn.

He stuck his head through the feeder, in between its lower, flat trough and the v-shaped hayrack above. Did he think he could get out through the feeder?

Poor Havana! I came to his rescue by untying the gate next to the feeder; that way he could walk on a thin strip of slightly less muddy ground. I spoke encouragingly to him, which gave him the confidence to make a break for it.

He did have to cross some sticky, deep mud, but was soon on the other side and went trotting into the field, whinnying to his herd.

BITING AND REARING
Sunday, 9 December 2007

It has been very cold, wet and windy, all weekend.

I need not have worried about Havana though; he keeps warm by playing 'biting and rearing'.

This is how the game goes (it's very simple):

First, Havana selects a potential playmate and nips the other horse's front legs.

Next, the other horse reciprocates by nipping at Havana's front legs.

Finally, both horses rear.

From what I've seen, there seems to be no limit as to how many repetitions of this game Havana finds entertaining!

The trouble was that Ben didn't really want to play.

He did a bit of leg nipping, but no rearing – which is a good job, as he could squash Havana if he came down on top of him.

Each horse's innate characteristics were clear: Ben, being Shire, is of a docile breed; Havana is half-Thoroughbred, so much more excitable and, as he is a year younger than Ben, he's likely to be more playful anyway.

DEFENCE
Tuesday, 11 December 2007

I don't know what goes on in Havana's head …

He had just started eating his lunchtime feed from the bucket I was holding, when he took a step back and bucked at the wall.

The only explanation I can come up with is that, because it was very sunny, he saw his own shadow behind him and thought it was going to steal his food.

Perhaps he has now matured enough to defend his food rather than let other horses, including imaginary ones, take it from him.

Wednesday, 12 December 2007

My theory may be right …

Havana did the same thing again today, when the sun was in a different position: he turned, jumped backwards and bucked at the back wall, where my shadow fell.

THEFT

Saturday, 15 December 2007

*H*avana is getting cheeky.

He was next to Ben, eating at the big bale. As I checked his legs, by running my hand down them, I noticed his ears were back, flat (indicating aggression). He doesn't usually react like this to having his legs checked.

I watched Ben lift his head out of the very deep hole he had made in the hay with his nose. As he did so, Havana darted his head under Ben's neck and snatched a mouthful of hay.

This happened each time Ben raised his head – and each time Havana's ears were back, flat.

I decided to have a look on Ben's other side. There I found Freddy – also with his ears back, flat.

Havana had been using Ben as a protective barrier against Freddy, whilst stealing Freddy's hay!

Sunday, 16 December 2007

Ben has moved to other stables, hundreds of miles away.

I am worried about whether Havana will now feel the cold; Ben gave off a lot of heat.

I expect Havana will miss him.

"… stealing Freddy's hay …"

ROLLING
Friday, 21 December 2007

*H*avana is mad – or at least has no fear!

After he had eaten his midday feed, he was so excited by a smell in the straw, that he frantically dug up his bed by pawing it with his front foot – then proceeded to roll on the spot.

This time I was not worried about colic; it was obviously the smell in the straw that made him want to roll – not discomfort.

Nor was I worried about him becoming 'cast' (wedged against the wall and unable to get up); his bed has good banks and he is so little that there is plenty of space.

Also, and very fortunately, the house was full of burly men who were fitting a new kitchen, so even if Havana had been cast, there was plenty of available muscle power to get him back on his feet.

One roll was not enough; he got up, pawed the straw again, and had a second roll.

He would have gone for a third if I had not clipped his lead rope onto his head collar and insisted he stood up properly and walked out of the stable.

How brave of him to roll in a confined space, with a person standing right by him. I'm so glad he trusts me.

BIG TREE
Christmas Eve 2007

*W*hat a little star!

Havana walked up the lane with Mrs B. and me all the way to the big tree on the right – that's about twice as far as to the telegraph pole on the left.

He was quite happy and would have gone further, to the end of the lane, if he'd been allowed.

The other horses were in the front field and he stopped to talk to them on the way.

He's still 'mouthing' in submission to older horses – but is very inquisitive. It helps that there is a high, thick, spiky hedge between them.

Rollo was there; he's only a year older than Havana and friendly towards him.

On the way back from the big tree Havana was rushing. He was a bit anxious; but when he could see Faith and Flower in his own field he relaxed and slowed down.

"… all the way to the big tree …"

RUGBY TACKLE
Christmas Day 2007

*R*icky and I walked over the fields to give Havana his midday feed.

We brought him into the stable and, after his feed of mix and sugar beet, he had a treat – a 'Christmas apple'.

He was so polite; he is not used to apples, so I had cut it into eight slices – he ate each one individually, and very carefully.

In the tack room there was a Christmas present for Ricky and me, in a bright red, very shiny carrier bag.

After we had finished feeding Havana, Ricky was carrying the bag as we walked back across Havana's field. The strong sunlight reflected by the bag made it glow like a burning ember.

In Ricky's words, Havana, "rugby tackled" him for the bag. He was very excited and barged into Ricky – trying to grab the bag in his teeth.

When Ricky swapped the bag to his other hand, Havana darted to the other side to continue his assault. He was fixated with the incandescent bag!

In an attempt to quell Havana, we took out the contents and let him put his nose in the bag, but his excitement did not abate.

As it was such an impressive bag and I was short of Christmas wrapping, I intended to re-use it. I didn't want it to get ripped, or dirtied by Havana's nose, so I folded it up and put it down the front of my jacket. As far as Havana was concerned, it had vanished.

He was still very excited when we reached the electric fence and got under it into the next part of the field. Havana could not follow, so he walked back and forth along the fence watching us, with his head high – confused about where the shiny bag had gone.

Eventually he began to graze.

(P.S. I gave Havana a 'Christmas apple' after his feed for a few more days. His impeccable manners didn't last though; by the third day he got all eight pieces into his mouth before starting to chew them!)

MY HAT
Thursday, 27 December 2007

*S*ince I started wearing my brown 'fur' winter-hat, Havana has been fascinated by it.

He behaves as if he thinks it is an independent creature – rather than something I have chosen to put on my head.

Whenever possible, and particularly when I am bending down or picking-out his hooves, he makes a beeline for it with his teeth – more out of exploration than aggression.

To try to satisfy his curiosity today in the stable, I took off my hat and held it at arm's length for him to sniff. He did so, but that wasn't enough; he repeatedly butted under my outstretched arm and then got the hat in his teeth. As the hat didn't cost much and would be washable anyway, I let go of it.

Having given it a vigorous shaking, Havana dropped the limp brown fur-fabric onto the straw and – just to make sure it was really 'dead' – pawed it with a front foot before standing on it. He then appeared to forget about it.

After I had retrieved the hat from the straw, I discovered from the label inside, that it's not washable. One part of it didn't smell very nice ... but I expect that will wear off.

(P.S. The next day my hat was as interesting as ever to Havana. Perhaps he thought it had come back to life!)

TIED UP
Saturday, 29 December 2007

*H*avana doesn't really enjoy the frustrating experience of trying to eat hay from a tightly stuffed haylage net (which has far smaller mesh than a hay net).

He moves his teeth around the net with his lips curled back – trying to find an easy bit to pull out – in an agitated way, which suggests he can't understand why I haven't just put the hay loose on the floor so he can eat it normally.

The haylage net is actually a decoy.

The real purpose of the exercise is to get Havana used to being tied up.

His lead rope is tied to the string on the same ring in the wall as the haylage net, but he seems unaware that he is prevented from walking round his stable – and anyway, why would he want to walk round his stable when there's hay to be eaten?

The ingenuity required to get a mouthful of hay so preoccupies Havana that he doesn't seem at all bothered that he's tied up – and certainly doesn't panic about it.

WAITING
Thursday, 3 January 2008

*F*or the first time, Havana was waiting expectantly, by himself, behind the barn where I feed him.

Also for the first time, I got a special whinny – of relief and recognition – when he saw me.

That was rewarding; it made me feel very wanted!

FURRY BOTTOM
Friday, 4 January 2008

*H*avana had some more visitors today: Samantha and Danielle, who are eight-year-old twins, and their mother Diane – my neighbours.

I brought him into the stable for his midday feed; his manners were impeccable.

I don't know who was more interested in whom. Havana certainly seemed fascinated by the matching pair of blonde girls (in shocking pink anoraks) looking over his door and, after he had finished eating, he was very keen to sniff them.

To see over Havana's door both girls needed to stand together on a bale of straw. As they are not used to horses, there were delighted squeals each time Havana stuck out his nose and either Samantha or Danielle toppled harmlessly off the bale – only to be promptly scooped-up and returned to their vantage point by their mother.

This entertained Havana even more than it entertained the girls! From his perspective, on the stable-side of the door, Samantha and Danielle must have appeared like skittles; automatically popping-up again every time they were bowled over.

Eventually, by sticking out his nose very gently, Havana was able to sniff these new people and have his muzzle stroked.

It made Samantha and Danielle giggle helplessly when – demonstrating the luxuriously thick, winter coat on Havana's rump by burying my hands in it – I enthused about his "furry bottom"!

I don't think Havana could believe his luck when I went back later to get him in.

By 7.00 p.m. it was dark, wet and windy. Everyone was in the top muddy paddock, nearest the yard: Freddy and Toffee, Faith and Flower – and Havana, standing by himself by a tree, dozing – resigned to a chilly night.

He could have gone into the barn, or round the back of the barn; both would have been warmer – but he obviously didn't want to.

Within minutes, he was in the snug stable.

I felt like a traitor as he very sweetly stuck out his nose when he saw the syringe of wormer. He had got used to the 'decoy' syringes of apple juice which I had given him for a few days after his last worming (a very helpful suggestion from Jennifer).

Now, he automatically tried to suck syringes, but this one contained poison – at least that's what it tasted like! (I know; I tasted a bit on the tip of my tongue and spat it out thoroughly afterwards).

Poor Havana, I did feel sorry for him. He looked confused by that particular syringe, but I quickly gave him his feed to make him feel better – that worked.

As the cold darkness closed in outside, Havana settled down to a mountain of hay and a thick straw bed. He did look cosy.

PHONES AND ZIPS
Monday, 7 January 2008

*H*avana gets more adorable by the second; today he demonstrated his interest in technology!

Whilst I was giving him his lunchtime feed, Ricky rang me on my mobile phone.

When Havana had finished eating, I put the phone to his right ear so Ricky could talk to him. Havana stood with that ear immobile, locked onto Ricky's voice, whilst his left ear rotated slowly, like a radar antenna scanning the stable.

Horse's ears point to what they are thinking about and Havana's attention was very clearly split – between listening intently to Ricky's disembodied voice with one ear and using his other ear to pick up any acoustic information with which to locate Ricky's physical presence.

When the phone call ended, Havana didn't concern himself further with 'the strange phenomenon of the invisible Ricky'; he was content simply to get on with our usual routine.

When I did eventually turn him back out into the field, he was evidently in a mood for still more fuss – and stayed with me by the gate.

Havana has always been fascinated by the sturdy, plastic zip on my jacket and often tries to grip the tab between his front teeth. I discourage him because this usually leads to nipping.

This time, as he was being so gentle, I let him continue his investigation of my zip. He was entertained by the fact that it moves – and when it moves it makes an interesting, crunching sound.

He discovered that he could zip it down and zip it up – with accompanying sound effects – repeatedly, which is very amusing if you are a little horse!

Havana was even more intrigued to discover that, under my zip-up jacket, I was wearing a zip-up fleece. He did have a go at that zip too, but it has a tiny tab and was done up to my throat (as it was a cold day, and I had flu) so for my own safety, I had to call a halt to his game of 'unpeel the person'.

He really is an intelligent lad.

PRIVILEGE

Saturday, 12 January 2008

What a privilege that Havana is so relaxed with me.

After all the rain yesterday, today was bright and sunny so he was in a much better mood.

When he had eaten his midday feed, I followed him into the paddock. He was playful; the warm sun on his coat had cheered him up.

I stood on the bank as – with huge confidence – he got down and rolled in the dry peaty soil immediately below me.

When he stood up, he wanted to start a game of nipping legs, but I reminded him that you don't play horsey games with people – because their skin is thin and bites hurt them.

I squatted on the bank, at Havana's eye level.

He calmed down as I rubbed his forehead; he yawned a lot – and his eyelids drooped.

Eventually, we both dozed … with our noses together.

His nose is so tiny, and delicate; the jet-black hair on its tip contrasts with the golden hair at the sides. It's beautiful.

He was content: breathing out, as I breathed in. We stayed like that for about fifteen minutes.

I am very fortunate that he is so gentle, relaxed and accepting – to have his trust is an honour.

EDWARD

Sunday, 13 January 2008

*O*ur friend Edward came to see Havana today; we had planned to walk down the lane.

As it had been so wet, all of the horses from the front field, by the lane, were in their stables in the yard.

In front of the new bungalow that is being built, there was the most enormous puddle; the whole path was submerged.

Edward went first. Havana stayed on dry ground and watched Edward wade through the water.

For a while, Havana considered Edward (who was now standing on the dry ground on the other side of the puddle) and then, with a little encouragement from me, he very bravely walked straight across the puddle.

That's the first time he's ever walked into such a lot of water.

He didn't want to go up the lane at all though – why should he?

It was spooky and windy and all of the horses had deserted their field by the lane for the yard. If they were not there, then Havana had every justification for assuming there must be a reason why they were not in their usual field – and the reason could be 'some sort of danger'.

All in all, he was very sensible for saying he definitely did not want to go up the lane!

We did go into the wood for a while, but Havana was unsettled there too.

He didn't want to go back into his own field either and pawed the ground to remonstrate – but some food in a purple bucket changed his mind.

A RAINY DAY
Thursday, 17 January 2008

*M*r B., my father, came to see Havana today.

He had not seen him for a few weeks and, as he arrived first, he went down the footpath in the field – with his camera.

When I arrived, Mr B. said that Havana had grown so much that, to start with, he was unsure whether he actually was Havana!

We had all intended to go for a walk down the lane, but it had started to rain heavily.

Whilst Havana was eating his feed, he was as enthusiastic about it as ever. He probably uses more calories pawing the ground with his front legs, as he gobbles up the mix and sugar beet, than the food gives him!

After Havana had eaten, Mrs B. also arrived.

I tied Havana up, picked-out his feet, and groomed him – as he voraciously snatched hay from the net. I hadn't groomed him for a while; he was good, but still hyperactive.

The electric light in the stable was not working and, because it was raining so heavily, the natural light was quite gloomy – which made Havana's coat appear to be the most opulent dark red.

Eventually, he started to yawn; huge, all-consuming yawns, as if he was fighting sleep … *and losing.*

Mr and Mrs B. went home for some lunch.

That was a shame because, after going through the 'hyperactivity – sleepy cycle', Havana emerged calm, settled and very affectionate.

We stayed, happily, in the stable together for another half-hour, with Havana getting a lot of love and hugs, which he absolutely soaked up.

WEATHERBYS
Friday, 18 January 2008

I rang the foal registration department of Weatherbys, to check on how Havana's registration on the 'non-Thoroughbred register' was progressing.

As that line was engaged, I decided to speak to the 'stallions department' whilst I was waiting – to ask whether horses' heights are recorded.

I wanted to know how tall Sharpo and Treeline, Havana's Thoroughbred grandfather and grandmother, were.

I was informed that Wheatherbys don't keep this information as:
"If a horse wins races – it doesn't matter if it's 14.2hh!"

What I did find out was that Sharpo was born in 1977 and died in 1994.

He raced over short distances: five to six furlongs – winning seven races and being placed in seven.

Whilst he was at stud, from 1983, his 'progeny' – i.e. Havana's (and Cayman's) father, aunts and uncles – won three million pounds.

I can't wait to gallop Havana when he's old enough – I know he'll fly!

MISUNDERSTOOD
Saturday, 19 January 2008

I don't think Toffee is 'bad'.

I think that, historically, people probably have not treated him very well, which has affected the way he behaves, and now he is 'misunderstood'. I think he wants to be loved.

Today it was so wet that everyone was under the barn. As usual, Toffee and Freddy – but mostly Toffee – monopolised the gap between the hanging tarpaulin and the wall, where they can pull hay from the big bale behind the tarpaulin.

When Toffee had eaten enough hay, he moved towards the side of the barn where I was standing; he came and stood close by my side – it was as if he wanted to be with me.

I very gently, and respectfully, stroked his neck, and then his forehead – which seemed to relax him.

Faith is similar; she is aged seventeen and has had a hard life – having a foal each year. She is very independent and it seems she is not used to interacting closely with people.

Throughout her life her job has been to have foals. When she came to the farm, in-foal with Flower her last foal and with Rollo (her previous year's foal) still suckling, she had been neglected.

How fortunate Faith and her foals were to have been rescued by kind people.

Again, I am very respectful of Faith and try hard not to impose myself on her; but when she does allow me to stroke her forehead, under her forelock, this simple comfort seems to be the most luxurious treatment she has ever received – her relaxation indicates that she does really appreciate it.

I wonder what Toffee and Faith think of all the attention that Havana gets (and now takes for granted). I wonder whether they are envious of him – or sad that they have not received more kindness from people.

QUICK LUNCH
Tuesday, 22 January 2008

*S*ometimes I do wonder about Havana!

Every day for nearly four months, he has had a midday feed and has got used to the routine. Today, as I did not have a lot of time, I decided he would have a 'quick lunch' behind the barn instead of going into his stable.

The horses were all down at the bottom of the field, grazing. I walked to the top of the field and stared hard at Havana's rump whilst I slowly counted to ten, then turned and walked away – nothing!

I walked halfway down the field and stared at Havana's rump again. Everyone else, starting with Faith, noticed me and put their heads up – even little Flower; but Havana just kept on munching grass. If I had been a predator, I know which furry rump I would have leapt on!

As I wanted to feed Havana by himself, quietly behind the barn, I did not want the others to notice him leaving the big field – but now there was no chance of that. When Havana finally noticed me, he looked surprised.

As we walked up the field, everyone else, led by Faith, came with us.

In the muddy paddock, Havana then decided it would be fun to provoke and antagonise Toffee, who must be at least thirty years old and is 'the boss'. Havana's disrespectful sparring, from the higher ground of the dry bank, made poor Toffee over-exert himself, resulting in wheezing and heaving sides.

When Toffee decided it was time to put this upstart firmly in his place – by running at him with his ears pinned to his outstretched neck, then turning and kicking-out with both back legs – Havana decided to come and stand by my side for protection, putting us both in a dangerous position.

Eventually, poor Toffee went into the barn with the others.

Havana was standing expectantly by the gate, on a 'safe island' of old trodden-in hay, in the sea of mud.

I stayed near the barn, calling him to come to me so we could go round to the back for his feed. But Havana didn't move from the gate; he was determined to go out of it, rather than through the mud.

My attempts to encourage Havana to come to me alerted Toffee to the fact that 'something was going on'. Toffee knows about our feeding place at the back of the barn and he is old enough and bold enough even to challenge a human if he decides that *he* would like to eat Havana's food. If cornered by Toffee behind the barn, Havana scarpers!

As Toffee was clearly 'clocking' us, and for a quiet life, I put on Havana's head collar and led him out of the gate – so he could have his feed in the stable after all.

So much for trying to be quick today!

CASTRATION
Wednesday, 30 January 2008

Poor little Havana was castrated yesterday, under the barn.

Sue gave him a general anaesthetic. She said that, as he is so well handled, he could have had the operation standing (under local anaesthetic and heavy sedation), if he was taller.

However, she was concerned that he was rather little for her to work under, and decided that the operation would be best performed with him lying down – for which a general anaesthetic was needed.

As we were on the subject of height, I asked Sue how big she thought Havana would grow. I was pleased when she said 16hh, although I do think that anything over 15.2hh will be a bonus.

When Ricky and I checked him in the field, in the dark at about 8.00

p.m. last night, he came straight to us – even though we were shining a very powerful torch. He seemed fine.

By this morning the pain relief must have worn off.

He was grazing miserably by himself and didn't want to talk to me. He was in pain. I knew because all he wanted to do was bite me and he doesn't normally do that – he's grown out of it. He bites to tell me there's something very wrong.

It was like yesterday morning; he was biting vociferously then to tell me he was hungry.

He had not been allowed any breakfast before his operation and only a meagre amount of hay overnight. Biting me was his way of letting me know, in no uncertain terms, that he was starving!

TRUST

Friday, 1 February 2008

*W*hat an amazing experience I've had today – something I have never experienced before!

It was so bright and sunny that I decided to walk to Havana.

As I came up from the stream, I could see Flower sitting down at the top of the field; Faith was grazing by the side hedge a bit further down, and Freddy was grazing on the opposite side. I could not see Havana or Toffee, so I assumed they were in the barn.

When I got much closer to the top of the field, I was surprised to see that Havana was sitting near the top hedge; he had been so well camouflaged as to be invisible.

He was asleep – with his eyes closed – in a pool of bright, hot sunshine. His coat was all puffed-up, so he looked even furrier than usual. He could not have looked more contented.

I decided to sit with him, so I approached very gently and called him quietly, so he was not startled when he did finally realise I was there.

He woke up enough to notice me and was not at all bothered when I sat down, close to his shoulder. The ground was not dry and there was a lot of poo about, but I didn't mind; it was such an honour that Havana allowed me to sit with him.

The sun shining directly onto us was so hot that I could hardly manage to touch Havana's black mane.

After a while, I could tell from his heavy breaths and the way his neck swayed towards me that Havana really wanted to lie flat to get a good sleep.

I encouraged him by speaking softly and gently stroking his neck.

It was not long before he keeled over, flat, with his head across the tops of my outstretched legs – and his eyes shut.

As I stroked his jaw, I could hardly believe what was happening.

Even when I had to readjust my legs to get comfortable, Havana just raised his head a few inches and then rested it down again.

There was nowhere on earth I would rather have been. It is humbling to have the trust of such a beautiful animal.

HORSE HEAVEN
Sunday, 3 February 2008

I climbed over the bales and, when I saw the cosy scene in the barn, went back to the car for my camera.

Havana was in horse heaven! Snuggled up in the corner, *sitting* on hay *and eating* hay, he looked adorable.

Flower was sitting down close by, with her mother keeping watch over her. Toffee and Freddy were on the other side of the barn eating from more piles of hay. Outside was very cold and the wind made an eerie sound as it whistled through the wooden slats on the upper part of the barn wall.

The second time, I clambered over the bales (that way you avoid the mud) and down the high fence into Havana's part of the barn, moving quietly so I didn't disturb anyone.

Havana looked up sleepily. Toffee and Freddy looked a bit surprised, but it was easy to sit down on the hay with Havana. As I stroked his neck, he put his muzzle down to the ground, so the weight of his head was on his front teeth, and closed his eyes. We stayed like that for about twenty minutes, then, quietly, I went off to get Havana's lunch.

By the time I had made the bucket of feed (with antibiotics and pain relief), Havana and Flower were both eating hay, standing up. Havana followed me out of the barn – over a series of 'safe islands' in the mud – to the paddock at the front of the house; he did not need to have his head collar on.

I shut the paddock gate, in case anyone else wanted Havana's lunch. As I sat on the stile holding his bucket, Flower was watching from the barn, over the sea of mud.

When Havana had finished I opened the gate again, and he went for long drinks of water from several different buckets behind the barn: first the blue one, then the green one, then some from the red bucket.

In the green one I saw a carrot; I pulled up my sleeve and plunged my arm into the icy water to retrieve it for Havana. As far as he was concerned, a carrot just 'appeared' on the ground – which was a nice surprise!

He then waded back to the front of the barn and it was not long before he had negotiated with Faith to be allowed back into 'his' snug corner.

He's obviously feeling much brighter today. I think the pain from his castration has gone; I'm glad.

"… 'his' snug corner."

MUD FEVER
Saturday, 9 February 2008

*A*t this rate, I'm going to run out of superlatives, but I have to say that Havana is an angel!

He let me wash his legs for the first time ever, then dry them and put on soothing cream – for his mud fever.

I didn't know that he had mud fever until yesterday.

I have been checking the backs of his fetlocks regularly and thinking how amazing it was – considering how much mud he has to wade through to get into the barn – that he didn't have mud fever. Then yesterday in the stable, I noticed what looked like a graze on the *front* of his offside front fetlock.

When I looked closer, I saw that the hair right across this area was thinning out, and there was a bald patch on the side of his other front foot too. In the mud caked to his offside hind foot, which has a white sock, there was a flash of pink, bare skin.

Poor little thing; no wonder he had protested yesterday when I used straw to clean off the worst of the mud.

I tied him up loosely, with a hay net, and he let me use a huge, drippy sponge to wash away the mud.

He did do a bit of hopping about when I washed his back feet but, when I rested each foot on my knee, he obviously felt more secure and stood still.

Other times I held his foot up at the back; it was as light as a feather – he was doing a sort of horsey arabesque.

Havana was quite excited because Gill and her farmer husband, Tim, had come to see him – he likes having visitors. Gill had not seen Havana since she came with me to North Wales to visit him, when he was only six months old. Tim had not seen him before; they were very impressed.

In particular, Gill commented on his beautiful fine head – and his big knees. Gill is a riding instructor and has looked after many horses;

it was a relief to have her reassuring, practical, advice on mud fever.

After Gill and Tim had left, Havana was very settled, having had his 'lunch', a lot of hay, and ever such a lot of fuss. I thought it was important that his legs were dried thoroughly so the cream would stick.

I had three different grades of 'leg-drying equipment': an old green towel, an old flowery sheet and a roll of kitchen paper.

I did not know whether the towel or the sheet would be more absorbent so, whilst I tested the towel on Havana's front leg, I left a screwed-up piece of sheet on his rump. He didn't mind.

The towel worked quite well, so I very carefully blotted all four legs with it. When I had finished, I hung it on Havana's back like a saddlecloth. That was the first time he had *ever* had anything on his back. He didn't seem to notice, so when I had finished with the sheet, I also put that on his back on top of the towel ... still no reaction.

He clearly didn't mind seeing something green, with something flowery on top of it, on his back – or maybe he didn't even bother to look! What a lovely nature he has.

The kitchen paper mopped up the last of the dampness, and then I gently smeared a lot of cream onto the front of each fetlock.

Havana was not totally sure this was a good idea as it smelled strange – but he is used to me doing odd things, so was not really all that bothered.

He looked so sweet, with four bright, white, cream socks – but he got a shock when he investigated a front foot and got cream stuck to his nose.

He was very relieved when I put him back into the field by the dry route. All I had to do was turn off the electric fence and take him into the front paddock, which leads to his field.

We have been that way before and, given a choice, it's the way Havana asks to go! He has been right all along; it's better for horses not to have muddy legs.

"… cream socks."

TOFFEE
Thursday, 14 February 2008

*W*hat could have been in Havana's lunchtime feed to make him so cheeky and disrespectful to Toffee – who is so much his senior?

No sooner had Havana finished eating, than he was trying to get Toffee's head collar in his teeth and nipping at his chest and shoulders.

As Toffee was provoked into trotting round in circles to try to get rid of this nuisance the game was made even more exciting, and it quickly escalated into circuits of the big field at a flat-out gallop from Havana, and with running bucks from Toffee.

Poor Toffee; after the second circuit he came up to the muddy paddock, where he stood wheezing and coughing. You can see from the rapid, shallow movement of his sides that his breathing is obstructed.

Why does he let a young upstart wind him up? I think he really does still enjoy playing!

As for Havana, he was nowhere to be seen; doubtless flying round the big field on yet another reckless circuit.

EVIL EYE
Friday, 15 February 2008

*I*t was only the fourth time that Havana had ever had his legs washed, but he let me use the hose pipe ('yellow snake'). It seemed to reassure him if I held his foot up as I hosed his leg. He was brilliant.

My very knowledgeable and experienced friend, Jennifer, was with me: she was concerned about the livid salmon-pink skin visible in Havana's white socks on his back legs. I needed no more cue to ring the vet.

Some more antibiotics and some corticosteroid cream were prescribed; they would be available for me to collect from the local branch surgery this afternoon. It was agreed that Havana needed to stay out of the mud. So, he would remain in the stable today, then be in at night and out in the front paddock (via the dry route) in the day. That way he avoided the mud by the barn.

When I arrived in the evening with the medication – and a purposeful demeanour – poor Havana's disconcerted expression told me that, as far as he was concerned, he had already had his legs done once today, which was quite enough!

I tied him up, with a net of hay for distraction.

By the time I had finished putting cream on the last fetlock, he was trying to stand on one front leg and one back leg. When he found that he couldn't, both front legs came off the ground at an alarming height.

I decided it would be unfair to test his tolerance any further and told Havana that I had finished.

With his eyes narrowed, in a very accusing way, he stood looking at me as if he had been betrayed. It's a look Mrs B. calls 'the evil eye' and I have not seen him do it for a few months now – not since he was quite little. It's as if he was saying:

"I really, *really* HATE you!" It hurts me to see him upset.

I gently stroked his forehead. In no time, his eyes were sleepy and his beautiful little golden and jet-black muzzle was pressed tightly into my shoulder as he let out some very big sighs.

He was reassured that I had not really been attacking him. We were friends again.

FIRST BIRTHDAY

Sunday, 17 February 2008

*I*t's Havana's first birthday!

An important milestone; with juvenile ailments and accidents, I've been all too aware that not all foals make it to their first birthdays. But here he is, robust and rumbustious – a sturdy, strong and bold yearling; full of enthusiasm for life, exploration, questions and games.

"Hello, I'm Havana! – and I'm *brave*."

"What's that?"

"What does it smell like?"

"Can I eat it?"

"Let's play!"

A party, to celebrate Havana's three-hundred-and-sixty-five days, was imperative.

Our friends – human and equine – were all invited. There was a shiny, multi-coloured banner over Havana's stable door proclaiming: "1 TODAY" and a string of birthday cards.

A theme ran through Havana's birthday presents: fruit – vegetable – fruit *and* vegetable. Bags of immaculate even-sized carrots from the supermarket, bunches of 'foliage on' organic carrots, gift-wrapped varieties of apples far too expensive to feed to horses (the equine equivalent of tasting vintage champagne). Nothing was deemed by his friends to be too good for Havana.

However, had this been a competition at a horticultural show, then the accolade 'Supreme Best in Show' must have gone to our friend Laraine for her exquisite gift – in a small wicker basket and meticulously arranged by our local greengrocer – of a colourful selection of perfect apples and juicy pears, complemented by an orderly group of four pristine carrots.

A buffet was set out on the lawn opposite the back field, where the horses were. My culinary speciality is chocolate cake, which I have been perfecting since I was seven. I was so happy to make a huge one for this very special occasion.

Sparkling wine (in practical plastic cups) flowed – absorbed effectively by the decadently gooey birthday cake.

Edward and his mother were first to arrive; Claire (on foot) helped Lisa – on her Friesian mare Klaska, and Sarah – on Hattie, to juggle drinks, cake and *reins*.

All of the horses had been grazing out of sight, down the bank. However, as more people arrived – and possibly because he seems to be helplessly drawn to visitors – the gathering attracted Havana, who appeared with Flower on the other side of the fence that separates the lawn from his field.

Havana was curious.

Circulating amongst guests, my concentration was only occasionally directed towards him, but I did notice that he was standing close to Alison W. and Sarah (Harrison's person), who were deep in conversation by a stout fence post.

Havana doesn't like to be excluded.

I was then distracted for several minutes, before I moved closer to Alison and Sarah and noticed a big lump of squashed chocolate cake on top of the fence post.

I assumed it had been put there for the birds to eat, but was surprised (and rather offended) that someone had not liked my delicious cake.

However, slightly closer inspection revealed the cake had been rolled in soil!

Now I got it: Havana – doubtless with outstretched neck, inquisitive muzzle and imploring, hungry-looking eyes – had asked one of our cake-eating guests (all of whom would readily have understood his gesture): *"Can I have some of that?"*

But, upon Havana's wish being granted he obviously decided – as he often does with unfamiliar food – "It's *not* food!" and spat it straight out onto the earth by the fence.

Oh well, there was more than enough cake to go round, so no one was deprived.

When my gaze next fell on Havana, I could also see that Alison and Sarah were standing facing each other, still talking intently.

No one noticed Havana's neck stretching over the fence and his muzzle getting closer … and closer … to Sarah's plastic cup. Lured by the sweet aroma of the celebratory wine, Havana could not resist plunging his petite nose right into it.

Perhaps he had not anticipated the contents being wet – or perhaps he just didn't like the taste. Whatever the cause, Havana appeared startled, with wide eyes, and snorted as if trying to rid himself of something offensive. He stood for a moment, with his top lip curled-up, concentrating hard on absorbing more sensory information about the substance in the cup, and then – apparently having decided it *definitely was* 'poison' – flew off at a thunderous gallop, straight down the field to join the rest of the herd. Flower instinctively did the same and neither was seen again, at close quarters, for the rest of the afternoon.

No doubt Havana was happy – grazing peacefully on reliable grass! – and unaffected by curious and unpredictable textures and tastes.

Our human friends – all connected by their shared interest in horses in general and, today, Havana in particular – were happy to drink, eat and talk with each other.

The privilege of grazing on the lawn was also extended to Klaska and Hattie – so they were both content too.

"Havana doesn't like to be excluded."

WOLF
Tuesday, 19 February 2008

*Y*esterday I asked Jan, who gives Havana his breakfast and tea, along with the other horses in the field, whether Havana gets all of his feed now.

The reason I started giving him a lunchtime feed was because, when he was younger, he could not defend his food from the others.

He ate so slowly that they always finished before him.

Then, as the least dominant – although not the youngest (Flower is younger, but she has her mother's protection) – Havana was obliged to stand back, hungrily, as Faith, Toffee, or Freddy finished *his* food!

I was relieved, and amused, when Jan told me that Havana now wolfs his food down before anyone else and then shares theirs! His soaked sugar beet (which he now likes) and mix is much easier to eat quickly than their dry cubes and chaff.

Today I had a practical demonstration of what a voracious little dragon Havana has turned into.

I gave him his lunchtime feed, containing his last dose of antibiotics, in the field. I wouldn't normally do this, but there was only Flower in the field with Havana and she usually stays out of his way whilst he is eating.

Just in case, I took one of his 'birthday carrots' to give to Flower as a decoy.

Jan was about, so she decided to give Flower one of the ready-prepared buckets of feed from the tack room.

The minute Havana had finished his own feed, he made a beeline for Flower's – scaring her off as he did so.

Eventually though, he let Flower eat from *her* bucket, with him.

They looked sweet!

There was hardly enough room for them both to get their noses into the bucket at the same time, but they managed it.

As we have finished the course of antibiotics and as Havana now obviously does get his breakfast and tea, I think I'll cut out his lunchtime feed. I'll increase the size of his breakfast and tea though, so he doesn't lose out.

I measured him with the steel ruler and he seems to be 14hh, which isn't bad at twelve months! I'm certain he'll be big enough for me.

YELLOW AND GREEN CREATURE
Thursday, 21 February 2008

How can anyone find a yellow and green plastic feed sack so entertaining?

Havana is still in the front paddock, to keep his feet out of the mud. This means he can't get to the big bale of haylage in the field, so I took him – and Faith and Flower, who are with him – some sacks of haylage.

I try to teach Havana by giving him new experiences.

So, after I had emptied out the third lot of haylage, I left the sack on the ground for Havana to investigate.

Poor little Flower was apprehensive about the billowing, crinkly thing on the grass but Havana was obviously fascinated.

After he had spent a few minutes pawing and sniffing it, he made a concerted effort to shred the sack by standing on it very firmly with his front feet and trying to tear it with his teeth.

It was made of such thick plastic and he had pinned it so taut against the ground, that there was nothing for Havana to get his teeth into; but his tenacity did make me think that, really, he wants to be a dog!

He was so determined that I feared he might manage to tear off a large piece of plastic and swallow it.

I decided I needed to remove the sack.

This was easier said than done when there was a frenzied little horse standing on it. During a lull in his attack, I distracted Havana by calling to him. I then gently pushed his shoulder – unbalancing him – so he stepped off the sack.

Next, and all in one movement, I reached down, picked it up and quickly folded it into an innocuous, flat parcel.

As far as Havana was concerned the strange yellow and green creature, which he had to dominate, had gone away.

I let him sniff the neatly-folded plastic square, but I don't think he recognised it. That was a relief. It has crossed my mind that if Havana had wanted to 'tackle me' for *his* sack, then I was not dressed for a fight, as I was wearing neither my hat, nor my body protector.

Fortunately, a foal's attention span is short and Havana soon decided it would now be a good idea to get on with the more serious matter of eating grass.

ICE
Saturday, 23 February 2008

*H*avana is easy to impress!

Overnight, ice had formed on the water trough (which is really an old bath). I didn't notice until I saw Havana drinking; he wasn't actually *drinking* – more 'sipping'. I thought that was odd as he doesn't usually drink like that.

When I investigated I could see why. There was a sheet of floating ice covering the surface of the water. A little water had seeped up the sides and that was what Havana was sipping.

As I picked up the entire ice sheet, it snapped in two. The loud crack frightened Havana, who jumped away as half of the ice splashed back into the water.

He wasn't frightened for long though, and came back to try drinking again.

As I lifted out the second half of the ice, his wide eyes and sweet expression told me he was *very* impressed that I had sorted out his water trough. He drank … and drank … and drank.

I felt like a hero.

YUCK!

Wednesday, 27 February 2008

*H*avana was eating his breakfast. His mouth was full and there was mix and soaked sugar beet all over his muzzle.

Why did he get such an *imperative* urge to sniff my ear?

Feeling the cold, wet, bits of feed going straight down my neck was really horrible.

DRAGON-HORSE

Saturday, 1 March 2008

*H*avana was feeling playful this morning as I turned him out.

Rollo, who is nearly two, was standing in the gateway of the front field. As we went past, Havana insisted on stopping to talk to Rollo and, in no time, they were biting the crests of each other's necks over the gate; that's another way of starting a game.

I told Havana that they couldn't play properly with a gate there and, anyway, it wouldn't be long before all of the horses from the front field were put into his field, then he could play with Rollo all the time.

Once in his own field, Havana made straight for Flower; nipping her back legs, just above her hocks, to get her to play. It was clear *to me* that Flower did not want to play, but Havana kept on biting her legs anyway.

I felt a bit sorry for Havana, having no other 'boys' to play with, but more sorry for Flower who has to put up with his rough games.
In the evening, I decided there was a game that Havana and I could play,

which might entertain him. I would jump over the half telegraph pole, lying on the ground at the top of the field, and he could follow me.

I greeted Havana near the gate and asked him to come with me, as I purposefully walked towards the telegraph pole.

Both Havana and Flower followed me out of curiosity, but stopped a little way from the pole. To encourage them, I ran and jumped over the pole a few times – first one way, then the other.

Both little horses stood together, watching me, with incredulous expressions. They had probably never seen a person behave like this before, but no amount of calling, coaxing, or sending mental pictures would persuade Havana to join in. He just looked at me as if he was trying to work out what on earth I thought I was doing.

Eventually, I decided this was probably not the time to teach Havana to follow me over jumps, so I walked back to him. By this time he was grazing.

As I stood by him, he cheekily nipped my shin as if to say:

"OK – if you want to play, we can start by biting legs!"

I was just explaining, again, that you must not bite humans, because their skin is thinner than horses' skin – and it hurts them – when both Havana's and Flower's attention was suddenly distracted.

They trotted forwards and then stopped abruptly, shoulder to shoulder, with their heads high. It was starting to get dark, but – following their gaze down the field – I could see someone walking towards us along the fenced-off footpath up the side of the field, while a light-coloured dog ran on ahead.

Almost immediately, Havana put his ears back to 'aerodynamic setting', stuck out his neck like a goose and charged down the field – aiming for the dog. The poor dog turned-tail and ran back in the direction of his owner as Havana continued to canter after him.

The reunited dog and owner then quickly retraced their steps along the path whence they came and out of range of the little horse-dragon, who stood triumphantly watching their retreat.

As I walked up to Havana, intending to tell him off for his antics (*although I was really rather proud of how magnificent he looked!*), he looked at me this time, as if to say:

"Now *that* was a game!"

SUNRISE
Monday, 3 March 2008

*H*avana stayed out last night – for the first time in two weeks.

The electric fence in the big field has been moved, so Havana, Faith and Flower cannot get into the muddy paddock, and the hair is starting to grow back on his fetlocks.

When Havana was in the stable at night, and Faith and Flower were out, there were some very cold nights.

As the sun rose and warmed the morning, Flower liked to sit down for a reviving and much-needed snooze; but Havana, having had a cosy night, wanted to play.

He pestered poor little Flower, standing right over her and biting her neck and front legs until she got up.

This morning, having also had a chilly night, Havana was sitting down snoozing in the sun – with Flower.

He let me sit with him; there was a lot of deep sighing and his sleepy eyes just could not stay open.

Now, maybe Havana will be a bit more considerate towards Flower!

RHINOCEROSES
Sunday, 9 March 2008

*H*avana's world has been turned upside down.

His 'nursery' has been invaded by horses the size of rhinoceroses – four of them – along with Rollo, who is smaller.

As Ricky and I approached the field, on the footpath from the church, we could see a lot of horses careering about. Notably, one little, lithe horse was galloping the largest circuits at the perimeter of the shifting group.

As we got up to the top of his field, Havana was relieved to see Ricky and me and came to stand by us.

The dried sweat on his neck, shoulders and flanks showed there had been an earlier spate of galloping laps; behind his front legs was wet again from this latest exertion and his sides were heaving like bellows.

His natural inclination to run back to his group, Faith and Flower, only got him into more trouble. Faith appeared to be in season, which was driving one of the big horses – the dapple grey, Prince – mad with excitement. To him, this little male upstart who was with Faith had to be dealt with by 'running him off', so he chased a *very frightened* Havana round the field for a few more circuits.

Havana flew! It's a good job he is so light and nimble.

After Havana had broken the electric fence by running into it (fortunately where its first post could harmlessly pop out of the ground) and all of the horses had got mixed-up into the wrong fields, Prince was caught, taken from the field and put into a stable to simmer down for a while.

I did feel bad leaving Havana, but learning to fight his own battles is an important part of belonging to a herd – it's not something I can do for him.

By teatime, they had all settled down a bit and Prince was back in the field – but they were in two distinct 'camps': 'The Nursery Camp' – Faith, Flower and Havana – and 'The Big Horses' Camp'.

There was no chance of my getting Havana out of the field for his evening feed, as the big horses were occupying the territory by the gate.

It was safer for Havana to do without a feed than to risk being kicked, but I did reassure him he'd get some extra breakfast!

KISS
Tuesday, 11 March 2008

*H*avana wasn't in a rush to go off down the field as I turned him out after breakfast.

He was in a 'fussing mood' as he gently investigated the chinstraps on the riding hat I was wearing.

I am cautious about horses' teeth around my face. There are times, for example when Havana is in a playful mood, when I would not allow it but, today, he was so gentle as his tiny, velvety-soft, black muzzle worked its way around my jaw.

I can only assume he was fascinated by the warm air I exhaled; but as his muzzle made its way under my nose and across my mouth, his investigation ceased – with his lips welded to mine.

Time stopped.

Exquisitely, eternity held us in the loveliest 'horsey kiss' as my whirring mind struggled, inadequately, to cope with my amazement.

A PLAYMATE
Wednesday, 12 March 2008

*L*ast night, rather than being segregated into two gangs, 'The Big Horses' and 'The Nursery', the horses were grazing, spread out all over the field.

I was glad they had settled down.

This morning it was different, Havana was the sole representative of 'The Nursery' in the field. Faith and Flower had both been put into stables because the vet was coming to give them their injections.

It was a bit much for him – his confidence had completely evaporated.

When I arrived to give him his breakfast, he was waiting, uneasily, by the fence opposite the house – as near as possible to Faith and Flower in their stables.

The other horses were a bit farther down the field.

Havana seemed very relieved to be leaving the field with me.

After breakfast, when I returned him to the field, I did feel sorry for Havana. I know he has to learn to stand up for himself, but he's so little.

Rollo came up to him and I encouraged Havana to play with Rollo, although I knew he did not feel at all playful.

Rollo seems to be drifting towards membership of 'The Nursery'. After all, Faith *is* his mother and Flower is his full-sister.

What a relief it was when, finally, after Havana's evening feed, he and Rollo were grazing with their noses side-by-side trying to eat the same piece of grass – and taking turns to act as windbreaks for each other.

At last! Havana has another 'boy' to play with. Flower will be glad.

BEAUTIFUL
Friday, 14 March 2008

*I*t was on the dark side of dusk when I got to the stables this evening.

I went straight to the tack room to get the feed ready and then walked to the fence.

Appearing magically out of the gloom, halfway down the field, I could see a beautiful horse – graceful, elegant and lithe – making his way deliberately towards me.

He was taller than Havana.

I was unsure who he was; there aren't any horses like this in the field.

As he got closer, I called: "Havana?"

He whinnied to me.

He had grown since this morning *and* become even more beautiful.

OVERINDULGENCE
Saturday, 15 March 2008

*W*hat a scare Havana gave me!

This morning Ricky and I walked up the field from the church. As we approached, we could see all of the big horses standing resting in the top corner and Flower lying down near Faith. They were all there – except Havana.

As we got closer, I became more and more anxious; I concentrated on looking along the top hedge as, sometimes, Havana is camouflaged. No – he definitely wasn't there.

I was starting to panic when – amongst the remains of the haylage bale – I noticed a little, golden-brown, triangular shape. Could it be Havana's ear? I hardly dared look.

As we got closer still, I could see Havana lying flat-out on the haylage – his eyes were closed. I thought he was dead. I was frightened to call his name in case he didn't react and really *was* dead.

"Havana!" Nothing. Again, louder and more urgently:

"HAVANA!" Thank God! He lifted his head an inch or two. I knelt down in front of him. The eye that I could see half-opened and then slowly closed again, but he sat up.

I hugged his furry little neck as we pressed our foreheads together. His breathing was laboured.

I sat back to get a better look at his face; his half-closed eyes, bemused expression and tight facial muscles spelled out one thing: colic.

I stroked his forehead and spoke gently to him. I was very worried.

It often helps to have the opinion of someone who is not burdened with worry and 'worst case scenarios'. Ricky cut into my thought process, which had just about got to colic surgery.

"They're all the same!" he observed.

He was right. All of the adults were standing motionless, which was unusual; even if most were resting there would invariably be one or two still grazing. Flower was lying so flat-out that she might have been ironed onto the field, except for her 'medicine-ball belly'.

Then, it dawned on me! The big bale of haylage was only put into the field on Wednesday evening. It *had* been about four feet high; now there were only about three inches of it left on the ground … they had all stuffed themselves.

The effects of this over-indulgence were felt most by Havana and Flower, as their bodies are so much smaller than the adult horses'.

Havana was actually lying on the evidence! He reminded me of the intemperate oaf who ends up asleep under the table after a party, cradling an empty whisky bottle.

Now that I had a cause, I felt relieved – and a bit annoyed.

Assuming the demeanour of a no-nonsense school matron coming across the debris of a sixth form party that had got out of hand, I told Havana:

"We're going for a *walk*!" I left him sitting on the haylage and went off to get his head collar.

When I came back he showed no inclination at all to get up.

One way to make a horse want to get up is to lift its uppermost hind leg straight up. That didn't work. Havana is so biddable that he was quite happy to sit there with his back leg up; I really don't think he knew what I meant.

I decided that if I 'unfolded' one of his front legs (horses get up 'front legs first'), he could have no doubt – that worked.

Havana stood, bleary eyed, like someone with a hangover ejected from bed too soon.

He was so bloated that even his back looked as if air had been pumped into it. Poor little thing.

Unenthusiastically, Havana walked with me to the yard, where he was probably expecting his usual breakfast of mix and sugar beet. Instead, we continued in a smart walk up the lane. He didn't really want to go up the lane and kept stopping for grass. I let him graze, grass is good.

After some strange gurgling sounds from his belly and two elephantine mounds of poo, Havana's expression was getting back to normal, he looked much brighter.

We walked round the yard for a while and I decided it would be alright to put him back in the field, where he would graze and walk about.

I hoped he had learned his lesson about haylage – but no! Within minutes, like an addict, he was back amongst the adult horses around the remains of the bale.

From the way I marched straight to him, he must have known *exactly* what I meant. I didn't have the head collar, so I got hold of a hank of mane halfway along his neck and, with my other hand on the front of his nose, steered him down the field to where Faith and Flower were now grazing – sensibly. I was surprised he put up no resistance at all, he was as easy to move as a lamb.

As Ricky and I walked away down the field and up the next one, I kept glancing over my shoulder, but Havana was grazing peacefully.

Maybe he really had learned his lesson.

EMPEROR

Monday, 17 March 2008

*H*avana was about as bothered by his second-ever hoof trim as an ancient Chinese emperor having a weekly manicure.

I tied him up, behind the first row of stables, with a hay net. Stuart, the farrier, agreed that, although it was five months since his first trim, there wasn't much to take off.

Havana systematically munched at the hay as Stuart, apparently effortlessly, rasped all four feet.

Once, when Stuart had Havana's front leg extended forward – his hoof balanced on his knee – Havana decided to sniff the back of Stuart's head but, apart from that, Havana was completely unconcerned.

After he had finished rasping, I asked Stuart how long it should be before the next trim, bearing in mind that I might start walking Havana more. He said:

"Same again – they might have a growth spurt. Does he paw the ground a lot with his nearside front foot?"

Stuart must have noticed that hoof was more worn. I said it *is* the foot he uses most often to 'make a point'. I also told him how, whilst he eats, Havana paws the ground and waves each front leg about enthusiastically because he loves his food. I said I don't discourage him; it's probably something he'll grow out of but, for now, if I hold the bucket at arm's length, I can *just* keep my shins safe!

I remarked on the fact that Havana's knees seem to be bigger than his feet.

"There's plenty of timber in him!" was Stuart's positive reply.

I think this means that Havana is a strong little horse, with plenty of bone.

HEAVY DOG
Thursday, 20 March 2008

*A*s if I needed it, I had clear proof today of just how much Havana has grown.

Last time he stood on my foot it felt like having a heavy dog standing on it. This time it definitely felt like a horse! (My foot was in his way – it wasn't his fault).

To give him his evening feed, I had to pull him away from the mineral-lick that is tied onto one of the fence posts; I've never seen him licking it before.

With fresh grass rushing through them at this time of year, horses are susceptible to mineral deficiency. This week, I have noticed that both Havana and Flower seem a bit stiff in their back legs as they walk, which can be a sign they're not getting all the minerals they need.

It's wonderful how, given the opportunity, animals medicate themselves. Havana is obviously sorting himself out.

EXAM
Good Friday, 21 March 2008

*F*or the first time, I invited Mrs B. to groom Havana this morning. My invitation was the equestrian equivalent of asking my mother: "Would you like to hold my baby?"

Havana stood in the front stable, tied loosely and pulling at a hay net, as Mrs B. gave him a very 'no nonsense' grooming.

I felt like an examiner, standing in the corner by the door.

Actually, I was concerned that Havana didn't do anything silly and hurt Mrs B.

"I've groomed horses more troublesome than him!" was her characteristically dismissive response to my concern that she was grooming a horse aged twelve months, not twelve years.

I need not have worried as Havana was a credit to me; probably rising to the occasion because Mrs B. was grooming him as if he were an adult horse!

This morning reminded me of the word: 'equanimity'. It suits Havana so well – just as it had suited Cayman.

The phrase: "Oh, alright then!" seems to sum-up the approach of each half-brother to the demands people make.

BRAVERY
Easter Monday, 24 March 2008

*H*avana is too brave!

I put him out this morning, after he'd been in for worming since Saturday night.

He was eager to get out to play. Before I'd even taken off his head collar he was trying to start a game with Flower, who had come to greet him in the gateway. No polite nose touching – just straight into 'grabbing-withers-in-teeth'!

After I'd done the stable, I went back out to the field to check Havana, only to find him trying to play 'nipping and rearing' with Prince who, at five, is the youngest of the adult horses. What was Havana thinking of?

It was Prince who had made him run for his life when the adult horses came into the 'nursery' field only two weeks ago. Prince must weigh three times as much as Havana.

Undeterred, there was Havana, repeatedly lunging at Prince's neck, getting a fold of skin in his teeth and holding onto it until Prince reacted by biting him – at which point Havana would either rear, or sink to his knees in submission.

When Prince got really exasperated, he turned and bucked. There was a sickening, dull thud as a hind hoof made contact with Havana's breastbone. It must have hurt, but Havana nonchalantly trotted round Prince in a large circle, before renewing his assault on Prince's neck.

Watching made me anxious, but I know that if you are a young horse, this is how important lessons are learned about your place in the herd.

Thankfully, Prince soon went off to eat haylage with the other adults and Rollo, so Havana had to make do with playing 'biting withers' with Flower.

ORNAMENTS
Tuesday, 25 March 2008

*T*his evening Havana could not have looked sweeter!

He extricated himself from the banquet around the haylage bale and walked decisively across the field to me, with a scattering of ornamental hailstones on his rump and a 'secondary forelock' of haylage looped over one ear.

"… ornamental hailstones … and a 'secondary forelock' of haylage"

DIPLOMACY
Thursday, 27 March 2008

*N*egotiations for a place round the new haylage bale are worthy of The United Nations.

Havana's disrespectful attempt to barge straight in was instantly rebuffed by the 'elder statesmen'.

Anyway, he could not have been *that* hungry as he had only just finished his breakfast.

His over-sycophantic attempt at conveying submission by 'mouthing' did not wash; and even his strategic alliance with Faith failed – with both being chased off by one of the Beauties. (In the herd there are *two* black mares with white stars and they are both called Black Beauty. As they originally had different owners that's not as silly as it sounds!)

When I went back into the field to say goodbye to Havana after I'd done the stable, I was shocked to see a one-inch-square area of hair missing from the point of his nearside shoulder – he had obviously not got out of the way of Beauty's teeth fast enough.

He *will* learn diplomacy … or he'll end up looking very tatty!

ANYONE FOR TENNIS?
Friday, 28 March 2008

*H*e really is asking to get 'duffed-up'.

When 'fluffy, fat little spoilt boy' emerged after breakfast from a luxurious night in his cosy stable, it was evident from the way the others were standing – heads down, in a sodden row along the wire fence, like Victorian London Hackney carriage horses – that they had had a miserable, wet night; and it was *still* raining.

Why then, did Havana think it would be a good idea to try to agitate someone – *anyone* – into a game?

He could not have been more annoying to the other horses if he'd bowled up asking: "Anyone for tennis?"

DEMONSTRATION
Saturday, 29 March 2008

*H*avana has been in for a few nights, as it's been so cold; I can tell when he'd rather stay out though.

On Wednesday night, he brought Flower to the gate with him to tell me he'd rather stay out with her.

On Thursday he brought Flower *and* her mother, Faith, to emphasise the point.

Yesterday, Flower and Faith came again and, once he was outside the field, he refused to move from the gate for a while in protest at being removed from his friends.

Tonight, the protest was the same as last night. However, to make it even clearer that he really didn't think he should be going in, he again refused to move and this time added very demonstrative pawing the ground, with an extravagantly high knee action.

It was a good five minutes before he decided he *would* come with me after all.

CHEEKY
Wednesday, 2 April 2008

*H*avana clearly doesn't heed my warnings that he must be respectful to the adult horses.

This morning his offside hip was missing some hair, probably from another bite for being cheeky.

I'm teaching him to eat from a flat bucket on the ground, without waving his front feet around and sending it flying.

Previously I've been holding his feed bucket, but it's time he learned.

He's doing quite well.

ELATED
Friday, 4 April 2008

*W*hat an amazing experience!

I brought Havana in from the field this morning to give him breakfast.

When I put him back into the field, we stood by the gate.

I had just taken off his head collar; it was very warm and sunny and Havana obviously wasn't in a hurry to go off to eat grass, so he stood facing me as I tickled under his jaw.

Then he put his muzzle onto my shoulder – up against my neck – and closed his eyes.

We stayed like that for such a long time that I felt as if my spine was about to collapse, as I had the full weight of his head on my shoulder.

Very gently, so as not to disturb him, I shifted my weight slightly. Havana then moved his muzzle from my shoulder and planted it firmly on my right cheekbone – pressing quite hard.

I had time to realise that he wasn't going anywhere.
I made my own mind very still.

It was then completely filled … *with Cayman.*

I was aware that, although Havana's body was there in front of me, it was an empty shell. Havana's spirit *was not there,* only Cayman's – and it was *immense.*

Cayman looked exactly as he did when he was twelve: 17hh, white, and very kind.

I had been worrying a lot and feeling anxious. Now I felt reassured, really loved and comforted.

In my mind, I told Cayman that I knew he was there and I loved him.

After what seemed like an eternity, Havana detached himself from me, went over to the nearby water trough, had a long drink, then walked purposefully off down the field.

I was left stupefied: rooted to the spot and conscious of an aura filling my body.

All of my worry had gone and I felt elated.

CONFIDENCE
Saturday, 5 April 2008

*H*avana is so brave!

This morning, we went exploring in the front field. A couple of weeks ago, he had seen the blue tarpaulin lying by the barn for the first time; he had been very wary of it, breathing heavily and not wanting to go too close.

The second time, he noticed some tasty grass right by the edge of the tarpaulin and – keeping a close eye *and ear* on it – managed to nibble the grass.

The third time, he made straight for the grass.

After he had eaten for a while, I tested him by asking him to walk forward.

There was a two-foot strip of tarpaulin right in front of him that I assumed he would have to walk on – but no! He briefly assessed the situation before, disdainfully, taking a long, elegant stride right over the offending piece of tarpaulin.

Today, he was so unconcerned by the tarpaulin that, when I deliberately walked over it so it made crunching noises, he happily joined me – but quickly became exasperated because it hadn't grown any grass.

He tried pawing it to see whether that revealed grass. When it didn't, he obviously couldn't see the point in hanging around on it any longer, so walked across its crunchy surface to the grass on the other side, as if the blue tarpaulin was no more than a minor inconvenience.

What lovely confidence he has.

CALM
Wednesday, 9 April 2008

*W*hen I arrived this morning to give Havana his breakfast, I got a lovely 'greeting whinny' from him as he looked over the stable door.

Then I was waylaid and talked to Jan for a few minutes.

Havana could see me standing in the yard – and I clearly *wasn't* getting on with making his feed.

Rather than becoming agitated and 'weaving' (swaying from side-to-side), or whirling impatiently around his stable, Havana just stood there very sweetly … watching.

His calmness and self-assurance are lovely.

This evening in his stable, I noticed how Havana is getting longer from nose to tail and what good bone he has, particularly his thigh.

He's so beautiful.

STEPLADDER
Thursday, 10 April 2008

*T*onight Havana met his first stepladder.

He was confidently bowling along to the yard to have his evening feed in the stable, when there it was standing in the middle of the yard – as shiny as you like!

Havana stopped dead; put his head up high, widened his eyes, and flared his nostrils. He obviously didn't trust this creature.

To get to the stable he had to go past the stepladder, so I needed to reassure him that it was not going to hurt him.

The long lead rope enabled me to keep hold of Havana as I strode up to the ladder and stroked it, while reassuring him that it was a "nice ladder", even a "lovely ladder".

Incredulously, Havana watched me enthusing about the ladder – and clearly not being attacked by it – which gave him the courage to walk a few paces closer, still with a very quizzical expression. Using his own momentum, I encouraged Havana to circle the ladder, which he did, warily.

It had still not attacked him – nor even moved – and still I was stroking and praising it.

Finally, only about five minutes after first seeing it, Havana was brave enough to sniff the ladder – very gingerly at first. Then, with a bit more encouragement from me, he gave it a thorough, investigative sniff.

The next morning the ladder had gone but, even if it had still been there, I really don't think Havana would have given it a second glance.

He's quick to learn.

BEETLE
Friday, 11 April 2008

Today Mrs B. came to check on Havana's progress and, as usual, he was a complete star.

As it was pouring with rain I had mucked out round him after breakfast; he was not at all bothered by the intrusion of the fork – with the unnecessarily long handle.

I had also groomed him.

When Mrs B. arrived he looked angelic; beautifully groomed, in the clean stable and pulling at his hay net.

We chatted, one on each side of him, and he seemed lulled by our voices.

When it stopped raining we went exploring in the front field.

This time, Havana had no hesitation in trampling over the tarpaulin. As we were about to leave the field, he stopped by a ten-foot-high mound of fresh earth (the spoil from drainage excavations in the muddy paddock).

I decided this was a good opportunity to see whether we could have a game of 'follow-my-leader' up one of the 'giant molehills'.

Havana watched me stride up to the top of the mound nearest the gate.

He was at the full length of his twelve-foot lead rope; a gentle tug and some encouraging words from me had him bounding onto the top of the mound too. As he came up, I moved down the other side a little way to make room for him.

The top of the mound was very soft soil. It was inevitable ...!

Despite the fact that he had just been groomed, Havana's knees buckled ... he sank down ... and rolled.

Not a good idea on top of a mound of loose soil!

There was nothing around him from which to push off so he could get back onto his feet.

Like a beetle on its back, all four legs flailed in the air as he slid on the flux of loose soil until he was halfway down the mound.

He managed to gain some traction and, finally getting on his feet, stumbled to the bottom, looking surprised and obviously thinking:

"*That doesn't usually happen when I roll!*"

Although he can do some really clever things, Havana *is* still a baby.

"That doesn't usually happen when I roll!"

LAZY
Monday, 14 April 2008

It was like trying to get your lazy teenage son out of bed!

In fairness to Havana, he *had* probably been up all night grazing and eating hay – and most of the other horses *were* lying down.

It was 9.30 a.m. and I had come to give him his breakfast but, for that, he needed to get up and walk with me to the yard.

It would cause a riot if I attempted to feed him in the field – the other horses would notice and want breakfast too.

Havana clearly could not see the sense in getting up when he was happily dozing, with a full belly. Why should he want to move?

He's so used to me and so totally unphased by anything I do to him, that my whole armoury of tricks had little effect.

I tried: unfolding his front legs … he carried on dozing; lifting a hind leg … the same; lifting his tail … he didn't notice; tickling his tummy … unconcerned; rocking him, by pushing his hip … he just rocked back and forth.

He was quite happy to be mauled and most of the time his eyes weren't even open.

Eventually, I pressed some bits of apple between his teeth.

The brain activity caused by food slowly woke him up until he could actually get to his feet. He then followed me obligingly to the yard where, now fully awake, he did enjoy his breakfast.

HOT POTATO
Wednesday, 16 April 2008

*T*oday was freezing! The wind was really sharp.
Most of my horsey clothes were in the wash because they made me feel as if I had fleas.

I got absolutely frozen in the yard at Jennifer's farm – probably because I didn't have enough clothes on.

By the time I got to Havana to give him his late breakfast, I was worried that he would also be cold.

I needn't have worried; with his coat all puffed-up he was like a fluffy, hot potato. He's so much better designed than I am! I had to hug him *a lot* to get warm again.

He didn't seem to mind warming me up; it was very effective and I soon felt much better.

MAGICIAN'S RABBIT
Friday, 18 April 2008

*A*s I walked across the field I could see all of the horses grazing around the two enormous, cylindrical, haylage bales by the hedge; all *except* Havana!

Where was he?

I scanned the horses again as I got closer, but still *no* Havana – I was getting worried.

Suddenly – like a rabbit popping-up from a magician's top hat – there he was, blinking at me with a sweet, surprised expression.

He had been standing directly behind a bale – so it totally obscured his body – with his entire head down the 'nose hole' in the centre. From a distance, his neck is about the same colour as the haylage so that was invisible too.

He must have been in a world of his own, with the sound of his munching amplified in the 'nose hole' and all external sound muffled by the thick walls of the bale. No wonder he didn't hear me approach.

He looked so surprised to see me in front of him; as if *I* had just appeared by magic!

TRANCE
Monday, 21 April 2008

I thought it was about time Havana learned to do 'big boys'' grooming, outside; that is being tied-up to be groomed, without a hay net to occupy him.

I gave him his breakfast in the usual place behind the stables. When he had finished, he looked expectantly at the space on the wall where I usually tie his hay net, he seemed surprised that it wasn't there. He looked quizzically at me, as if I might have made a mistake and forgotten his hay.

I told him I had not made a mistake. To settle him, I rubbed his ears and his forehead. As he lowered his head, I put my forehead against his and we stayed like that for a while.

Eventually, I noticed Havana's eyes were closed. He was in a sleepy-trance. As we really did need to get on with grooming, I quietly called his name.

He hauled himself out of his slumber with a languorous stretch: arching his neck ... pulling his head in towards his chest ... growing by at least two hands ... and stretching out a hind leg.

I did some grooming, but then couldn't resist resting my face on top of his head between his little velvety ears. In no time, we both had our eyes closed.

Another nap later, I roused Havana and I could hardly believe it when his second, luxurious, arch-necked stretch proved conclusively that he *had* fallen straight back into his second sleepy-trance.

I led him back out to the field.

After I had taken off his head collar it was clear, from the way he stayed close to me, that he didn't want me to rush off. Some more gentle forehead stroking produced sleepy-trance number three.

I did have to put the head collar away in the tack room, so quietly extricated myself from him to do this.

As I got into my car and drove off, Havana was still standing, droopily, by the gate – immersed in a sleepy world of his own.

I love his tranquillity.

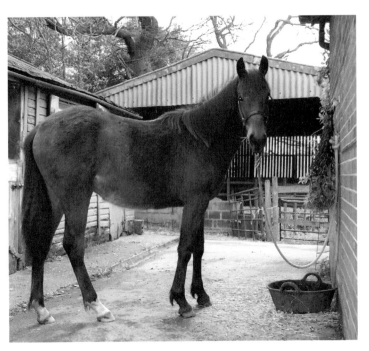

"… where I usually tie his hay net."

ESCORT
Monday, 28 April 2008

*H*avana got *twenty* out of ten this morning for exploring in the front field – he was brilliant!

I had intended to groom him before we went exploring, but it was raining; so he had his breakfast in the stable and then, because his back was still damp, I decided instead to give him a good scratching, with both hands, down his neck and around his ears.

He's got so much loose hair; he really enjoyed being scratched – and it re-bonded us just as much as grooming would have done.

In the front field, Havana's manners were impeccable.

First we went through the barn, past the trampoline. The ground under the barn is having last winter's muck scraped off it, so the cleared areas looked different, but Havana wasn't bothered.

We came out in the corner of the field, walked round the muck heap and then, very bravely, Havana strode diagonally right across the open field to the big log on the far side.

He walked by my shoulder on a loose rope; he wasn't rushing or frightened. He seemed totally in command of the situation, escorting me, rather than relying on me for confidence. I was very impressed.

He was rewarded with ten minutes' grazing, whilst I sat on the big log.

After that, he walked positively to the mound of earth in the corner by the gate and enjoyed going up one side and down the other side with me – without trying to roll.

He seems to have got the hang of that game now!

As he was so confident, I asked him to walk along the lane with me; that was effortless.

Apart from a brief stop to look over the fence at the four horses in the field – and a bit of grass when he decided they weren't really very interesting – Havana marched along right to the end of the lane: *'the outside world'!*

I was so pleased with him that he was rewarded with more grazing in the gateway at the end of the lane.

He would have continued walking with me out onto the quiet, narrow road, but I decided he had done enough for one day. I don't want anything in 'the outside world' to frighten him and dent his confidence.

His brain is obviously developing fast; it won't be long before we do go exploring in 'the outside world'.

RESCUE
Thursday, 8 May 2008

I don't think Havana realised how much he'd grown.

I brought him into the stable for worming, but the lure of the new straw bed was too much for him. The instant he was in, his knees buckled and he was rolling.

Last time he did this in the stable it wasn't a problem as he was littler – but not any more!

As he tried to roll to his right, the wooden wall stopped him abruptly: he was stuck. He couldn't continue the roll to the right, nor could he roll back to his left, because every time he tried to push off from the wall his hooves just slipped along it.

After a few tries he just lay there, all four legs in the air, looking up at me.

It's a good job I regularly approach him in the field when he's sitting down. He's used to me standing over him, so doesn't panic; but he did seem a bit confused now that he was upside down too.

This was serious. Havana was 'cast': a potentially fatal position for a horse.

When he is the right way up, a horse's stomach, intestines and other abdominal organs are in the right place, allowing his lungs to function. He can breathe – and all is well.

When you turn a horse upside down, the weight of his stomach and other organs on his lungs prevents them working properly and he has difficulty breathing. If he *can't* get up – and there's no one there to help him – he will eventually suffocate.

Thank Goodness Havana was neither elderly and arthritic, nor alone!

I kept calm and was just thinking about requesting some urgent muscle power – in the form of Den (the farmer) and his adult son – to help me push Havana away from the wall, when he started to wriggle again.

It was easy to see the problem; the clean, new straw was slippery. Havana's back and rump couldn't dig into anything firm. There was no solid point from which he could roll onto his side and so get back on his feet.

So much for my banks of straw around the edges of Havana's bed. I'd done them as I always did, about a foot wide, but now their inadequacy was clear. To be effective, they would need to be wider than the length of a horse's legs to keep him completely off the wall.

I encouraged Havana:

"Come on boy – you can do it! Do some more wriggling – *come on!*" It worked! Havana put all his effort into one huge wriggle of his young athletic back, and was suddenly standing up.

He did look surprised – and ever so sweet; standing blinking at me, with straw in his ears and his forelock. Poor little thing, he'd given himself such a shock.

Havana's tribulations were not over yet though.

He had come in for worming – so *worming* was what we had to do. Two syringes of apple juice went down very easily; next came the end of an old syringe of wormer – just a few millilitres that needed using up. It had gone chewy and was easy for Havana to spit out, but equally easy for me to pick up from the straw and push back into his mouth.

He obviously did not like the taste but, by clamping my hands round his nose and lower jaw, I managed to keep his mouth shut long enough for it to dissolve. He got another syringe of apple juice as a reward, but it wasn't over. I still had to get the major part of the dose, from a new syringe of wormer, down his throat.

Some squirted up the outside corner of his mouth as he objected by throwing his head up, but it was only token resistance and he quickly resigned himself, so most of the wormer did go on his tongue.

More apple juice reassured him I was not really trying to poison him.

Havana must have thought everything was conspiring against him tonight, when – from nowhere – big, biting midges swarmed around him. It was warm and they must have been attracted to the light in the stable.

Liz to the rescue!

I remembered there was some 'human' insect repellent in our bucket of grooming things. I thought if it was good enough for Ricky and me, then it was good enough for Havana.

He didn't mind the noise of the spray and in no time the invisible force field around him was evident. The midges hovered, but could not land.

I often feel that Havana thinks I rescue him from things; it's a really rewarding feeling.

Tonight, he seemed not to blame me for giving him a slippery straw bed, wormer and midges.

Instead, I felt that he was grateful for reassurance when he was upside down, apple juice, and a magic, midge-repelling force field.

He settled down happily for the night … with a huge mound of haylage.

WHINNYING

Sunday, 11 May 2008

*N*ot all horses are equally vocal. Some whinny often, others almost never. The sounds of horses' whinnies are as individual as they are, and they don't all whinny about the same things.

Last Friday, Havana had to stay in his stable after having been wormed. As there wasn't much to do he had decided, in the afternoon, to sit down for a while in the middle of his bed and snooze.

His appreciation – when I arrived unexpectedly to entertain him – was evident in the sweetest whinny, bursting with relieved surprise, which greeted me.

Today, everyone was grazing towards the bottom of the field on the fresh grass where the electric fence had been moved.

I didn't want to disturb Havana so, after I had checked him, I walked away up the field, deliberately not looking back so as not to attract his attention.

When I was three-quarters of the way to the gate, I *did* look over my shoulder and saw Havana resolutely making his way up the field after me.

I thought this was very sweet, so walked faster to get to the cow parsley growing up the farm lane, and quickly gather some for him to eat.

Havana got to the top of the field but – being unable to see me anywhere – had stopped, confused about where I had gone.

When he saw me coming back through the gate – with a huge bouquet of cow parsley – he whinnied in amazement that I *was* still there and was bringing him one of his favourite tasty plants!

I felt shocked as I realised that in something as individual to horses as whinnying, what they whinny about, and what their whinnies sound like, Havana is so similar to Cayman.

These were exactly the sort of situations in which Cayman had whinnied and, when Cayman whinnied, it was his expression of exactly the same emotions. In fact, I don't remember Cayman doing any other sort of whinny!

'Relieved surprised' whinnies are characteristic of each of these sons of Falconwood – although, why should I be surprised?

FROG

Monday, 19 May 2008

I must not forget that Havana is only fifteen months old.

He resisted temptation beyond endurance as we walked across the front field, from the barn to the log.

He had already investigated the trampoline in the barn; he was sure that under the blue plastic strips around its edge he would find something to eat, if only he could position his teeth at just the right angle.

I had discouraged him; the padded strips are a safety feature and the two boys who play on the trampoline would not appreciate the padding being rearranged by a food-fixated little horse.

We were just coming back from the log to the gate when – all of a sudden – Havana was not by my side.

He had propelled himself upwards and outwards, so he was suddenly at the end of the rope, twelve feet away from me.

Poor little thing, his excitement at walking in a big field – with grass up to his knees – had brimmed over in one big, excited leap.

He looked a bit startled, as if his legs catapulting him twelve feet away had surprised even him!

To keep the excitement under control, we walked a few tight circles on the way to the gate, just so neither of us got any more surprises.

After that, walking the length of the farm lane to 'the outside world' was very straightforward.

The luscious long grass and cow parsley in the gateway by the road at the end of the lane was a dream-come-true for Havana.

The people at the farm next door had put their bottles and cans out in a big green box for recycling. When Havana saw it, he was not at all sure whether to trust it. But it didn't move and, after he had settled himself with a lot of lovely grass, he decided to go over to it and stick his nose in amongst the contents. The box did not retaliate in any way, so he knew it was not something to be bothered by.

I always hope that a car will come quietly along the road at the end of the lane while Havana is grazing in the gateway. He needs to know that cars go along roads – so far though, no cars.

A lethargic frog took its time … to hop … slowly … across the road towards us; Havana didn't mind that at all.

PLAYTIME
Thursday, 22 May 2008

*T*he midges were very annoying this evening.

All of the horses were around the gateway, stamping, swishing their tails and kicking under their bellies.

After I had put insect repellent on Havana, by spraying it onto my hand then stroking him all over (which he now prefers to having it sprayed on), I told him there was no point in standing around the gate getting cross with the midges; we might as well go down the field and play a game.

He must have agreed, because he followed me happily down the field. The others must have agreed too, because they all came as well!

In the top corner of the field, there are two, upright, sawn-off telegraph poles and one 'lying-down' one. The upright poles are for the horses to rub against when they are itchy, as there aren't any trees in the field.

Unfortunately, the trunk of the big, old, oak tree – whose canopy provides so much shelter for the horses – is actually on the other side of the barbed wire and sheep netting fence, so inaccessible for relieving their itches.

In practice though, itchy horses will make for whatever relief is nearest, when they are afflicted with an aggravating tickle. So, despite the thoughtful inclusion of telegraph pole 'scratching posts' in their field, it is very often the fence posts which bear the brunt of half-ton itchy rumps, so they are incessantly loosened, or even snapped off at the ground. Maintaining horse-proof fences is a constant battle.

I thought that we could play at jumping over the lying-down telegraph pole.

To encourage Havana, I energetically trotted up to the pole and jumped over it. Havana looked surprised.

Then, I trotted back over the pole, towards him. Now he looked bemused.

To reassure him, I sat down on the middle of the pole and drummed my hands on it. This attracted his attention sufficiently for him to walk over to investigate it.

I stood up again – clearing the way for Havana to step over the pole – and called to him, encouragingly.

He decided the best way to get to me was to walk around the end, but that didn't work because I quickly repositioned myself on the other side, facing him. Undeterred, he very patiently walked around the other end of the pole to me.

By this time, Rollo, who is a year older than Havana, had become curious about what we were doing and walked up to the pole. With a little verbal encouragement from me, he picked up first one front foot, then the other, then his back feet – and walked over the pole.

I thought how fortunate I was to have two young horses on whom to try out my experiment; having Rollo to compare Havana with was helpful.

It was quite clear that Havana is not yet mature enough to sort out what to do with the pole – or at least to do it *my* way.

I do know that Havana is good at following though! He was ever so good at our next game, readily following me in a figure-of-eight: in and out, and round, the two standing telegraph poles, which are about ten feet apart.

Havana's figure-of-eight earned him some cow parsley and a tail scratch.

Again, Rollo came up to see what we were doing. Some provocative mutual nipping soon resulted in both horses trotting off down the field, side by side, alternately biting each other's withers.

Now it was *real* 'horsey playtime'!

CARS
Saturday, 24 May 2008

*S*ue, from Gunstone Hall stables, came to see Havana again today. She is Alfie's person; Alfie is her first horse – a kind, dark bay, 16.2hh, Thoroughbred cross Draught – who now lives in what was Cayman's stable.

I had visited Gunstone shortly after Cayman's death and introduced myself to Sue. She told me that when she first brought Alfie there, the tragic circumstances of the stable suddenly becoming free were explained to her.

The whole yard had been in mourning.

The day after Cayman had been rushed away to Liverpool University's Equine Hospital for colic surgery, the husband of one of the horse owners arrived at the yard to collect his wife and daughters. Sensing the sorrow hanging over the entire place, seeing unusually sombre-looking owners going about their morning stable routines, then being met by his tearful family, it is easy to see how he drew the (thankfully mistaken) conclusion that a person must have died, rather than one of the horses.

Everyone loved Cayman.

Sue's complete sensitivity and – although she had never met him – her genuine respect for Cayman, meant that we immediately became friends.

I was particularly touched when Sue told me, at our first meeting, that when she and Alfie 'moved into' Cayman's stable, she could feel it was "full of love".

Sue said she had been surprised at how quickly Alfie had settled in his new stable, and at how contented he was there; she felt the atmosphere in the stable reassured Alfie that this was 'a good place'.

I was glad that Sue, knowing our full story, was keen to keep up-to-date with Havana's development and that she was kind enough to visit us.

As Sue and I walked down the farm lane, chatting, Havana walked ever so nicely beside us to 'the outside world'; only stopping once to have a look at the horses in the field at the side of the lane – whilst nibbling some cow parsley.

As usual, Havana's reward was to graze in the big gateway at the end of the lane, where there is a lot of long grass and more cow parsley; he was quite relaxed there.

I was just telling Sue that Havana was very good, but I didn't think he knew he was actually grazing by a road that cars used, because we had never seen one, when a car approached and stopped right by us! Its driver wanted directions to a house which neither Sue nor I knew.

Havana acknowledged the car by briefly putting his head up as it approached, but decided not to let it interrupt his grazing.

Sue and I were agreeing that it had been a very good introduction for Havana to the idea of cars on the road, when – out of nowhere – cars appeared from *both* directions. They only avoided hitting each other because one screeched to a halt on the gravel at the end of the farm lane where we were standing.

Havana didn't even look up from the grass!

OAK TREE
Wednesday, 28 May 2008

*T*his evening it was pouring with rain, but warm.

The row of bedraggled horses were standing side-by-side, heads down – under the big oak tree near the gate.

I approached very gently … and quietly … so as not to disturb anyone.

Havana was at the far end of the row. I could see that although his eyes were open, they were glazed – he was in a trance.

I was standing two feet from his nose before he noticed I was there.

His dazed blinking and arched-neck stretch as he roused were lovely.

I felt so privileged to be permitted by the herd to join their row, next to Havana, under the tree.

What a joyous experience for my senses to smell 'warm, wet horse', and listen to big, round, raindrops plopping onto the canopy of shiny oak leaves above; with each leaf radiating its own, early-summer, green light.

It was an honour to be part of the sheltering group – equine *and* human – all equally embraced by the mystical energy of the tree.

In no time Havana slid back into drowsy slumber, standing by my side, eyes open … but fast asleep.

"… under the canopy of the big oak tree …"

WILD CHILDREN
Thursday, 29 May 2008

*H*avana had never seen 'wild children' in his field before.

The sight of two brightly-coloured ones – skipping down the field to meet him – was all too much. He tried to run away and very quickly got to the end of his twelve-foot rope; fortunately, I was holding onto it tightly.

After I had stopped Alex and Hattie cascading towards us, by shouting to them to: "STAND STILL!" – I walked to Havana, speaking quietly, and stroked his forehead to reassure him that he need not be worried about these cavorting children.

I told him they were young people – just as he is a young horse – and, like him, they enjoyed playing and jumping about.

Havana was soon more reassured, but still stood close to me, his head high, incredulously watching Alex and Hattie.

I encouraged him to walk up the field with me to meet them but he was reluctant; he didn't feel *that* brave!

Instead, he stood watching them intently as they approached him – quietly this time.

By the time they had reached Havana, held out their hands for him to sniff and then stroked his nose, he had decided children were probably not frightening after all.

We all walked up the field together and were joined at the gate by Mr and Mrs B.

After Havana had had some food and settled down with a haylage net, he was quite happy for Alex to groom him.

"… children were probably not frightening after all."

SPLINT
Friday, 30 May 2008

*P*hew – Jennifer has put my mind at rest! She is so knowledgeable and helpful.

I had been worried about Havana's leg.

On Tuesday, I noticed a longish, shallow lump on the inside of his near fore, halfway between his knee and fetlock. When I first saw it, he was standing with the others by the water trough.

It must be human nature always to think the worst when you care so much. Havana has such delicate, Thoroughbred legs – and is in a field of hefty Cobs; I feared his leg was broken.

As I watched – not actually wanting to see him move for fear of what it would reveal – he turned from the trough *and walked away normally.*

Thank goodness. What a relief!

In an instant, I had squeezed between the horizontal rails of the fence, into the field, and was running my hands down both of Havana's front legs simultaneously; he didn't mind at all.

No cut, no heat, no tenderness – in fact, the lump felt like *bone.*

Havana's excited canter around the field as I was leaving confirmed no lameness either.

This didn't seem like a 'call the vet' situation. I was baffled.

The next morning, Havana's leg was exactly the same and when I picked-out his hooves he had no difficulty standing with his weight on the 'lumpy' leg, whilst I picked-out the other foot.

I left a telephone message for Jennifer. She had been at the Stafford County Show and returned my call as soon as she got home:

"It sounds like your boy's thrown a splint." I said that I thought horses only got splints from too much work on hard ground.

"A horse I once entered for the Highland Show developed a splint the size of a golf ball overnight – the night before the show!" was Jennifer's informative response.

"Is he having a growth spurt?" she asked. I said that I didn't really notice him growing because I see him twice a day, but my father – who had just seen Havana after about six weeks – thought he had "shot up".

I was so grateful for Jennifer's kind advice that Havana would "grow into" his splint.

There really is no substitute for experience!

MORE FRESH GRASS
Saturday, 31 May 2008

The electric fence has been moved back a few more yards.

Most of the horses were grazing along the new strip of fresh grass; Flower and Rollo were sitting down – but where was Havana?

I don't worry as much as I used to when I can't see Havana as he's always there – it's simply a matter of finding him.

Spotted! Yes, I was sure that what looked like a golden, over-sized medicine ball, just protruding above the long grass, was Havana's belly … and it was.

As I got closer I could see him lying flat out, having stuffed himself.

He's become so used to me approaching when he's lying down that he didn't even raise his head. He was in 'grass heaven', occasionally pulling a mouthful of lush grass which happened to be close enough to his muzzle to require no effort.

This was an ideal opportunity to look in his mouth.

A few days ago I had noticed nasty-looking (but healing) ulcerations at each inner side of his top lip. As he was lying down, I had the chance to run a finger along his, unusually inactive, bottom teeth. Sure enough, on the bottom corner tooth, corresponding with the worst ulcer, I felt a sharp point.

Oh dear! Poor Havana. Although they are only milk teeth – which will soon fall out and be replaced by permanent ones – I think we need the dentist. A dental examination will be a bit scary for such a baby, but Geraint is very gentle and we don't want any more ulcers.

Eventually, Havana rolled luxuriantly and then got up. Doing an enormous poo gave him room to carry on mowing the long grass, without a care in the world.

UNFRIENDLY NEIGHBOURS
Sunday, 1 June 2008

I decided to show Ricky how brave Havana is at going down the farm lane to graze in the gateway at the end.

Ricky walked with us to the gateway and, as soon as we got there, Havana's nose vanished into the long grass. As all seemed well, Ricky then marched off down the road for a twenty-minute brisk walk whilst Havana grazed.

Ricky had only gone about fifty yards, when two rough-looking skewbald horses came careering up the field at the side of the other farm lane, which is parallel to ours.

They had seen Havana and stood by their fence, whinnying in a way which, to me, did not sound very friendly.

Immediately, Havana's head went up high; next, his whole body was in the air, with his front legs flailing. He struck my chest with a front hoof but, fortunately, I was wearing 'riot gear': body protector, hat and gloves, so was not injured.

Havana took the initiative to *'get to a safe place, quickly!'* by walking, very purposefully, back down the farm lane. It's a good job we use a twelve-foot rope, which enabled Havana to tow me to safety with him – and that he doesn't kick!

Halfway down the lane, his 'eating instinct' got the better of him, when he spotted some particularly appetizing leaves in the hedge. This enabled me to regain some control by getting up to Havana's shoulder.

As I led him – in a more conventional way – he was still very agitated and light on his feet. Each time I felt his energy level about to overflow into another attempt at flight, I turned him in a very tight circle.

We circled our way back to the yard and then, to prove that I really was in charge, we walked around the house and back to the start of the farm lane, before I opened the gate and let Havana back into his field.

I half expected him to gallop off to the bottom of the field and the security of his herd but, instead, he had a drink from the trough, then came back to me – to have his rump 'scrumbled' (roughly massaged) – before calmly walking off down the field, apparently none the worse for his fright.

GAMES
Wednesday, 4 June 2008

*T*his evening, I decided that Havana might like to play some games.

It was a beautiful, golden evening; the horses were relaxed, spread-out, grazing at the bottom of the field. As I approached, Havana left the others – and the grass – and walked up the field to meet me. This boded well for games; he was obviously ready for some entertainment.

Having his head collar put on confirmed, to him, that we were going to 'do something'. He looked alert and keen to find out what we would do.

Together, we walked to the top corner of the field where the telegraph pole 'scratching posts' are.

I don't know what the horizontal pole is really for – perhaps it just never got put up – but Havana and I found a good use for it. The pieces of carrot that miraculously appeared in the grass, on either side of the pole, encouraged Havana to step neatly over it in both directions.

We did this a few times.

As I didn't want Havana to get bored, we then moved on to something else: I would teach Havana to back-up, by standing a few feet in front of him and wiggling the rope attached to his head collar.

The idea is that when the rope turns into 'a snake', and the person on the other end of it scowls angrily, the horse feels uncomfortable, so takes a step back.

That's the idea … but Havana's approach was different.

He's so confident that, when the white rope started to gently ripple towards him, he didn't react. As the ripple turned into a more energetic wriggle, Havana's only reaction was to look at me quizzically, as if to ask me what I thought I was doing.

The effect of my 'angry face' was simply a disconcerted expression from Havana, as if he was thinking, "*There must be some mistake!*"

He obviously did not consider it remotely possible that I would either be sending him away from me, or being unfriendly towards him.

I love his self-confidence!

We'll have to work on this exercise ….

ELEPHANTS
Thursday, 5 June 2008

It was like watching a herd of elephants.

This morning was warm, and one of the Beauties decided that it was time for water. Languorously, she led the way, with the other Beauty following her, up the gentle incline of the field to the trough. Grace, the mare who grazes by herself, fell in behind with Prince, in the slow procession. (Faith was in her stable).

Next Rollo, and then finally – almost as an afterthought – Havana and Flower, who had been grazing together right at the bottom of the field, could not resist the unconscious effect of the whole herd moving, so joined in at the back.

There isn't room for everyone to drink at once. When the two Beauties had drunk their fill, they peeled away – leaving Grace. In an orderly fashion, Prince and Rollo replaced them.

By this time, Havana and Flower had arrived at the top of the field.

They know that, as the two junior members of the herd, they must wait their turn. They didn't even attempt to go near the trough – loitering instead to one side, near the gate – until Grace, Prince and Rollo moved off and they could drink in peace together.

There is no substitute for Havana being in a mixed herd like this; not only is he learning 'how to be a horse', but also the manners he is learning from the older mares make my job, as his human teacher, so much easier.

MINERALS
Friday, 6 June 2008

*T*his evening, I saw behaviour from Havana that I have never seen from a horse before.

He found a patch of light soil under an old tree stump, with what looked like a rabbits' burrow under it, and was intent on eating small quantities of soil.

He really was swallowing it! I could hear the 'glug' sound made by his throat due to the effort of moving something so dry down his gullet.

If Havana did not have access to a mineral lick, I would have understood why he was eating soil; but there are two mineral licks roped to the fence, near the water trough.

Hunger could not be the cause; there is so much grass that he could not possibly be hungry.

Curious, I licked my finger, stuck it in the soil and then put it in my mouth (probably not hygienic or sensible), so I could taste what Havana tasted.

It was very gritty (no surprise!) but did not taste of iron, salt or anything I recognised.

I was none the wiser, and it took a lot of spitting to eject the grit.

I'll just have to trust that Havana knew what he was doing; his determination certainly suggested that he did.

Possibly, he just could not be bothered to walk all the way up the field to the mineral licks.

However, what I prefer to believe is that he was again manifesting his marvellous natural instinct to self-medicate.

Whatever he needed is very likely to have been in that gritty soil.

RUDENESS
Monday, 9 June 2008

*H*avana looked surprised as he walked to the gate this morning as it was the first time he had ever seen me in a dress.

The weather was so hot that long, pale bits of me, which he had never seen before, were sticking out each end of my sundress. He was particularly intrigued by the ones at the bottom; my bare legs.

As soon as I was in the field, Havana felt compelled to investigate thoroughly.

Shoving your nose up her dress really is not the way to greet a lady!

Having established how my legs smelled, Havana very inquisitively gave my chest and shoulders a slow, systematic sniff, eventually – when he was satisfied he had sniffed enough – resting his muzzle in the middle of my chest and closing his eyes.

He's irresistible when he does this.

In turn, I rested the side of my face on Havana's forehead and gently stroked both sides of his jaw as we stood peacefully together in the sun. However, the rumbustious monster inhabiting Havana's body this evening – when Judy came to visit – bore no resemblance to this morning's little angel.

Judy is not at all used to horses. Upon seeing us, Havana detached himself from the grass and made a beeline for 'the visitor'.

He always does this. I suppose he already knows that I'm going to be nice to him, so it's in his interests to make an impact on the person he doesn't know.

'Impact' is the word! Havana confidently bowled straight up to Judy and gave her a *friendly* bite on the top of her arm, depositing a mouthful of half-chewed grass on the sleeve of her pristine, cream cardigan.

I was horrified at his rudeness.

Sensibly, Judy decided to go up the field out of Havana's reach. To distract him, and prevent a further assault on Judy, I scratched Havana's rump whilst she retreated.

Sensing that this visitor probably did not want to play with him, Havana went back to grazing.

Judy was very understanding. Having brought up two girls, she rationalised that young horses:

"…like children, have different moods, at different times of day."

I still felt rather ashamed that Havana had been so rude. But, in his defence, I reminded myself that he is only very young, he was 'at home' in his own field and it is good that he is so confident – even with people he doesn't know.

I decided, however, to get him into the stable tomorrow and spend a while grooming him – for a bit of discipline – just to remind him how to be polite around people.

FILLIES

Friday, 13 June 2008

*T*his evening, I had the loveliest demonstration of the pacifist nature of fillies, compared with young geldings.

The midges were biting and Havana was a bit fractious. He marched deliberately up to Rollo, who was grazing, and provocatively nipped his shoulder; the cue to start a game.

Rollo obliged by nipping Havana's shoulder and a game of 'nipping and rearing' developed.

It was quite a sedate game; as if both young horses were playing by set, gentlemanly rules that regulated their movements. Each took turns to nip, rear, nip, and then bow down on one knee – with no one getting hurt.

However, this game was obviously too sedate for Havana, who felt equal to a larger opponent.

Prince, who, with summer grass, must now weigh four times as much as Havana, was his next target. Havana was sparring ... again, a nip on the shoulder.

Prince, tolerant of this little pest who wanted to play, kindly reciprocated with a nip, but thankfully no rear, which could have squashed Havana flat.

Once he had Prince sufficiently engaged in the game, Havana enticed Rollo to re-join it, with another nip.

All three took turns at nipping, with the two younger horses rearing and kneeling too.

Eventually though, Prince and Rollo tired of playing and went back to the more rewarding occupation of eating grass.

Poor Havana had no one to play with except Flower, who had been grazing peacefully, out of the way of the over-energetic males.

Havana's attempt at inciting Flower to a game of 'nipping and rearing', by biting her shoulder, produced a very different result from his identical approach to Rollo and Prince.

Instead of starting to 'fight', Flower very sweetly began nibbling Havana's mane, as if to pacify him by saying:

"No, I don't want to play fighting, but mutual grooming will be nice."

So, that's what they did ... and Havana settled down.

What a difference there is between young geldings and fillies!

"… mutual grooming will be nice."

MICK AND BRUCE
Sunday, 15 June 2008

*L*ast Wednesday, I had taken Havana halfway down the farm lane to look at the big, rough, skewbald horses on the neighbouring farm – from a safe distance.

It hadn't helped that the grass and weeds on either side of the lane had been sprayed with weed killer, turned brown, and wilted – so there was no food at all to distract and placate Havana.

To make him feel better I had taken some carrots which, as far as he was concerned, miraculously appeared on the lane, right at the point where he could see the other horses and they could see us.

Ricky had also been with us, so, the combination of two of his people, *and* carrots, had made Havana less concerned when 'Mick and Bruce' (I had invented appropriately tough names for them) whinnied their threats and insults at their spindly-legged, little upstart of a neighbour.

We hadn't tried to go any further down the lane; I hadn't wanted to ask more of Havana, or to frighten him – this was enough.

Today we did ever so well!

Havana, Ricky and I walked right to the end of the farm lane. As a precaution, I asked Ricky to stand between the entrances to the two parallel farm lanes, so he was between Havana, and Mick and Bruce. I hoped this would make Havana feel protected.

When, like two vigilantes, Mick and Bruce came storming over to investigate, Havana ignored them – concentrating instead on the abundant grass in the gateway.

I had an idea: I asked Ricky to pick some of the long grass and cow parsley from the side of the road and offer it to Mick and Bruce. If Ricky was friendly to them, I thought they would be friendly back – which would comfort Havana.

My idea worked. Even after they had eaten all of the grass and cow parsley, Mick and Bruce stayed by their fence – allowing Ricky to rub their foreheads and stroke their ears.

Everyone felt calm.

Havana evidently felt so safe that he decided to go and talk to Mick and Bruce.

When we got closer, I could see that 'Bruce' is actually *a mare* (sorry Bruce!).

Havana was appropriately deferential; 'mouthing' his submission and inferior status to her.

With Mick – a gelding who looks about Havana's age – Havana was on equal terms; so blowing and sniffing each other's nose was the appropriate greeting.

Introductions over, Havana's attention was diverted by the large, green uncovered box, containing plastic for recycling, which had been put out for collection. Without hesitation, Havana turned his back on Mick and Bruce – who were obviously now his friends – and shoved his nose in amongst the interesting, multi-coloured plastic bottles.

As we walked back down the farm lane, even Mick's excited cavorting across the field (probably because he had had fuss from Ricky *and* cow parsley) did not distract Havana from walking sensibly with his people.

POO
Thursday, 19 June 2008

*W*hat a very obliging little horse!

Today was the day when I should have wormed Havana but, for the first time ever, I decided to have a 'worm egg count' done by the vet, to find out whether Havana actually needed worming. For this, I had to take a sample of poo to the surgery.

Last night I went to check Havana in the field, armed with a washed-out plastic pot, but no poo was produced.

Today was 'D Day'; I really needed a poo sample. I thought about putting him in the stable for a while so I could capture a poo; but as there was no hay left, there wouldn't be anything for him to eat.

I stayed in the field – watching … and waiting … for him to do a poo – for about an hour, but with no luck.

I gave up, and was walking off up the field, through the long grass of the herd's 'dunging area', when Havana lifted his head from grazing and purposefully walked after me.

I don't know whether it was the unconscious effect of walking through the long grass of that particular area that caused it but, miraculously, Havana stopped, lifted up his tail and did a huge amount of poo.

He's never seen me so overjoyed at this routine event, let alone eagerly scoop the poo into a 'tomato and basil soup' pot!

Havana's expression reminded me of another of his truly sweet characteristics: the way he can look both extremely surprised by, yet totally accepting of, the very peculiar things I do.

CAYMAN DREAM
Friday, 20 June 2008

$\mathcal{I}$ knew that when I got the result of the worm egg count Havana would probably need to be wormed.

I was concerned about what to feed him whilst he was in his stable as I had been told not to use the last big bale of haylage – and did not know where I could get a small bale of hay.

* * *

I dreamed that Cayman (who was dark grey) was eating – possibly grazing – in the immediate area outside Havana's brick stable block.

He was letting me know that there *was* food there, all around – that he was content to eat this and I should not worry.

P.S. When I got the result of the worm egg count the following week and needed to bring Havana into his stable to worm him, I had a brainwave.

I would fill his hay nets with *grass*, which I would pull up from the bottom of the field on the other side of the electric fence. The grass is about a foot high here, as the horses cannot get to it.

So that's what I did on Havana's first night in.

After that, Den opened the last big bale of haylage for Havana – it's under the barn next to the stable block.

Just as Cayman had let me know, the food that Havana needed was close by and there really was no need for me to worry!

WORMAL
Tuesday, 24 June 2008

*W*ell – 'Wormal', as Ricky calls him, has certainly wormed his way into Ricky's heart!

This was the last evening, before leaving to work in Dubai for three months, that Ricky was free to come with me to see Havana.

Our early-summer evening visits to Wormal have been lovely.

Ricky appreciates the opportunity to discharge the frustrations of his business day with a brisk fifteen-minute walk, up the hill to the church, down the path through the fields on the other side, under the electric fence and straight into Havana's field.

Often, Havana sees us approaching. His bright, interested expression is a joy – making even Ricky, who is not really very 'horsey', feel happy.

It is an honour to have Havana walk to the fence to meet us. He'll regularly go straight to Ricky, rather than to me. I'm not offended. I think he does this because he knows that I'm definitely 'his person', whereas Ricky is a bit of a novelty, so more worthy of investigation.

Usually, after greeting Havana by stroking him and pulling his ears, which is blissful for Havana (although a 'head-shy' horse might seriously object!), Ricky continues to walk up the field, down the farm lane, along the road at the end and back again, for more exercise.

Whilst Ricky is walking, I check Havana for lumps, bumps, cuts and bruises; and then either 'scrumble' his rump, talk to him, or just stand and watch him grazing, depending on what mood he's in.

This evening, when Ricky said goodbye to Havana, for the first time ever I saw genuine tenderness in the way he scratched under Havana's jaw. The alert little horse had pricked his ears forward and poked-out his muzzle, so Ricky could scratch 'just the right place'.

As Ricky looked into his dark, bright eyes, I know he felt sad to be leaving. I'm sad too – but very, very glad that I've got 'Wormal' to keep me company and to fill my heart with love.

BENDY LEGS
Wednesday, 25 June 2008

A mirror image of the thickening on the inside of Havana's nearside fore cannon bone appeared ten days later on the offside. At first, I had been reassured that it was happening to both legs; this made me think it was meant to happen. However, over the next three weeks, no amount of comparing diagrams in books with Havana's front legs could convince me they were the right shape. In fact, quite the opposite; where they are supposed to go in, half way down, they go out!

I decided it was time to call the vet.

When Sue arrived I apologised, saying I may be wasting her time and this was probably as stupid as when I once asked her why his 'wee' was white, to which she had replied:

"That's horse wee, it can be different colours."

Sue didn't think I was stupid. She said I had done the right thing and that

Havana's unusual condition may be caused by mineral imbalance – and not helped by galloping around on hard ground on "bendy little legs".

I would need to give him 'balancer' in a small feed each day and it might take six months before there was any improvement. No ordinary balancer either; we're going to have one which is for Thoroughbreds and comes from Ireland – so it must be good!

I had got Havana in at 9.30 a.m., having rung the surgery for an 'expected time of arrival'. Sue was obviously in demand as it was about 3 p.m. when she arrived. It was good for Havana to be in the stable though, just to remind him of stable etiquette.

To entertain him whilst we were waiting I did all of the usual things, like grooming and picking-out feet; also some rump scrumbling and peaceful time, when I sat quietly in the corner of the stable whilst Havana, after sniffing me, looked out over the door.

I had decided not to measure Havana until autumn but, as there wasn't much to do, I could not resist getting the retractable steel ruler out of the grooming kit bucket.

Havana is suspicious of it, as it makes some curious noises and is bright yellow, but after a while he did allow me to stand the ruler, set at 14hh (his height on his birthday in February) by his shoulder. It was clearly too short! I was pleased.

Optimistically, I pulled the ruler out to 14.2hh – which was only *just* over-optimistic; so I decided that, unofficially, he's probably about 14.1½hh.

Employing a rule of thumb I learned from Alison the other day, I then measured the length of Havana's leg, locked the ruler and held it at the top of his leg, pointing upwards. This is supposed to indicate a foal's eventual height.

I got 15.3½hh; but it's a bit unscientific because I'm not exactly sure which bits count as 'leg' (I measured from elbow to fetlock), or what age the 'foal' should be when you take the measurement.

Anyway, Havana didn't mind all this measuring and it did kill some time.

The speed with which he galloped off to join the others when I finally turned him out could not have helped his legs.

In the morning when I had rung the surgery, I had asked whether they had received the results of the worm egg count; but they hadn't. Sue said they should have, so when I got home I rang again, and was told:

"Yes, worm him – he has strongyll ova (worm eggs)."

As I needed to keep Havana in overnight after worming, and as I was going to Dubai for two weeks with Ricky on Friday night, I needed to worm him *tonight*.

I left it as late as possible to get him in again. I went at 9 p.m., so he could have maximum grazing time.

Poor Havana must have thought I was being deliberately cruel when I went down the field with his head collar and asked him to leave the grass and his herd and walk with me up the field.

He made it quite clear that he did not think my idea was at all sensible and he wanted to stay in the field and eat grass.

I employed every tactic I could think of: moving Havana's feet by turning him in tight circles and sending him mental images of us both walking happily, and eagerly, up the field. Each time I gained some ground he protested by reversing the same distance.

Not to be outdone, I turned him round and backed him in the direction I wanted him to go – up the field. He's too bright! He soon worked out what my trick was all about and firmly planted his feet.

I must confess that, as it was approaching 10 p.m. and I was getting hungrier and hungrier, I did resort to just pulling, with my back to him as if he was a heavy load.

At first Havana stood his ground, but then – after each protracted haul – he moved one grudging pace forwards.

I didn't like doing this to him so I stopped.

We stood looking at each other.

I was nearly fainting with hunger. Havana looked cross and

confused, but then that expression evaporated, to be replaced by an air of mental exhaustion and vulnerability. My irrational demands and our battle had troubled him, which made me feel sad.

Fortunately, the herd started to move slowly towards the top of the field.

Flower came to sniff our lead rope, and then sniff me.

I pulled up some long grass and held it just out of Havana's reach. For him, food works every time! He probably thought that Flower was going to get the grass, so walked a few paces towards me. The grass was tickling his nose, but he had to move forwards to get it into his mouth. Flower was still with us and, thankfully, our impasse had ended; he decided to carry on walking with me to the gate and into the stable.

Poor Havana, as expected, really didn't like the wormer, but a feed took away the taste and he settled down for the night.

I was so glad to be able to go home – to my own very late dinner – safe in the knowledge that Havana's 'strongyll ova' were being chemically annihilated and would not mature into anything more troublesome in his gut.

I reflected upon how it's not always easy to do what's best for him, or to persuade him that illogical procedures and foul tastes *are* actually in his best interests.

FARRIERY GAMES
Friday, 27 June 2008

*H*avana behaved abominably yesterday morning – I'm really ashamed of him.

He was so over-energetic that Stuart, the farrier, could not trim his hooves.

I can understand why he behaved like this though. It's summer, he's growing fast and has a lot of energy.

On Wednesday he was required to stand in his stable for six hours, which he did without complaining. Then, just when he thought he was out to graze for the whole night, I made him come back into the stable.

Yesterday I went to him early – about 6.30 a.m. – which, given that it gets light far earlier than that, isn't at all early for Havana. I gave him more haylage, but didn't let him out of the stable.

When I returned at 11 a.m. he was probably hopeful that, this time, it was to turn him out, but it wasn't.

Soon, Stuart arrived and, after fussing Havana for a while, ran his hand down a front leg and picked up a foot.

Having watched Havana start games with Rollo, Flower and Prince, I know that's one of the ways he does it; by nipping at their legs.

So, here was an over-energetic little horse, having his leg handled, and lifted. What was he to do but lift the other leg too – and his whole front end – into a low rear?

For him it was a great game – but not one appreciated inside a stable by two humans. We'd stayed in the stable, as I thought going outside might be too exciting for Havana.

I was not having this!

I quickly stuffed some haylage into a net and tied it outside, behind the stables, which was where Havana last had his feet trimmed; I hoped that, by association, he would remember how to behave.

I marched him round, not giving him time to consider going to the field, and tied him up.

Again Stuart lifted a foreleg and, again, as if by a new law of physics, the other one came up too.

Another tactic was required. I reassured Stuart that, with his muzzle in a bowl of food, Havana would not notice what was being done to his feet. I was concerned that he might think he was being rewarded for misbehaving, but I was running out of ideas.

Whilst in the tack room getting the food, I took the opportunity to put on 'riot gear'. Stuart was relatively unprotected – in the usual farrier's upper-body summer outfit of just a vest.

How Havana managed to rear and paw the air, with his muzzle still in the food, I don't know. It all happened so fast after the 'leg-nip' cue from Stuart.

An attempt by Stuart to trim a back foot resulted in Havana aiming a cow kick at him – something he had never done before to a human.

Stuart quietly stood back to allow Havana to calm down, although I'm sure there are some farriers who would have been far less charitable!

That was enough. I didn't want Havana to get any more practice at this behaviour. It was unacceptable, although I *could* understand why he was doing it.

He had too much energy but, at fifteen months, he did not have the mental development to do anything with that energy, other than what he was doing.

I think Stuart was surprised when I suggested that, for fear of injury and as I needed to be on a plane to Dubai on Friday night, not in hospital, I'd like to reschedule Havana's hoof trim.

There was no real urgency. Despite Havana's antics, Stuart had skilfully managed to re-shape the only hoof with a bit missing, the rest could wait a couple of weeks.

I'm sure the way I stuffed Havana unceremoniously back into his stable – without fussing him at all – and told him that I was disgusted by his silly, dangerous behaviour, left him in no doubt that I was displeased with him.

I might have felt better if Stuart had accepted my offer to pay him regardless.

It was very kind of him to waive his fee completely, even though he did say that Havana's behaviour was "worse than the first time he had his hooves trimmed".

I reassured Stuart that, before the next appointment, Havana would have been out at grass playing with his friends for weeks, so should not be so full of beans. To be on the safe side though, I will do plenty of 'feet practice' with the little monster.

This morning, when I finally turned him out after almost forty-eight hours in his stable, Havana's facial muscles were tense and his eyes were very round – he was distressed.

The speed with which he flew down the field showed his relief at being free again.

I won't see him for two weeks now. I'm sure that *he* won't be bothered and by the time I come back we'll be friends again.

In the meantime, he'll be loved and well cared for by Mr and Mrs B.

CAYMAN DREAMS
Sunday, 29 June 2008, Dubai

I dreamed that the front fell off a long row of wooden stables and all the horses (whom I did not know) went galloping away, except for one big one who did not run far.

He ran in a circle, stopping with his nearside by my right shoulder, so standing by my side.

It was Cayman and he looked as he did at three years old, very dark grey.

It was comforting and reassuring to have him standing close to me.

As with my last few Cayman Dreams, this dream was not as strong as the early ones; it was like a normal dream.

It followed immediately after a disturbing dream.

Mid-May 2008 (recorded 1 July 2008)

I was surprised to have a Cayman Dream because, since having Havana, I have not had any.

Unlike most other Cayman Dreams, it did not involve any activity; it was very simple.

Whilst I was asleep I was aware that Cayman was there; a big, dapple grey, reassuring presence close to me.

It was not a strong dream and at the time I did not record it, which is why I am unsure of its exact date. However, as I have recently had two further Cayman Dreams I feel it should be recorded.

MRS B.'s DIARY
Saturday, 28 June – Saturday, 12 July 2008

*W*hilst I was in Dubai my mother, Mrs B., very kindly agreed to look after Havana.

Knowing that I was keeping a diary of his development and not wanting anything to be missed, she helpfully decided to record her own (and Havana's) version of his activities:

Saturday 28th
Too busy eating to talk.

Sunday 29th
Ditto.

Monday 30th
'Mares and Foals in a Landscape' under the oak tree. Havana came to say "Hello" with Rollo and Flower, then went off to graze.

Tuesday 1st
Ditto.

Wednesday 2nd
"Really exciting! Rollo broke the fence and we all escaped onto the bog."

Thursday 3rd
New grass – very busy eating.

Friday 4th
All under the oak tree. Very sleepy – big yawns.

Saturday 5th Sunday 6th, Monday 7th
Manic grazing.

Tuesday 8th
"Ate my minerals with my bucket *on the floor*!"

Wednesday 9th
Havana's table manners are improving.

Thursday 10th
Very good table manners.

Friday 11th
"A nasty black mare kicked me, but Mrs B. made me better."

Saturday 12th
"I was very good, and my leg is OK."

SEA HORSE
Sunday, 13 July 2008

I couldn't wait to see Havana again!

I got back from Dubai very late last night, but the three-hour time difference worked in my favour so, by UK time, I was up bright and early.

What a lovely sight met me when I walked to the field gate.

I could see that all of the other horses were grazing; but there was Havana, sitting contentedly a little way from the gate in the early morning sun.

For the first time, I noticed how big his eyes have become and how his nostrils flare out from his delicate, narrow nose. I could see the ancient Arab ancestry, from both his Thoroughbred and Welsh bloodlines, so clearly.

In profile, his face looked just like the face of a sea horse.

I decided to test him, to see whether he recognized me after two weeks.

As I approached quietly, I could tell he hadn't a clue who I was but, as I was moving gently, he didn't feel threatened so didn't move.

As I got closer, I crouched down to reassure him that I wouldn't harm him; finally, when I was next to him, I sank down so I was sitting right by his front legs.

Then, for the first time, I spoke.

I could almost see his brain whirring. As his eyes widened and became round with surprise, his face brightened – illuminated by amazed recognition.

I could not have asked for a lovelier welcome, or have stopped myself leaning forward and embracing him so his forehead was flat against my chest, my arms were round each side of his head and neck, and my cheek rested between his ears.

I closed my eyes and that's how we stayed for ages, locked together in so much love.

Finally, I decided that poor Havana must have been nearly suffocating with his muzzle buried in my fleece jacket, so I straightened up to give him some air. I don't think *he* was in any hurry to rearrange our position though, and it certainly felt as if we would still be there now if I had not moved.

I had brought some chopped-up apple, so Havana ate that off the ground before finally deciding to get up.

I moved a little way away to allow him to unfold his legs – and what a shock I had when he did get up ... *and up*. His rump must have been two-and-a-half inches higher than when I had last seen him. I could not believe how tall and lanky he had become – his back legs, especially, had shot up.

Suddenly, all of my anxieties about whether he would be big enough for me vanished. I realised that he is very quickly growing into the finest and most beautiful horse I have ever seen.

What a privilege that I will ride him.

He's going to be magnificent – I can't wait.

And his colour! This morning his coat glowed with red-gold intensity inherited, two generations back, from three chestnuts and one bright bay – his grand-sires and dams.

BAD MANNERS
Saturday, 19 July 2008

*P*oor Havana – today I got it all wrong!

When I arrived, everyone was waiting by the fence at the top of the field. Havana looked happy to see me and left the others to go to the gate. By the time I had collected his head collar from the tack room, he was standing expectantly in the gateway and was keen to walk towards the stables with me. I led him round to our tying-up place at the back of the stable block.

We needed to do some 'feet practice' after his last disgraceful performance, and we only had a week before Stuart would be coming back to trim his hooves again.

Tied-up by the wall, Havana was downright rude and disrespectful; turning his face first one way and then the other, regardless of where I was standing. He continually barged into me as I tried to settle him with a relaxing grooming session; even rubbing the top of his tail had little effect.

I was very disappointed by his bad manners.

"You've missed your breakfast! Is it okay if he has some?" Jan appeared from nowhere, startling Havana.

I thanked her for her very kind offer and accepted on Havana's behalf.

As he eagerly tucked into the bucket of chaff, Jan explained:

"I always give them a bit of breakfast …"

I had not known this!

"… the others are eating theirs now."

I was so relieved to find out the cause of Havana's terrible manners.

He had been waiting by the fence, with his herd, *for his breakfast.* When I arrived, he was eager to come with me because he thought he was going to be fed before everyone else!

When I proceeded to tie him up and start grooming him, he had to tell me – in the only way he knew – that I'd got it all wrong.

To add insult to injury, he could probably sense the rest of his herd were eating – whilst he wasn't – which is practically the worst thing that can happen if you're a horse.

After wolfing down his breakfast and with order restored, Havana stood to be groomed and have his feet handled, effortlessly.

LISTEN!
Sunday, 20 July 2008

I decided that, as it was about three weeks since we last walked to the end of the farm lane, we should do this today.

I was by myself, although someone else usually comes with us for safety. I could tell that Havana was not interested; nevertheless, I persisted.

We got to the gateway at the end of the lane, where he usually enjoys grazing, but this time he was unsettled.

Down the road to the left, some men were loading a lot of old tyres into a van.

I tried to reassure Havana that the whole purpose of coming to the end of the farm lane was for him to see what was going on in 'the outside world' – and that grass was his reward.

He was unconvinced; he clearly felt that he needed to keep an eye on 'the outside world'. Although he was grabbing at the long grass as if it was about to vanish for ever, it was not placating him.

After about five minutes in the gateway, Havana decided he had had enough of 'the outside world' and started to march off home.

I was at the end of the twelve-foot rope, but quickly reeled him in so I was walking by his head.

His pace was increasing, so I circled him.

He came out of that manoeuvre faster than he went into it, completely defeating the object.

I circled him again, which only served to 'wind him up'.

Another circle lit the fuse and he was off! – cantering back down the lane towards his field gate.

The huge knot that I'd tied in the end of the rope was ineffective; Havana was too strong for me to hold.

I also learned a painful lesson: whilst it's sensible to wear gloves to protect against rope burn, it's not a good idea to wear *old* gloves with holes across the palm. I got a rope burn.

As I watched Havana slow slightly to an elevated trot, with twelve feet of rope trailing between his legs, I was not too worried; he was simply taking himself home where he felt safe. He did not feel at all safe in 'the outside world' today.

Later, I telephoned Lisa, my very knowledgeable sister-in-law, who is a riding instructor.

"Don't set goals about how long you want to walk him for, or how far you want to go. *Let him tell you what he wants to do.*"

Really, I *knew* Havana did not want to go down the farm lane today.

I didn't really want to go either; I felt nervous, as there was no one else with us, and I'm sure Havana could tell.

He's so young, at seventeen months, and I shouldn't expect him to do something one day just because he's done it on another day.

Today taught me that I must listen to what I know Havana is telling me, rather than ignoring him if what he's saying doesn't fit my plan.

Havana is quite entitled to have his own ideas and it's only when our ideas are the same – or when Havana's generous spirit means he doesn't mind going along with my ideas – that we make progress.

Mr B.
Friday, 25 July 2008

*A*fter Mr B. had visited Havana this morning, he was so keen to tell me about him.

It was very hot and all of the other horses were standing in the shade of the oak tree, swishing away flies with their tails.

Not Havana!

Havana was helping Den, who was walking along the wire fence, checking it and occasionally stopping to pull up the netting, or hammer in a staple. Havana followed him, walking when Den walked, and stopping when Den stopped.

Mr B. commented on how intelligent Havana is and how he reminded him of Cayman, who would walk along the fence by the footpath across his field at Gunstone, sociably following lone walkers, couples, dog walkers and entire hiking clubs.

Mr B. was clearly even more enchanted by Havana when, having given him some carrots on the ground (and then having his attention distracted by a quick chat with Den), he found Havana standing at his side, with one elegant front leg extended forward horizontally and poker straight.

He said Havana's outstretched leg was quivering with the strain of maintaining such an unlikely and demanding pose.

I explained to Mr B. that this is what Havana does after he has had some really enjoyable food. It's his way of telling us how much he enjoyed it and, probably, how much he would appreciate some more!

"… enchanted by Havana."

BIRTHDAY FEET
Saturday, 26 July 2008

*T*oday is my birthday and I have been worrying about the date ever since our last 'farriery fiasco'.

We have done a lot of 'farriery practice' in the past two weeks and I have concluded that Havana must have reached a particularly playful stage in his mental development. Although he has stopped actually rearing, the lightness of his front end – when extending a lifted foreleg forwards – makes him want to take the weight off the other foreleg too. This produces a movement like climbing up imaginary stairs.

When Stuart arrived I explained this and asked whether he could possibly trim Havana's front hooves with each front leg bent under his belly, as it would be if his hooves were being picked-out. I thought Havana might be less likely to mistake this leg position for an invitation to a game.

Stuart was very kind and gentle with Havana. He did do his front feet as I suggested and Havana showed very little inclination to rear. He jumped about a couple of times – having lost his balance when a back foot was lifted – but Stuart held on tight, so Havana learned he could regain his balance without putting his foot down. There was certainly no sign of any naughty cow kicks either.

I was so relieved to be able to give Havana a sliced apple as a reward and was grateful to Stuart for being so kind and adaptable with such a baby.

With great trepidation, fearing a response which did not bode well for Havana, I took the opportunity to ask Stuart about the extra bone on Havana's front legs. I was surprised by the matter-of-fact breeziness of his response:

"Oh, I've seen that before on young racehorses."

Knowing that very many young racehorses never make it to the track, I forced myself to ask the obvious question:

"What happened to those racehorses?"

Again, Stuart's reply was cheerfully authoritative:
"They were fine; they grew into their bumps."
I could have kissed him! – another huge relief.

MUTUAL GROOMING
Thursday, 7 August 2008

*H*avana is brilliant at coming to me.

All I have to do, when I go in the evening to give him his minerals in a bit of chaff, is stand at the top of the field and look hard at his rump, whilst I count slowly to ten, then walk away.

Suddenly alert, Havana raises his head from concentrated grazing and walks determinedly up the field with an increasingly anxious expression, as I retreat.

If I start to trot, so does Havana. Running gets him into a canter and we have a race to the gate, which is fun for us both.

I do sense that he suspects I've gone a bit mad, but he doesn't really care, because his bucket of chaff and minerals is always there by the gate, and that's the real attraction.

If he has left a particularly good patch of grass to come up the field to me then, as soon as the last mouthful of chaff is safely in his mouth (but not chewed), he unceremoniously turns on his haunches and canters off, back down the field, to resume grazing. I don't even have time to give him a goodnight kiss.

At other times, if the need to graze is less pressing, Havana hangs around for some fuss. Tonight he was so ecstatic at having first, the top of his tail, and then along either side of his spine rubbed, in small circles, that his urge to reciprocate with some 'mutual grooming' just had to be satisfied.

As I leaned forwards, working my way along Havana's spine towards his head, the top of *my* head was met by his gentle, but insistent, muzzle.

The circular action of his proboscis-like top lip systematically frothed-up my hair like candyfloss.

What an honour: *to be groomed by a horse!*

AN 'AT HOME'
Saturday, 16 August 2008

*L*ast time Havana was kept in for worming, it was quite a stressful experience for him; I was determined that this time, it would be better. In the hope of attracting some visitors to entertain Havana, I decided to let all of my 'horsey' – and some of my 'non-horsey' – friends know that Havana would be having an 'at home' day.

Also I had a family mediation book to read, so thought that if I camped at Havana's stable, there would be fewer distractions and I would read more than if I was at my house.

Having got Havana in and given him his wormer last night, I arrived at about 10 a.m. this morning, with my flask of hot chocolate, banana, Chelsea bun, mediation book … and carrots.

I gave Havana some 'Alfa' (chopped, dried alfalfa grass) for breakfast, picked-out his feet then took him out to eat grass around the field gateway. He was a bit confused about why I didn't just open the gate and let him go in to graze with the others. He snatched at some grass but didn't really settle.

Faith was grazing on the lawn. Havana wanted to join her, but Faith's dismissive demeanour told him that now her own foal, Flower, had been weaned, she really didn't want to be bothered with babies. Anyway, grazing on the lawn is a 'Faith only' privilege, the right to which must be deserved; it is not for upstart yearlings.

I thought that grazing in the wood might settle Havana, but that didn't work either. He investigated the muck heap, the children's slide and the asphalt path, but he did not settle down to graze.

Whilst I mucked-out his stable, I tied Havana up, with a net of lovely hay. He was not interested in it. The determination with which he pawed the ground told me he was quite exasperated at not being allowed to go out into the field with the rest of the herd.

I put him back into the stable with about a quarter of a bale of fragrant, soft hay, which did seem to placate him. Then I pulled the bench round from the front stables and set up camp outside his stable door. I was going to sit in the stable but, as Havana had been unsettled, I decided not to crowd him.

It was 11.30 a.m. and I poured myself a drink from the flask. Immediately, Havana's head appeared over the half-door. His muzzle stuck out enquiringly with nostrils flared, capturing the novel smell of hot chocolate. I put some on my hand (it wasn't really so hot!) but Havana didn't want to lick it; obviously, the smell was more interesting to him than the taste. As I don't usually feed him from my hands anyway, he may not even have realised that it was edible.

I settled down to read and Havana settled down to eat hay.

Every quarter-of-an-hour or so, he extended his muzzle towards me and, when I lifted my head from my book, explored my face with his lips. Not hearing the tell-tale sound of lips parting to reveal teeth, whilst his whiskers passed over my eyelids, I kept my nerve.

I don't know why he felt it necessary to keep examining my face, but I'm glad he did; it was a lovely experience.

About an hour later, our first visitors, Judy and Rita, arrived.

Judy described the scene – me sitting on the bench, Havana looking over the door – as 'a picture of contentment'.

Having been bitten by a playful Havana last time, Judy kept just out of his reach whilst we chatted.

Judy and Rita both enthused about what a beautiful horse Havana was growing into.

By 3.30 p.m., I didn't think we would have any more visitors, so I decided to go home for a couple of hours and leave Havana in peace.

Just as I was walking to the car, I met Alison W. on her way to visit and then, as we arrived back at Havana's stable, a phone call confirmed that Claire (Harley, and now Bella's person) had also arrived; a full house. Alison and I went into the stable while Claire stayed outside.

Havana was in his element, thoroughly entertained by all of these admiring ladies who kept telling him how lovely he was. Claire had fallen for his beautiful dark-rimmed eyes and his now cascading, shiny black mane – it was orange-tipped and vertical the first time she saw it!

I think by the time we had all, at last, left his stable, Havana was probably glad of some peace and quiet.

When I came back later he was sitting down, very sweetly and contentedly, in the middle of the bed. He got a lot more hay and another feed to settle him for the night.

What a night! At midnight, I was woken by the most torrential downpour. I could imagine Havana sitting snugly in his bed. I was glad he was in; he was probably glad too.

Sunday, 17 August 2008

When I led him out to the field early this morning, Havana seemed happy. I was relieved; my entertainment strategy had worked!

It was lovely to see him trotting down the field back to his herd, so purposeful and free.

ASSAULT COURSE
Saturday, 23 August 2008

I'm over the moon – Havana is 14.2hh and he's only eighteen months old!

I know I said that I wasn't going to measure him until the beginning of autumn, when Mrs B. says he'll be 15hh, but I just couldn't resist it.

I was grooming him behind the stables; he was being so good and standing up so nicely that I had to know to what height his new long and lanky legs had elevated him.

He's still a bit unsure about the yellow, retractable steel ruler. In my excitement, and forgetting my previous measurement, I set it at 14hh but that was obviously far too short. Another inch was not enough, and I was so happy when I realised that he'd grown to 14.2hh.

Just to make sure, I found a straight piece of wood and got Den, from under the bonnet of his van, to give me a second opinion as to whether I was holding the piece of wood perfectly horizontally across Havana's withers: I was.

To think that when I first met Havana when he was three-and-a-half months old and would not leave me alone, I said:

"Go away, you're too little!" *He knew* that he would grow.

I saw a thick, dark green towel in the tack room. After grooming Havana, I let him sniff it. I know it smelled horsey because I had seen Den rubbing Flower with it in the week when she had got wet and cold in the rain. Havana didn't mind at all when I put the towel on his back, just as I would put on a saddle.

Next, we went into the small area of woodland, past the muck heap. I had decided that we would do an 'assault course'.

Havana, still wearing his green-towel 'saddle', helped me to find a bright yellow oil drum and position it on the path, then he followed me as I led him briskly round bushes, under trees, through more bushes, round the unlit bonfire and back to the starting point – the yellow oil drum. I had thought he might be a bit scared of the oil drum, but he wasn't.

There is a caravan in the wood with a bench at one end; so I built in an interval – when I sat on the bench and Havana stood still – until I had counted to ten.

Then we set off again: round ... under ... through ... round ... along and, finally, round and round the oil drum in the tightest circles we could do.

What a total star!

Havana is so willing and flexible, and well on his way to being a 'handy horse'. I hope, eventually, he'll do our assault course by following me, *without* a lead rope.

GRAND FINALE
Saturday, 30 August 2008

*T*oday I decided to add another bit to our 'assault course'.

I thought that I could make a 'stream' for us to cross, out of plastic feed sacks. I remembered seeing some old ones last week, in a big oil drum at the end of the row of wooden stables.

First I groomed Havana, just flicking the dust out of his coat with a dandy brush, then brushing and combing his tail – he loves having the top of his tail combed. Brushing his mane gave me the opportunity to scrub the mud out of his ears; he loves that too – stretching out his neck and leaning hard into the brush.

I put more louse powder in the top of his tail; it was obvious from the broken, mussed-up hairs that he had been rubbing it.

I haven't seen any lice, but the powder is so fine that it sinks right through to his skin and would probably deal with whatever was making his tail itchy.

Next, I wanted to remind him that syringes inserted into the corner of his mouth don't always contain wormer. I had a bottle of apple juice, which Havana usually loves, and filled the syringe with that.

Despite squirting apple juice around his mouth, I could not distract Havana from the fact that this syringe was the same as the one which administered his wormer, which he hates. Despite the lovely apple juice, he was genuinely afraid; his eyes were round and his head high.

After a few syringes of apple juice had failed to convince him, I conceded that his brain was still registering: 'syringe – wormer – horrible' rather than 'syringe – *apple juice* – lovely', so I got his feed bucket and poured the remaining apple juice into it. Still he was not convinced, so I added some pieces of carrot, which he seemed to eat despite the apple juice.

Then, fly repellent. This time I used the spray rather than the usual roll-on. Havana wasn't too keen on the hissing noise, which I can hardly blame him for, so I squirted it onto my hands and put it on by stroking him all over, which he likes.

Feet followed; we're still perfecting our 'every leg position a farrier could ever request' routine. Havana is less likely to rear when his front leg is pulled forwards, but did still 'walk' out of this exercise by lifting his other front leg too. We'll keep practising.

By the time we went into the wood to make a stream, Havana probably felt as if he'd already had quite enough education for one day, but he was soon attracted to a large sheet of corrugated zinc. It was about three feet wide and four feet long, partially covered in mud and leaves and lying on the ground at the entrance to the wood.

Without hesitation, Havana put a front foot on it to investigate. Immediately he did so, a sound like a series of slinky metallic waves came from it and the opposite end flipped up, causing a pitchfork to fall onto it. A cacophony of percussion in an instant!

Havana was suddenly at the far end of his twelve-foot rope; his head high and his eyes surprised and indignant. Then, as if rebounding and with determination, he walked forwards and was just about to paw the zinc sheet with his front foot when I pulled him back, in case he injured himself on the sharp edge.

The plastic feed sacks that I had seen last week, and even the big oil drum that they were in, had vanished; but we did find some clear plastic bags and one white one.

Havana helped me to lay out the plastic bags in a row across the path; although they crackled, he was not frightened of them – not even the white one.

To start our assault course I thought we could go: under the tree, through the bushes, round the bonfire (still unlit), down the path, and then … as a Grand Finale … *over the stream!*

Havana had other ideas – mostly to do with grass and eating.

As I tried to persuade him to walk forwards, he walked *backwards* along our newly-constructed 'plastic stream', then just stood there in the middle of it.

In ten seconds, he had proved that he had no concern whatsoever about standing on something unfamiliar that made crackling noises and shone strangely. This would have taken some horses hours – if not days or weeks – to perfect.

Havana had done it quickly enough to be rewarded with a further twenty minutes' grazing, before going back into his field.

MAD HATTER'S TEA PARTY
Wednesday, 3 September 2008

*I*t was like the aftermath of 'The Mad Hatter's tea party'.

Eight feed buckets: some red, some green – strewn along the top of the field by the fence – every morsel of their contents having been consumed without a trace.

When I arrived to give Havana his evening feed, I knew that he had actually already been fed.

So as not to over-feed him I did reduce the amount, but I still had to give him something to combine with his daily dose of mineral supplement, which helps his bones, and especially his bendy front legs, to grow strong.

Havana eagerly devoured a second feed. As he did so, I 'tidied up' by throwing the empty red and green buckets over the fence onto the lawn, so they could be collected and taken back to the tack room more easily.

I had given Havana his feed a little way down the field but, as soon as he had finished, he made straight for the fence. On the way, he noticed some chaff floating on the surface of a couple of large puddles and stopped for a moment to investigate how he might eat it.

Walking resolutely on, he had obviously concluded that it was not possible, even for him, to eat floating chaff; anyway, his attention was already on the feed buckets on the lawn.

As he craned his neck through the fence trying to reach them, it was plain that, had each one been miraculously full of food again, he would have eaten all of that too.

One feed, two feeds, *ten* feeds – to Havana they all say: "Eat me!"

MORE WAITING
Sunday, 7 September 2008

I'm sure Havana senses when he's going to be fed.

Yesterday as I walked to the tack room, I glanced down the field and there were no horses to be seen; they must all have been at the bottom of the field.

I got Havana's feed and was walking along in a dream, thinking I'd leave the feed outside the field and walk down to the bottom to get Havana. Suddenly, I noticed him waiting alone by the fence at the top of the field.

Today, we had a visitor; Sara had come to see Havana. Again, he was nowhere to be seen when Sara and I walked to the tack room. We spent a while chatting as I mixed his feed and were still talking as we walked back towards the field.

Suddenly our conversation was interrupted by a shrill whinny from Havana, who was waiting impatiently on the other side of the fence. I was amazed by this second, curious, 'appearance from nowhere'.

I told Mrs B. what had happened today and yesterday. She laughed and said that, on Friday, when she and Mr B. had gone to feed Havana, the rain was so heavy that they had decided to stay in the car, so parked opposite the gate until it eased off.

When they had arrived there were no horses at the top of the field. As they waited in the car, the windscreen misted up completely. After a while, when they wiped away the condensation, they were both astonished to see Havana standing by himself on the other side of the gate … waiting.

TRANSFORMATION
Tuesday, 9 September 2008

I don't know when Havana's neck transformed.

Today was the first time I noticed it – it was just *there*! Strong, muscular and powerful, and enhanced by the most beautiful cascading mane of thick, black, poker-straight hair; it was truly magnificent.

His tail had changed too; still with its delicious ripples, it is now thicker and heavier.

What a combination!

Havana has his Thoroughbred father Falconwood's beautiful lithe body and intelligent head, along with his Welsh mother Bonnie's prettiness and extravagant mane and tail.

Infinite beauty has mysteriously combined into the sweetest creature you could imagine.

HAY FEVER
Monday, 15 September 2008

*H*avana's nearside eye has been a bit runny.

I thought about putting some of my hay fever eye drops into it, but they sting me so much that I didn't think it would be a good idea to introduce Havana to having his eye treated, with something he would think was blinding him.

155

Having taken Mrs B.'s advice, I made up a warm, weak, saline solution and took it in a thermos flask to the stables.

Havana is so used to me stroking his face – and over his eyes – that he hardly noticed when I bathed his eye a few times with a couple of saturated cotton wool pads while he was eating his evening feed.

Eating was clearly his priority. So what if some salty water was running down the side of his nose?

I'm sure this treatment was far less traumatic for Havana than my hay fever eye drops are for me!

MORE TICKLY- TAIL
Tuesday, 23 September 2008

I've given Havana a couple of dustings of louse powder during the summer.

Today, I could tell from the mussed-up hair at the top of his tail that he'd been rubbing it again, probably on the gate – it is obviously very itchy.

He was even more insistent than usual when he presented his rump to me to have his tail scratched.

I remember it was about this time last year, just a few days after I had brought him from North Wales, that I noticed Havana rubbing his tail a lot.

Then, I had been worried he might have 'sweet itch' (an incurable and miserably irritating equine skin condition) and would rub off all of his mane and the top of his tail, reducing both to a spiky, raw mess. My poor old pony, Shandy, did this thirty-five years ago, before many of the present-day means of alleviating the symptoms of sweet itch were developed.

Why do I always imagine the worst? Anyway, now I know Havana doesn't have sweet itch, it's just 'tickly-tail-time-of-year'.

When it gets colder and the midges die off, Havana's tail will be fine.

I must try to worry less about Havana!

GRASS
Wednesday, 1 October 2008

*T*oday the horses moved into the front field.

I had been telling Havana for ages that, when he was 'bigger', that's where he would live. He had only been in the front field before for walks, when he had had to be very well-behaved, and was rewarded with a few minutes' grazing.

My caution arose from an incident on about the second day I had Havana when, with the courage of ignorance, I had marched him smartly to the far end of the field. He had walked very nicely but then – realising he was surrounded by about eight acres of mouth-watering grass and being only seven months old – his excitement had completely overflowed into an exuberant jump into the air, with his front legs waving.

I had thought him so little, that his ability to land an energetic front foot on my shoulder had surprised me. Fortunately, I had on my body protector so I just felt the impact, rather than any pain. Ever since then, I have led Havana in the front field in a defensive and disciplined way.

So, when I took off his head collar and told him:

"Off you go Havana – this is where you live – go on!" I expected him to tear across the field of long grass, as his dream had now come true.

But no, like an overprotected only child with impeccable manners, he very sweetly dropped his nose and started eating right where we stood, about two feet from the gate.

I thought 'the penny would drop' and he would suddenly explode in the direction of the open field, but still nothing.

One of the Beauties was in the middle of the field. Prince and another Beauty had gone in just ahead of Havana, but still his frightfully good manners prevailed, as he grazed determinedly by the gate.

Den approached with the next relay of horses: Grace and Rollo; Havana would get squashed by them if he didn't move.

To encourage him, I walked towards the middle of the field, calling him to me … still nothing. I went back to fetch him.

This time he did realise he was not 'on a walk' and that he could graze out in the middle of the field. A sudden surge of excitement made him trot energetically to the others, then his head went down, as if his nose had lead in it, and some very serious grazing commenced.

As Ricky and I walked along the top hedge, re-checking the boundaries of the field, we heard a solid 'thump'.

It appeared that, from nowhere, Havana's excitement at being surrounded by so much grass had just got the better of him and he had expressed it by 'double-barrelling' Rollo under the jaw, with both back legs. He had then immediately resumed grazing, as if nothing had happened.

Surprisingly, Havana's unprovoked, and doubtless painful, assault didn't seem to disrupt Rollo's grazing either!

The next morning, the size of the horses' bellies indicated that they had all spent the whole night grazing non-stop.

REFUGE

Tuesday, 7 October 2008

*T*he way that Havana gets *exasperated* is ever so sweet.

About three weeks ago, it seemed as if it had been raining forever; all the other horses were standing in the not-very-effective shelter of the big oak tree by the gate. As soon as Havana saw me approaching, he marched purposefully towards me, like an envoy for the herd.

Rainwater trickled irritatingly down from his nearside shoulder to his knee. He stopped in front of me and, with an engaging, annoyed expression, stamped his nearside hoof in frustration. I'm sure he expected me to 'do something' about the rain.

It was the same today. Now that the horses are in the big front field, I gave Havana his evening feed in secret, under the open barn where the rest of the horses could not see us. The wood is immediately behind the barn and there is standing water in that part of the field.

I could feel the midges biting my head – and it hurt. Havana was so infuriated by the carnivorous insects that, the minute he had finished eating, he attempted to relieve the irritation of their bites by rubbing every bit of himself, all at once, against me.

Whilst I was flattered that Havana viewed me as a source of refuge, he is getting so much bigger, stronger and heavier, that a nine-stone human is not a very effective scratching post.

I felt as if I had let Havana down by being unable to sort out this particular problem. I told him that soon it would be dark, so the midges would go and that, anyway, it would not be long before they would all be killed by the frost.

Havana went off to resume grazing with the other horses; evidently, his enjoyment of the long, lush grass quickly overcame his insect problems.

THERAPY
Wednesday, 8 October 2008

The horses had all been on the front field for about a week. It had been intended that they would go on to it later in the year when the grass would be less rich but, because a lot of large, earth-working vehicles were now installing drainage in the back field, the horses had to be moved.

What horses do – for most of every day – is eat, so Havana's belly had got bigger and bigger.

The light was going as I fed him under the barn. I held his feed bowl firmly with both hands, at about my waist height, to prevent him sending it flying with his exuberant front leg pawing.

As Havana stood in front of me I could feel heat radiating from him and, as I felt his forehead, neck, shoulders and chest, they were all warm and damp. Either he had a raging fever, or he had just finished playing a galloping game. His enthusiasm for his food suggested he did not have a fever.

When Havana had finished eating, I decided that – to be sure why he was so hot – I needed to find his playmate. I went to Rollo first. It's usually Rollo with whom Havana plays 'rough games'.

But Rollo was not the culprit, his neck and chest were cool and dry. I was surprised to find that Havana's playmate had been Flower, whose pretty face makes her look a picture of innocence. However, the fact she was practically steaming was a dead giveaway that she and Havana had been doing some serious galloping just before I had arrived.

It occurred to me that giving Havana his feed had probably not been a very good idea. I walked back to him and, sure enough, on closer examination he did look pretty bloated – higher up his ribs than just a fat, 'grass belly'. In fact, he looked as though he had been pumped up with air.

Was I imagining it, or did his facial muscles look tight, indicating pain? Oh dear, he may have colic!

Havana's solution was simple: he just needed to get on with eating grass.

"Oh no you don't! We're going for a walk!"

I marched Havana to the top of the eight-acre field and back down to the bottom. We were halfway up the field for the second time, when Havana decided to question my unusual behaviour – by stopping.

I was glad Ricky had come to feed Havana with me; he walked across the field towards us with a torch. It was pitch-dark as we stood in the field and I examined Havana's bloated belly by torchlight.

I couldn't take any chances, so I telephoned the vet.

It's funny how just knowing the vet is on her way makes you feel better. It evidently made Havana feel better too, because as soon as I ended the telephone conversation he lifted his tail and produced what seemed like half-a-ton of poo.

After that, he really did not see the point of having to leave the field of grass. He told me so by refusing to walk with me towards the gate.

For a while I humoured him: turning him in tight circles – first one way, then the other – to keep his feet moving and, I hoped, to confuse him into walking where I wanted him to go.

Havana is so beautifully supple that he is almost able to reach his tail with his nose, without moving his feet; but I did manage to propel him round, rather like a dog chasing its tail.

This was all very good, but we were not getting nearer to the gate. It was becoming quite urgent, as it would not be long before the vet arrived and I wanted her to see Havana in the light of the stable rather than in the darkness of the field. I decided to back Havana towards the gate, as he is good at backing. Sometimes I am even able to back him by looking hard at his rump and squaring my shoulders in a very assertive manner.

But tonight, Havana wasn't keen on doing much backing.

The next trick in my repertoire was to poke his chest with my finger; this produced a couple of backwards paces, which soon petered out.

Further finger-poking had little effect, so fingers had to turn into 'teeth', which 'bit' (pinched) Havana's chest. This produced several more backwards paces but, again, they evaporated as the lure of the long grass re-entered Havana's mind.

When my 'biting' of Havana's chest became more insistent, he willingly engaged in what he thought had become a game, and nipped my shoulder each time I 'bit' his chest.

There were several such exchanges and he didn't really hurt me; in fact, I thought it was very sweet that Havana wanted to play a game with me, but we were still not at the gate.

I had to resort to bribery.

I asked Ricky to go to the tack room for a bucket and to put a very small amount of 'mix' – which would produce a good 'rattling' sound – in the bottom of it.

When Ricky reappeared with the bucket, Havana immediately recognized the sound of food and couldn't follow Ricky quickly enough.

It's a good job we had practised 'assault courses', because the area around the gateway was covered with builder's rubble. Having picked our way over that, with Ricky shining the torch like a cinema usherette, we had to negotiate fruit trees, tree stumps and the washing line before, thankfully, reaching the stable.

We had been in the stable about two minutes and Havana hadn't really finished sniffing and exploring, when the vet arrived.

It wasn't Sue, our usual vet, but Sally – who was covering out-of-hours cases.

She took to Havana straight away. He has that effect on people; with his bright, open expression and his very sweet, good manners.

With her stethoscope, Sally listened to Havana's gut and diagnosed spasmodic colic; his heart rate had increased, indicating discomfort.

Havana is very used to having needles stuck into his neck, so the intravenous injection of muscle relaxant was probably less annoying to him than last night's midge bites.

He was so unfazed by the injection that he started searching for something to eat. It was then that I realised I should have taken him into the stable with a wood shavings bed, not the one with the edible straw bed.

So, as Havana followed me, we picked our way in the dark, around heaps of bricks and scaffolding, to the little wooden stable with the shavings bed.

Once again, I had cause to be thankful that we had practised walking round the building site and that Havana is such an intelligent, trusting little horse. By the time we got into the second stable, Sally was thoroughly impressed, declaring:

"I can see what a bond there is between the two of you."

We chatted while Havana settled. His face became more relaxed and he was content to stand, dozing, listening to us talking.

He had a hen for company – roosting on the beam in the next stable.

It was 8 p.m. and Sally said that I should check Havana again at midnight and then at about 6 a.m.

Ricky and I stayed with Havana for another twenty minutes before turning out the light, to encourage him to sleep, and creeping out of the stable.

I went to the house to let Jan and Den know that Havana was in and there would be some coming and going later and in the early hours of the morning.

When I got back to Havana's stable I couldn't see Ricky anywhere; but then, in the gloom, I could just make out the most tranquil, wonderful sight: Ricky was standing close to Havana's shoulder, one arm protectively over his neck, the other hand gently stroking his forehead. This really was a sight I thought I would never see.

Ricky explained that Havana had started yawning and sighing, so he went into the stable to comfort him.

Historically, Ricky could not have been described as 'horsey' but, somehow, Havana has changed that!

Afterwards, Ricky told me incredulously:

"Whilst I was standing in the stable with Havana, for the first time in months all my business worries went away!"

I let him know that Havana could have taken his worries away, as horses have the power to do this, and that 'Equine Facilitated Therapy' is a recognized form of healing.

I went back to the stable to check Havana at midnight.

He was lying flat out, having a really good sleep. I was sorry for disturbing him, but I had to put on the light to make sure he was alright.

He was angelic as he sat up, dazed; with wood shavings in his beautiful, glossy, black mane and stuck to one side of his neck.

At home once again, I set my alarm for 5.30 a.m., but I didn't need to.

Normally a heavy sleeper, I awoke at 5.15 a.m. and by 5.30 a.m. I was in the stable.

Havana looked adorable, sitting in his cosy wood shavings bed. He was obviously fine.

Back at the farm at 8.30 a.m., I gave him breakfast of a small amount of 'Alpha and mix', made very sloppy with a lot of water, then put him out on the 'starvation paddock' with Toffee and Freddy.

Poor Havana thought I was being so cruel by not putting him back out in the front field, with its lush, long grass, and he really didn't think much of Toffee and Freddy as playmates.

He paced around the perimeter of the small paddock, whinnying to his friends in the front field.

No one whinnied back – they were all too busy eating grass!

INJURY
Sunday, 19 October 2008

*H*avana didn't really seem lame, so I don't know what alerted me.

It was 'just a feeling' but, as he started walking across the field towards me, I sensed there was something wrong with his nearside front leg.

Urgently, I went into the field to meet him. An adrenalin shot of panic speared my chest when I saw the three-inch-long, salmon-coloured gash – set off by the short, shiny black hair on the inside of Havana's knee.

He'd had a kick.

My mind went totally blank. Then, my first thought, which I am embarrassed to confess, was to phone my mother, Mrs B., to ask her what to do!

Havana obviously had confidence in me however, as it was with a particularly purposeful air that he walked by my side, back to the gate – clearly certain I would 'sort out' his knee.

164

As we walked, some useful ideas did float, miraculously, into my head: 'saline' … 'irrigate' … 'antiseptic cream'.

By the time we arrived at the stable, I had a strategy.

Havana had no problem at all in allowing me to examine his knee.

It was a relief to see that the wound didn't appear to have any visible dirt in it; also, when I lifted his other front leg, Havana was happy to put all his weight on the injured leg, and – although it was a bit swollen – he could bend it too.

I was relieved. Horses' legs are complex miracles of nature and are delicate – sometimes too delicate.

After washing Havana's leg – with probably far more saline solution than necessary, just to be on the safe side – I carefully dried it by pressing on big, flat cotton wool pads.

Then came the part I really enjoyed: I smeared on great globules of thick, antiseptic cream from a big pot. I felt the quantity I was applying must be proportionate to the benefit Havana would get!

When I led him back into the field, I'm sure Havana was walking in a proud, 'puffed-up' way; comforted and reassured by the luxurious attention that had just been lavished on him and confident – due to the smell of antiseptic, the coolness of his knee and the patch of thick, glaring-white cream – that his nearside knee was now 'very special'.

As he swaggered back to the other horses, Havana reminded me of a Premier League footballer who had just received dramatic, pitch-side treatment from the team doctor but was *really* well enough to have enjoyed all the attention.

MINTS
Friday, 24 October 2008

*I*t was 7.20 a.m.

I don't usually check Havana on weekday mornings now, as I'm on my way to work. Mr and Mrs B. do it after they have been to Mrs B.'s horse, Corris, who is at Gunstone – just a mile from Havana's stables. This morning though, I was going to a meeting which would not start until 10 a.m., so I could check Havana.

It was lovely to be in the field as it was getting light.

Horses are invigorated by the increasing light and busy themselves; the older ones by grazing even more determinedly, the youngsters by becoming playful.

Perhaps this explains why Havana thought I had chosen 7.20 a.m. as a good time to come to the field for a game of 'leg biting'.

The minute I was a neck's length from him, he had provocatively clamped his jaw round the front of my ankle (which didn't hurt) and was expecting me to make the next move by, somehow, clamping him around his fetlock.

When I did nothing but squeal in mock pain and push his head away from my leg, he must have concluded that I didn't understand the rules of the game. Sportingly, he gave me a second chance to commence battle by clamping his jaw round the same ankle again.

Whilst I was entertained by his antics, I did need to extricate myself from Havana's jaws so I could walk round him to check he had not injured himself in the night.

After giving his jaw a sideways shove, I was free. Quickly I walked all round him, checking his body and legs. Having established that he was fine, I stroked his forehead and then began to walk towards the gate.

Like a trainee dragon, Havana kept trying to get each of my ankles between his jaws as I walked. Despite the encumbrance of a baby horse attached to my feet, we did arrive at the gate.

Havana's bright, eager expression; ears forward, eyes wide, head alert, indicated that he expected something …

"No Boo – it's not tea-time! That's tonight, you'll have to wait."

I felt bad that I had not brought any food to give him. I know that Mr and Mrs B. always produce carrots. Havana was letting me know that he wanted something to eat.

I had no carrots. Then, I remembered that in the car I had some mints. I hurried to get them whilst Havana waited at the gate.

I don't usually feed him from my hands. When he was very young, he used to nip so badly that associating food with hands would have been a recipe for disaster.

But how could I give him something as small as a mint on the ground?

I broke my own rule and quickly slid a mint from my flat palm between his warm, velvety lips.

I don't think he knew how it got into his mouth. The effect was almost instantaneous; first a 'scrunch', then the raised head, then the very demonstrative outward-curled top lip of a horse who thinks his mouth is on fire.

A couple more 'scrunches' and the incendiary device was devoured.

Havana's excited, urgent expression told me he wanted to repeat the experience immediately.

His wish was granted, but only once; he was rationed to just two mints.

Adult horses love mints; their strong, hot taste is a novelty. It was amusing to see the curious effect that mints had on Havana when he tasted them for the first time in his life.

Another milestone!

Mrs B.'s BIRTHDAY
Monday, 27 October 2008

27 October has *always* been my mother, Mrs B.'s, birthday but, somehow, this year it has crept up on me.

I had planned to give her a special, hand-made birthday card, with a photograph of Havana on it.

So now it was 27 October and I had not even taken the photograph, let alone made the card.

I went to the field armed with my whistle. I thought that if I blew it, it would shock Havana into standing-up and looking very alert – and photogenic.

Havana was grazing.

After greeting him and explaining about birthday cards, I positioned myself in what seemed like the best place to get a good photograph of his whole body. Then, so as not to frighten him, I blew a very short, but not very loud, blast on the whistle.

Nothing! Havana did not even look up.

I blew a louder, shrill blast.

Without lifting his head, Havana stopped chewing for a moment to listen better, but quickly resumed eating.

Exasperated, I blew a loud, long blast.

Success! Havana raised his head from the grass … a bit. In fact, he stretched out his head and neck at a very *un*photogenic angle, just below horizontal with his back, and stared unintelligently into the middle distance.

He looked like a prehistoric stegosaurus.

I gave up and opted instead for an artistic close-up of his eye and forelock that I was able to take whilst he was grazing.

Havana has beautiful, deep, calm eyes and such a lustrous, 'blackcurrant-black' forelock that, thankfully, *Mrs B. thought her birthday card was lovely.*

"… blackcurrant-black forelock"

DORMITORY
Monday, 3 November 2008

*W*hen I went to give Havana his evening feed at about half-past-six, after work, it was already pitch-dark, but very mild.

I sensed that the horses might be near the far hedge; they were often there at this time. A quick sweep of my powerful torch's beam in that direction revealed a row of shiny eyes, like fireflies, apparently floating in the darkness at similar heights.

I quickly turned off the torch; I didn't want to dazzle them. It was easy to walk in the near-total darkness towards the row of familiar, dense shapes.

It was like a dormitory; everyone was sitting down, either dozing or asleep, whilst the mare, Grace, stood at the far end of the row, keeping watch.

This is how a herd of horses always sleeps. In the wild they would be preyed upon by lions and wolves, in fact by any large, carnivorous mammal with sharp teeth; so it's always a good idea for them to post a sentry to look out for danger.

The row of slumbering horses started with the babies: Flower, Havana and Rollo, in that order and evenly spaced.

Flower and Havana were both sitting neatly, with their front legs curled under their chests and their back legs to one side, their muzzles on the ground.

Rollo, however, was having a really good sleep and probably dreaming. He was flat-out and snoring – loudly – like a rough old engine.

Havana's long, furry coat and solid warmth were magnetic. As he raised his head to greet me, I quietly sank down onto my knees in front of him, put my arms around his chest and shoulders and buried my face in his soft neck. Havana rested his nose on my back. We stayed cosily snuggled-up together for ages.

Eventually, Havana lifted his nose from my back and arched his neck in a stretch; he was rousing. He had obviously decided it was time to remind me that *my* job was actually to give him his evening feed – and it was now overdue.

MORE FIREWORKS
Wednesday, 5 November 2008

*I*t's 'Bonfire Night'.

The sky is dank and cloudy, as in a "Hammer Horror" Dracula film. This atmosphere must have meant that, in the village, the fireworks displays were disappointing; but from Havana's field outside the village, the muffled bangs and muted flashes took on an eerie, other-worldly dimension.

The horses were not at all bothered; they were spread out, grazing in the middle of the front field.

Havana managed to sidle away, unnoticed by the others, to have his feed under the oak tree.

He rejoined the herd and resumed grazing as if *no* meal had just been taken.

Flower, apparently, has extra sensory perception when it comes to food; she made a beeline for Havana, sniffing his muzzle as he grazed. Her inquisition was obvious:

"What have you been eating?"

I was reminded of children and sweets. Poor little Flower; Havana had obviously just indulged in something scrumptious and she was jealous.

Energised by food, Havana became playfully provocative. He chose to spar with Rollo.

What a sight!

Two beautiful, fit youngsters silhouetted black against the misty darkness by the light of a silver half-moon.

Like mad March hares, they reared and boxed repeatedly, whilst endless fireworks exploded and then rained mauve, turquoise and pink sparkling trails through the sky above them.

A psychedelic dream … featuring two spirited horses.

The rest of the herd grazed peacefully.

MUD-TROUSERS
Tuesday, 11 November 2008

I could not help but laugh at Havana tonight!

He looked as if he was wearing mud-trousers.

His entire back end – rump, flanks and legs – was completely encased in a thick, solid crust of dried earth.

No doubt this is a very sensible outer garment when it's winter, you live outside and have fur to which it sticks.

What is so appealing is Havana's complete lack of concern; he was totally oblivious to his appearance.

This gives him a freedom that most people do not share, but may well envy.

WORMING
Friday, 14 November 2008

W orming usually happens every twelve weeks.

It can be very stressful for horses, and for their humans. Sometimes, it involves more than one human per horse.

Trying to deposit a syringe-full of unpalatable paste on the back of a horse's tongue can take ages. Both horse and human may become, at best, a bit agitated; at worst, absolutely terrified.

The paste can end up anywhere at all, on horse or human, and not always on the back of the horse's tongue.

Not so with Havana!

At the moment, I am worming him for a body weight of three hundred kilograms. This doesn't work out terribly neatly, as each hundred milligram syringe of the wormer I use contains enough paste for three-and-a-third doses.

Today, I had to use up the one third from the old syringe before giving Havana most of his dose from the new one. The wormer is kept in the tack room, where it stays pretty cold.

As I depressed the plunger, it delivered a 'blob of rubber' into Havana's mouth, which he promptly – and logically from his point of view – spat out onto the ground.

Horses have an instant reflex for ejecting anything they think might be poison.

As quickly as Havana had ejected the offending blob of rubber, I picked it up and pressed it onto the back of his tongue with my hand. Fortunately, it stuck and his attempts to spit it out were in vain.

It was easy to slide the fresh syringe into the corner of Havana's mouth and administer the rest of the, more liquid, dose.

I managed to worm Havana without even going into the stable.

His head was over the half-door, so I took my chance. Either he was so bemused at the speed of what was happening, or so confident I wouldn't harm him that he didn't even back away from the door.

He was like a sitting duck really – but such a sweet, trusting one.

A BABY HUMAN
Saturday, 15 November 2008

*T*oday Havana met his first human baby.

Mackenzie is six months old. His mother, my good friend Gill, practically – if unusually for a new mother – attired in her British Pony Eventing Team tracksuit, brought him in his very own 'armoured personnel carrier'.

The robust, high-tech, all-terrain pushchair, which appeared to run on a scaled-down version of knobbly truck tyres, was very effective for travelling over the building site in front of the stables.

We 'parked' Mackenzie in the stable with the straw bed, next to Havana's stable.

Above the low, solid partition, the stables are divided by two long parallel planks, each running from the front to the back wall. These planks are too high for a horse actually to get over, but he can see over them.

If the horse is smaller, he can peer through the twelve-inch gap between the two planks into the next stable.

In Havana's case, simply peering through was not good enough.

In order to get a better look at the strange little creature who was now in the next stable, Havana meticulously threaded his whole head and neck through the gap between the planks.

For Gill and me, it was magical to be in that still, peaceful stable, with shafts of midday winter sun beaming in, watching a beautiful, intelligent baby horse and an angelic baby human – his face illuminated by golden light – gazing intently at each other. Neither of them blinking and both with eyes like saucers.

It was impossible to decide which was the more amazed by the other.

IVY
Monday, 17 November 2008

*W*hy was I not one bit surprised when – on our way into the field through the little side gate and whilst I was fiddling with the chain – Havana took advantage of the opportunity to pull a long strand of cascading ivy from the top of the gatepost?

It's exactly what Cayman did, every time we went through the little gate at the far end of our favourite bridle path, 'The Long Mile'. He did it when my attention was either on opening or closing the gate, while mounted.

It was cheeky *and he knew it.*

For both Havana and Cayman, the result was a rebuke:

"No! Ivy is poisonous!" as I extracted the offending greenery from their mouths.

Neither horse resisted when I relieved them of their 'trophy', nor did they make any real attempt actually to eat the ivy.

I suppose my predictable response meant that – from an equine perspective – it was quite an amusing game!

SURCINGLE
Tuesday, 18 November 2008

*A*lthough Havana was not at all bothered, I was getting fed-up with the way the numnah kept sliding off his back when we went for walks. Also, I thought that it would be good to introduce Havana to the idea of having a strap around his chest, in preparation for when he would wear a saddle and girth. So, I borrowed Corris's surcingle (a broad, webbing strap that goes right round a horse) from Mrs B.

As Havana was eating some hay from the floor I quietly placed the surcingle on the hay for him to sniff. Its smell would help to reassure him that he needn't be frightened of it.

Havana was curious; the surcingle probably smelled of Corris. He sniffed it, warily to begin with, but then – when it showed no signs of reacting – he started pawing it, increasingly severely, with a front foot.

I rescued the surcingle, folded it in three and cradled it gently in my arms; again, to let Havana know that it was completely non-threatening.

For a horse, there is no distinction between animate and inanimate.

Everything is presumed to be animate, and therefore possibly dangerous, until proved otherwise. My treating the surcingle in this way showed Havana that it was not attacking me, so I hoped he would believe it would not attack him either.

He had gone back to eating hay, completely ignoring the surcingle.

I had already put the numnah on Havana's back. I suspect that he thought of it as something nice, designed to keep horses' backs warm whilst they went for walks or ate their evening feed.

The surcingle has beautifully crafted leather pads, about a third of the way along its length, which fit either side of a horse's withers and stop it from rotating.

I positioned the padded section, on top of the numnah, just behind Havana's withers, and very slowly allowed the remaining length of webbing to dangle down his offside.

Still no reaction. Havana was diligently munching his way through the hay and the sound of the circular, grinding motion of his lower jaw filled the stable. For Havana, eating is a serious business, to be concentrated on – very hard!

Then … the risky bit. In preparation, I gave Havana a good scratch behind each front leg and under his chest, just to remind him how it feels to have these parts touched.

He has never minded this at all; I am confident that he likes being scratched. So, standing by his nearside shoulder, I reached down for the dangling webbing band, pulled it around his belly and held it against his side, where it would be buckled-up.

Realising that 'a monster' had wrapped itself right round their body would be the point when other horses might 'detonate' and try to leap out of their skin to escape the clutches of such a deadly predator. Not Havana! – he just kept on munching.

This was better than I had hoped. I had expected some reaction, even if only a cursory sniff of the surcingle around his chest. He really is 'an angel in horse's clothing'.

Rather than just holding the straps in the 'buckled-up position', I decided that I could actually buckle-up one strap. There was no need to buckle-up both and, in an emergency (such as Havana suddenly deciding that he *did* have 'a monster' on him after all) two buckles would be more difficult to undo.

I was surprised that the hole the buckle slipped into was the same hole that Mrs B. uses for Corris.

Corris is Thoroughbred cross Fell, 15hh and fully-grown. Havana is Thoroughbred cross Welsh Cob, 14.2hh and only twenty-one months old.

I was encouraged that this boded well for Havana's growth prospects.

After he had eaten more hay and some pieces of apple I had brought as a reward, I quietly and carefully took off the surcingle. I felt a bit mean removing the numnah, as Havana's back was lovely and warm under it.

A good rub, in big circular movements all over Havana's back and chest, was another way of thanking him for the way he coped with his first experience of having something buckled-up round his body.

I hope that every stage in Havana's development, as he learns to become a reliable riding horse, will be no different from today. Actually, I have a feeling that nothing will change; Havana has such a lovely, calm nature.

DINING AND FURNITURE
Thursday, 20 November 2008

*T*onight, the matt darkness was damp and heavy.

Apart from Faith, who was standing alone a little way away by the hedge, all of the horses were settled around the big haylage bale in the corner of the field near the barn, contentedly pulling at the plentiful supply of succulent forage. Their warm breath created a fog around them.

The peaceful scene reminded me of an extended family gathering for dinner, each member knowing his or her place at the table, according to their status in the family. Beauty, the matriarch, was at the far side of the bale with the other two mature mares: Beauty ('number two'), and Grace. Next were Prince and Rollo and, directly opposite Beauty and under her watchful eye, were the babies: Havana and Flower.

As I gently approached the 'dining table', I sensed an air of frostiness from Beauty. I felt like an uninvited guest. I could feel the raised eyebrows of Havana's 'starchy' maiden aunts:

"We don't usually dine with strangers – let alone members of a different species."

I did not feel welcome.

Havana, not at all inhibited by his elders, very sweetly shifted slightly towards Rollo to make a little room for me to slide into the group, between himself and Flower. Although Havana is quite comfortable with a human at such close proximity, I knew that I must respect the tolerance of the older horses.

I kept myself warm by facing Havana, putting my head under his long, silky mane, my left arm over his neck and my right arm across his chest, as I sank down, leaning my back against the bale. It was a curious position but, as well as keeping me close to my personal 'furry radiator', it also made me fairly unobtrusive to the senior equine diners.

It was a great honour to be allowed around that table – an honour that I did not take for granted.

After a while, Havana stood back from the bale and looked at me – still leaning against it. His engaging expression told me it was now time for us to go into the stable for his evening feed, so he really did need me to move!

As we walked together across the field towards the yellow light of the stable, I marvelled at the ease with which Havana moves between the equine world, with its rigid hierarchy and codes of behaviour, and the human world, with its own set of rules. His transition seems effortless.

Once in the stable, Havana devoured his feed as if he hadn't eaten all day. It amazes me how much space there must be in his belly! Just as he was finishing, a vehicle approached and parked a few feet away from the stable. Curious, Havana stepped forward to look over the half-door. He was evidently fascinated to see a white pick-up truck stacked high with furniture. His fascination escalated as it was unloaded into the stable right next to his.

Havana watched, transfixed, as two men carried a heavy-looking chest of drawers past his door.

I was surprised he was not at all worried by the sounds emanating from the other side of the wooden wall, as the chest of drawers was clumsily put down and then dragged across the floor. Next came a table – again carried almost under Havana's nose and apparently dropped next door – a standard lamp, an armchair and a two-seater sofa.

By now, it might have sounded, to a horse less confident than Havana, as if there was a corral of monsters next door; but he was completely unconcerned by the bangs and crashes.

He was so intent on observing the men's activities, I am certain that, if he had been able to get out of his stable, he would have investigated the furniture on the truck by looking at it very closely, sniffing it well and possibly biting at it, for more information.

He would also have followed the men, as they went back and forth carrying various items, and would have looked into the stable next door to see where everything was being stored.

It's probably a good job Havana's stable door did remain firmly closed and his involvement was mental – not physical.

The men might not have appreciated having an inquisitive young horse as an apprentice but, given the opportunity, Havana would have become very involved in their task, not because he was trained or forced to, but because he wanted to.

That's just how Havana is and how he's always been. He doesn't see any reason not to interact with people.

SHORT CUT
Wednesday, 26 November 2008

*T*his evening, as I trudged through the mud towards the barn, I could see some of the horses around the haylage bale and other 'horse-shapes' standing inside the barn.

I recognised Havana's alert head; he was standing inside on the firm, dry floor at the far side of the barn.

His ears were forward, at an intelligent, forty-five-degree angle – he was concentrating as he watched my slow, squelching progress towards him.

I called him to me:

"Havana! Come on boy – come on!" Nothing. He didn't move a muscle and was clearly determined that I should go to him.

As I got nearer, Havana moved away from me.

Leaving the barn by the corridor of drier ground between its long, open side and the wood, he deliberately made his way to the garden gate and stood looking over it.

Havana was right! The garden gate is a short cut to his stable – *avoiding all of the mud.*

As the garden gate leads onto the lawn – with its well-tended shrubs and frequent lines of clean washing – it is rarely used.

Havana has only ever been through it once, nearly six months ago when the lawn was dry. Jan had encouraged us to go that way to save time, as the vet was waiting for us in the yard.

Today, we didn't take the garden gate route because Havana's increased weight would have meant that his hooves would leave waterlogged holes in the soft turf.

Instead, I persuaded a very perturbed young horse to take an absurd walk with me *through the deepest mud* in the main gateway.

There are times when Havana's intelligence astounds me.

I am sure there are also times when my illogical, human behaviour astounds Havana!

BUFFALO CALF
Sunday, 30 November 2008

*H*avana has turned into a buffalo calf overnight.

Today is bright and sunny, but very cold. The ball of chestnut-brown fur who approached me eagerly at the top of the field made me want to hug him.

Standing on end, his coat is so luxurious that you have to bury your face in it. Any part will do; Havana doesn't mind whether it's his neck, back or rump – just as long as it doesn't interfere too much with his grazing.

After he had allowed me to burrow my cheek into his rump for several minutes, Havana very clearly made the point – by waving an elegant front leg, horizontally in front of him – that when Mr and Mrs B. check him at this time in the middle of the morning they give him carrots: 'Where were his carrots?'

When I laughed at his clever communication, but did not produce any carrots, Havana wasted no more time before getting back to the important business of grazing. Compared to Mr and Mrs B., my inability to dispense carrots made it quite obvious that I was not really up to the job of 'mid-morning horse-checker'.

THE DEVIL'S WORK
Monday, 1 December 2008

*H*avana was upset and perplexed by what had happened to the – usually soft and sticky – deep mud around the haylage bale.

Overnight it had, strangely, set as hard as rock and was now a maze of irregular peaks and troughs.

He was disinclined even to attempt to walk over it but, when he did try, he adopted some very strange stances.

For example: he tried standing with no weight at all on one, bent, front leg and the other front leg down a deep hole, while his hind legs were straddled unnaturally wide, with each back hoof balancing, gingerly, on an icy mud-peak.

His very sweet, exasperated expression suggested he considered the frozen mud to be 'the devil's work', calculated, at best, to annoy and, at worst, to *trap* the feet of unwary foals foolish enough to try to walk on it.

Havana also seemed to find the adult horses' total lack of concern at this obvious peril quite incomprehensible.

Whilst he was trapped in this strange terrain, they simply got on with traversing it; from the field to the haylage – and back again.

The world of a foal is not so simple!

"… calculated to … *trap*… unwary foals"

WELCOME HOME
Thursday, 18 December 2008

*I*t had been like leaving a teenage boy 'home alone', but with a few mates and a daily delivery of take-away pizza, for two weeks.

Ricky and I arrived home from New Zealand at twelve noon. By 12.30 p.m., I was at the farm where Havana lives.

Mr and Mrs B. had looked after him superbly. The couple of phone conversations I had had with Mrs B. at the beginning of our trip had reassured me that Havana was fine and I had not needed to ring again; I knew he was in good hands.

My parents had a routine of feeding Havana each morning, after they had fed Corris at Gunstone.

They fed Havana by appearing at the top corner of his field at about 11 a.m. Havana quickly got to know when to expect them and was able to sidle away from the herd and have his feed over the gate, without any of the other horses noticing – until he had finished.

That way, it was easier, quicker and safer for Mr and Mrs B. than having to get him out of the field, which would have alerted the other seven horses. They would probably all have wanted to come out through the treacherous muddy gateway. Given that Mr and Mrs B.'s combined age is one-hundred-and-forty-six, this would not have been a good idea!

When I appeared in the field this lunchtime, I hoped that Havana might throw up his head, whinny and come trotting across the field to me; glad to see that I had returned and had not abandoned him. That would have been a lovely welcome.

A reassuring welcome would have been if he had put up his head and just walked towards me.

Not a bit of it! In fact, it was Flower who noticed me first and started walking towards me. That alerted Havana, who continued to graze until the last minute and then – in case Flower should reach me first and receive an edible reward – Havana walked quickly towards me, beating Flower by a nose.

The first thing I noticed is how much more solid he is looking; his legs in particular seem to be getting sturdier and stronger-looking. He is turning into a powerful horse. Havana's full winter coat, befitting an Arctic explorer, must add two inches to the depth of every surface of his body and this optical illusion adds to his bulkiness.

I put on Havana's head collar and walked him to his stable for his feed. He walked in a 'flighty' way; like a horse who had not been led very often, was not used to leaving his herd and had certainly *never* been that way into the yard before – a total little ruffian!

I'm not worried though. I am confident that, after a few days – when I have fed him, picked-out his feet, groomed and fussed him – Havana will remember exactly who he really is and what a lot of good manners and experience of being handled he has. So for today, I didn't make an issue of the fact that he was still mentally 'on holiday'.

Havana did give the game away himself though, by politely backing-up a good two strides, without hesitation, when I positioned myself assertively by his shoulder, facing his rump – before we left the stable after his feed.

This was the equine equivalent of the 'home alone' teenager coming out with:

"Thank you, my breakfast was lovely!" when what he really meant to do was grunt something incomprehensible and slope off ungratefully.

DRINKING
Tuesday, 23 December 2008

*T*he 'drinking hierarchy' is well defined in terms of seniority – and rigid.

As I appeared at the gate, Havana was already coming up the field, respectfully bringing up the rear in the nose-to-tail 'elephant train' of part of the herd: Beauty, Beauty, Prince, and Havana.

When he saw me, Havana peeled off and meandered towards the gate, as the two Beauties reached the trough, then he stood mid-way between the approach to the gate and the approach to the trough.

This told me that, whilst he knew he was expected to meet me at the gate, he also wanted to go to the trough. He had obviously joined the elephant train in the first place because he was thirsty.

The first Beauty (the one Mrs B. says: "definitely doesn't like children", meaning she has no time at all for Havana) finished drinking and moved away from the trough, allowing Prince to replace her.

I decided to try something; I wondered whether my presence would give Havana the confidence to step nearer to the trough.

I greeted him, put on his head collar and gently encouraged him forward in the direction of the trough.

He took just one step, clearly wanting to do as he was asked but reluctant to 'break the rules', probably fearing a swift bite or kick for any transgression.

When Prince finished drinking, leaving just one Beauty, there was plenty of room at the trough for Havana, but even my renewed encouragement (which enables him to walk under lines of flapping washing and over 'crunchy' tarpaulins), was ineffective.

Havana stood politely, like a pageboy at a wedding, in his prescribed position of respect – not stepping forward until Beauty had strolled languorously past, ignoring him, on her way back down the field.

I am glad for Havana's sake that, in his interaction with the two hefty matriarchs of his herd, his manners are now absolutely impeccable.

EBONY
Sunday, 4 January 2009

I can see Havana in the dark!

When I leave the stable, turn off the light and look back at him over the half-door contentedly eating haylage – his coat is lustrous.

Large, shining patches of silky hair capture the moonlight and reflect it back into the night.

Although he is truly (in the light of day) a bright, chestnut-bay, his coat has a magical night-time quality. It appears ebony-black; defining parts of his beautiful form … but indistinctly … so that he merges, mysteriously, into the soft darkness.

ASPEN
Monday, 5 January 2009

I have never been to Aspen, Colorado, in the winter.

Actually, I've never been at any other time either but this morning, in Havana's field, I *felt* as if I was there and evidently so did Havana.

I turned him out to a dense covering of powder snow, twinkling in the strong sunshine of a cloudless, intensely deep-blue sky. The bitter cold was exhilarating.

All of the other horses had spent a cold night out and were stoically munching their way through two big bales of haylage.

Not Havana! After a comfortable night in a stable and a good breakfast, he was ecstatic with excitement at this strange new world.

After quickly discovering that snow is not really good to eat, he was off – at full gallop – down the field.

On his return circuit, the earth rumbled as he approached uphill and then flew past me, like a racehorse exercising on the downs. At the top of the field, he slowed down to the most beautiful stallion-like, staccato trot: head and tail high, nostrils flaring and lustrous near-chestnut coat gleaming. Dark circles of sweat defined each eye and the base of each ear.

Now I know why cartoonists portray raging bulls as having horizontal lines, with clouds at the end, coming from their nostrils – that's exactly how the condensing breath from Havana's nostrils looked.

Not quite a raging bull, but a beautiful little dragon – breathing fire.

IT'S SNOWING!
Wednesday, 7 January 2009

Snow is still on the ground and Havana seems to have got used to it.

I turned him out and he quietly ambled off down the field to graze. The milky-grey sky was heavy with snow as I went back to the cosy stable to muck-out.

It wasn't long before I was aware of the sky's increasing presence, engulfing the yard – it was snowing!

I took the haylage net to fill from one of the large bales and, as I looked down the field, I was reminded of primary school children peering out of their classroom window into the playground. The excited cry: "It's snowing!" would ignite their building excitement, which would explode into joyous, shrieking activity as they tumbled outside at playtime.

Well, this was the horse equivalent!

Amidst the flurry of swirling snowflakes, Havana's youthful exuberance spilled over as he tried to start a game by running amongst his playmates: Rollo, Flower and Prince – who had all been grazing peacefully – and nipping their legs and shoulders.

In his own way, he was shouting: "It's snowing! It's snowing!" and he wanted *everyone* to join in his excitement.

HUMBLED
Thursday, 8 January 2009

I did really know that it was impertinent of me; but as Havana finished the last few grains of his breakfast, I thought that I could just take the opportunity – whilst he was standing still and I had nothing else to do – to feel his back fetlocks. I had to find out whether I needed to put on any more cream for his minor patches of mud fever.

My ticklish fingers, gently exploring his nearside hind fetlock – whilst he was concentrating on the exacting task of not wasting a single grain – must have been rather annoying for him.

His reaction made me laugh: slowly, and very deliberately, he brought his nearside hind-leg up, under his belly, forwards, and then out to the side in a sweeping, circular movement. It was the equine equivalent of the ballet exercise, 'rond de jambe en l'air', or 'round of the leg in the air'.

The reason I laughed was that this reaction was one hundred per cent Cayman's.

Havana was trying to 'scoop' me out of the way, to relieve the irritation of my 'tickling' his fetlock whilst he was trying to eat.

Had I been unfamiliar with 'cow kicking', as it is more commonly known, he would certainly have succeeded in removing me; but I had already moved quickly out of the way of his agile back leg.

When Havana had finished cleaning out his feed bowl to his satisfaction, he stepped decisively back and stood perfectly still, as if to tell me:

"You *may* examine my fetlocks now."

I felt ashamed of myself for imposing on him whilst he was eating – and humbled by his lovely manners, which, on this occasion were so much better than mine.

SCARED
Sunday, 11 January 2009

$\mathcal{O}$h Havana! Havana! Why does he scare me so much?

When I arrived to check him this afternoon, I was not surprised to see that two new haylage bales were in the field. Evenly spaced around the one nearest to the water trough – like iron filings drawn to a big cylindrical magnet – were some adult horses and two youngsters, all pulling eagerly at the succulent, aromatic fodder. Lower down the field, Faith had the second bale to herself.

With mounting trepidation, I scanned and re-scanned the first group, which included the two Beauties, Prince and Grace. From a distance, either of the two youngsters' bright bay rumps might have been Havana's but, on closer inspection, they were too fluffy and supported on legs sturdier than his. They definitely belonged to Rollo and Flower.

Was Havana sandwiched between two of the adult horses? No, he wasn't there. I moved quickly down the field to the second bale; perhaps he was out of view, behind it? Unlikely – he's bigger now and, even if he was directly behind it, I would see his ears and head over the top.

My anxiety soared. It was uncharacteristic of Havana not to be at either of the haylage bales; something must be very, very wrong.

I was scared. I checked my pocket; yes, my mobile phone was there and it has the vet's number programmed in. Would I reach the top of the bank, look down onto the lower part of the field and see Havana's body, lifeless, on the damp, cold ground?

Why do I worry so much? There he was! In solitary splendour – a beautiful, elegant little 'racehorse', head down, grazing contentedly.

As I approached, I don't know whether his slightly surprised expression was because I was earlier than usual, or because he sensed what, to him, would have been my totally incongruous panic.

What was there to panic about? The fence had been moved and, remarkably, as the night-time temperature had been well below freezing for the past ten days, had revealed a thick strip of short, fresh grass. If the others wanted to eat haylage, that was up to them!

Havana's methodical grazing continued unabated, whilst I discharged my anxiety by stroking his forehead, then scratching his withers and back.

I am sure that, whilst he was content to see me, he would not have liked me to ask him to leave the grass to go into his stable tonight.

As the forecast was for far milder weather, I had already decided to start leaving him out at night again. I know he likes to be out with the other horses best of all.

FROST
Wednesday, 14 January 2009

*H*ow could I have got it so wrong?

I knew the weather forecast had said Tuesday night would be cold, with a hard frost, and I had made a mental note to bring Havana into his stable for the night.

So why did I forget that yesterday was Tuesday?

I had brought Havana in for his evening feed and then, despite the fact that I could feel the temperature falling, turned him out again after he had eaten.

When Ricky arrived home at nearly 10 p.m., he exclaimed excitedly that outside was 'all frosty'. When I told him that Havana was out, he suggested we should go to the farm and get him in. I would have loved to but – worried that we would shatter the owners' peaceful night with our car lights and their barking dogs – thought better of it. I felt very, very guilty. Poor Havana would be so cold.

The second I woke up this morning, I pulled back the bedroom curtain, just enough to see that it was starting to get light and everything outside was glittering white.

In a minute, I was outside de-frosting my car. I had to resort to warm water on the windows, as cold water froze instantly.

Havana was standing near the top of the field. When he saw me his ears went forward, his expression was so sweet – and forgiving.

I got his head collar and went to him, but even though he would have known that he would be fed, he seemed not to want to move. Poor little thing, he had probably been standing dozing, legs locked, for so long in the cold that he had 'stuck' in that posture. Thankfully, the base of his ears was warm enough, as was his neck under his mane.

Eventually, I persuaded him to walk with me to the stable, where I gave him his breakfast. To start with, his rump appeared triangular – rising to a point on top and falling away each side – but as he ate, defrosted and relaxed, it became round again.

The breakfast worked. When he was half-way through, I knew that Havana was feeling better because he did one of his 'dog-stretches'. This involves him stretching out both front legs, rigidly, then bringing his nose into his chest with his neck arched and pulling his whole body away from his front legs. All the time, his back legs stay straight. The result is that his front end sinks down very low, to about my waist height.

This is another classic example of 'Cayman behaviour' and is what Havana usually does halfway through his breakfast. I knew that this must have been a particularly satisfying stretch, because it was accompanied by a deep, throaty yawn.

I was starting to feel a bit less guilty.

In case Havana wanted to lie down for a proper warm and restful sleep, I had put down the wood shavings bed, which had been banked-up around the walls. I got him some haylage to eat, reassured him that I would be back very soon and went off to Gunstone to borrow a bale of shavings from Mrs B., as our delivery will not be until tomorrow.

I had made a decision! That was it; no more messing about. Havana will be a horse who is stabled at night – at least until spring. He has a finer coat and a thinner skin than the other horses in his field.

He has always had a field shelter but, in the past few weeks since the building works started, the horses have been moved into the back field and can't get to the shelter. When it becomes warmer, it will get wetter. Rain can be worse for horses than cold so, until about the end of April, it will be better for Havana to get used to the routine of being in at night. After all, he needs most of his energy for growing – not keeping warm.

I knew that, given the choice, Havana would probably want to be outside with his friends and would prefer the shelter of a hedge to a stable.

They had all proved that, when they were in the front field. Even in the heaviest rain, the entire herd would be in the middle of the field grazing, when they could all have been warm and dry, under the barn. But that's horses for you; and it's why, sometimes, humans need to organise things for them!

I am glad that Havana doesn't seem to mind me organising him and I'm grateful for the subtle ways in which he lets me know he is content; a relaxed sigh, or a softening of the look in his eye, are precious endorsements of a human by a horse.

TRUFFLING
Saturday, 17 January 2009

I had decided it would be good for Havana to practise 'big boy's foot routine' every morning before leaving his stable.

Having his feet picked-out routinely might make the idea of having his front leg lifted far less exciting for Havana. This would enable Stuart, the farrier, to get on with his job, rather than having to deal with a baby horse who thinks his farrier wants to start a game of 'rearing' every time he lifts a front foot.

The stable is long and narrow. Havana's wood shavings bed covers the back two-thirds of the floor, which is bare concrete at the front. To make it safe for hoof picking, I needed to remove overnight manure from the front part so neither of us slipped.

I fetched the 'poo bucket' and my green rubber 'poo gloves' from the tack room. The bucket was instantly interesting to Havana. 'It might contain food!' When he found that it didn't, he turned his curiosity to the wobbly green rubber things I was holding. To investigate better, he took hold of a couple of glove fingers in his mouth. He seemed to find their elasticity, as he pulled, quite fascinating. As I did not want to pick up poos with fingerless gloves, I inserted my finger and thumb in the corner of Havana's mouth to persuade him to release his grip.

We established that Havana had no reservations about wobbly green rubber gloves when, dangling them in one hand, I 'walked' them from his nose and up the middle of his face, then made them 'dance' on top of his forelock, between his ears. He was intrigued – and not at all scared. As Havana stood looking over the half-door, I cleared up the poos from the front of the stable. Usually I muck-out after I have put him out in the field, but I decided it might be good discipline for Havana if I actually did all the mucking-out while he was in the stable, then did the feet picking last. So, I continued onto the wood shavings bed, squatted on my haunches like a truffle hunter and ferreted out the firm spheres of poo from the fluffy mass of wood shavings.

My activity had attracted Havana's attention once more and he began sniffing, then nibbling, my left boot. Intent on my 'truffling', I ignored him. It was only when I stood up that I noticed he had managed to undo my bootlace, despite the fact it had been securely knotted and tied in a bow with the bow-loops knotted together!

Havana had met the big sweeping brush before. As soon as it was in the stable, he clamped his teeth firmly onto its long wooden handle and we swept together. Soon Havana's attention moved to the large brush head and he grasped half of the bristles in his mouth, which stopped me from brushing.

To help him to investigate better, I stood the brush vertically, with the head uppermost. Havana's eager sniffing, and occasional pulling at a piece of haylage entwined in the bristles, demonstrated his appreciation of my co-operation.

We needed to get on.

I decided to try something; using a technique that my very talented friend, Jennifer, had taught me, I squared my shoulders and looked intently at Havana's rump. This is a predatory stance, it makes a horse feel uneasy and he usually backs away.

Sure enough, Havana took several steady and deliberate steps back, so he was standing on the wood shavings. He stood quite still, watching – as if from a safe vantage point – as I opened the stable door wide and swept out the remaining bits of dirty bedding.

I was impressed; many horses (both young, and old enough to know better) would have made a bid for freedom through the open door. What good manners he has.

Havana seemed to have been very entertained by our co-operative mucking-out session and I was enjoying it so much that I almost forgot to tie him up and pick-out his hooves. When I did, Havana showed just the same good manners and sweet nature.

I would never have imagined that mucking-out, with Havana's 'help', could give us such a wonderful opportunity for bonding.

Much like sharing any apparently dull or menial task with a companion, mucking-out with Havana was an unexpected and joyful way of building our friendship.

STORM

Sunday, 18 January 2009

There have been a few times when it has been obvious, from Havana's expression, that he thought I was completely mad but, last night, he had every reason to doubt my judgement.

Severe gales had been forecast and, right on cue, they started as I arrived at the farm. All of the horses were grazing but, as the wind got up, they became unsettled and in a moment were all careering up the field as if the wind was chasing them.

They were in rank order and the youngsters, Havana, Rollo and

Flower, were bringing up the rear. It was a game really; I could tell by his wide, but happy, eyes that Havana was excited to be running in the swirling wind.

With no difficulty, I put on his head collar and led him out of the field. Away from the herd, he was more agitated. The wind made a sheet of corrugated zinc clank against the fence and he over-reacted – head high, feet light.

Once in the stable, Havana's trepidation was justified; the wind was whipping into the rickety old building. With the half-door open, it was almost as windy as being outside.

The protective plastic on the newly-hung door of the house opposite the stable was fluttering with an eerie whistling sound.

Between snatched mouthfuls of feed, Havana put his head out over the half-door, clearly worried that he was confined inside while there was so much commotion going on around him.

Eventually, the natural sedative effect of a good, big feed started to settle Havana. He began methodically sorting out the loose haylage that was on the floor in one corner of the stable; spreading it out by pawing it with his front feet and selecting the tastiest bits to eat first.

It was then that I noticed it.

We had already used the stable on several occasions for worming, and Havana had been in nearly every night for about three weeks.

How had I failed to spot the danger?

A six-inch length of thick, grey electrical cable – at Havana's head height – was suspended between the corner and the light switch on the doorpost.

Just one inquisitive nibble and he'd get two hundred and forty volts. I couldn't leave him there.

In a split-second his head collar was on, he was pulled away from the carefully-sorted haylage, led into the escalating maelstrom of the night towards the whistling door and bundled into the empty stable next door.

It all happened so quickly that the sweet little creature had no opportunity to object.

Once safely in the next door stable, the surprise of his forced eviction began to crystallise. Havana paced around his new quarters, looking for a way out.

They didn't look right, they certainly didn't smell right, they were frightening, and the whistling door was now directly opposite. What was going on?

Had his human gone mad?

To make matters worse, Havana could see his own stable quite clearly, over the long parallel planks dividing the two stables. There it was – cosy and inviting.

At the end where his wood shavings bed was, he stuck his head through the gap between the planks and inhaled – it smelled of him.

He looked at me imploringly. Nothing made sense.

I transferred his water and haylage, but this time he just snatched mouthfuls as he paced round. The wind got stronger, whirling into the stables. I needed to shut both top doors in case Havana tried to use either as a way out.

With the doors shut, it was suddenly unnaturally quiet and cocoon-like and Havana started to settle down to eat haylage.

I was worried about him though, I knew he was confused and frightened at not being in his own stable.

I switched off both the inside and outside lights and pretended to leave but, once outside, I stood by the window for a while to make sure Havana did settle.

Although it was completely dark, I could just make out the rhythmical bobbing of the white star on Havana's forehead as he lowered his head to pull a mouthful of haylage, then raised it to eat.

I satisfied myself that he was as settled for the night as he was going to be. Short of staying in the stable there was nothing else I could do.

I woke very early this morning, waited for it to get nearly light and was at the stables before 7.30 a.m.

The wind had died down and Havana was the picture of a

contented youngster, as usual. I was relieved and he was thankful to have his breakfast early.

A piece of board was nailed over the offending electrical cable to box it in, making it inaccessible to Havana's teeth.

When I brought him into his own stable tonight, just as if nothing had happened, he seemed slightly puzzled, but glad that I had returned to my senses.

BONDING

Saturday, 31 January 2009

*A*nother bonding opportunity.

In fact, possibly an opportunity to make Havana believe I am a hero!

Whilst he was eating his breakfast in the front of his stable, a chainsaw started buzzing in the nearby paddock. To start with Havana was agitated by the incessant, piercing noise, but eating distracted him and I think my presence was a comfort.

The last few grains of mix were tricky to get into his mouth; horses tend to bite at even small amounts of food, rather than licking-up the last bits. Havana was concentrating hard on this task when – from nowhere – a terrifyingly loud, cracking sound split the air. It was followed immediately by a barrage of crashing and snapping.

Instantly Havana leapt to the back wall of his stable – as far away from the alarming sounds as possible. His eyes were huge and frightened, his nostrils were flared, and his head was at its highest.

I stayed right where I was, leaning on the doorpost, half looking into the stable and half looking out at the felled limb of a mighty old oak tree, which was now lying amid a mountain of shattered branches and dead leaves on the muddy paddock.

Havana looked at me from the safety of the back of his stable.

"It's alright boy, come on; it was only a tree branch being cut off. Come on, it's all right, come on boy." His confused expression indicated that he found my total composure incongruous.

Eventually, Havana's head lowered, his eyes softened and he walked forward to stand by my side and look out over the half-door at the mayhem of men, ropes and oak tree outside. His gaze was intent, but interested rather than frightened.

His confidence was being restored as we stood shoulder-to-shoulder.

I could not help feeling that Havana was impressed by my reaction to what was, for him, a very threatening situation. In the future, when we encounter situations that might frighten him, I hope this experience will help Havana to trust me, so he is less fearful.

BLISS
Wednesday, 4 February 2009

*M*y email to Jennifer.

"Hi Jennifer.

Inspirational thought for the morning:

We know that horses are authentic and that sometimes we might usefully follow their example … so, could this series of pictures of Havana, which I took yesterday, be a step-by-step guide to reconnecting with our inner bliss?

You can see him getting more, and more, *and more*, excited by the snow:
Walk, trot, roll. "Wow that was great!"

Walk

Trot

Roll

'Wow, that was great!'

He really has the right approach to life.

Love from

Liz X and Havana x"

HAYLAGE
Thursday, 5 February 2009

*T*oday, Havana let me know so sweetly that he really despaired of trusting a human to select his haylage for him.

At the beginning of the week there had been three big bales in the field. The one by the footpath – obviously the most delicious – usually had at least seven voracious horses around it at any time and had shrunk like a rapidly-melting snowman.

The one in the corner nearest to the muddy paddock must have been the second most appetising. Faith sometimes ate that one, either alone or with Flower. At other times, the two ponies, Toffee and Freddy, were at that bale.

Only very occasionally did anyone other than Toffee and Freddy go to the third bale, by the gate. But this morning it was the only bale left until the tractor came chugging into the field with a new bale of haylage impaled on its front loader – always a signal for excitement amongst the horses.

As soon as the bale was deposited on the ground most of them, Havana included, herded around the huge cylinder of moist, mouth-watering fodder. Then the tractor delivered a second bale, which evened out the competition for a place to stand and pull at each one. Even Toffee and Freddy deserted the third bale and joined the horses.

The problem with a tightly-packed new bale of haylage, still encased in a tube of plastic netting, is that you need to be a horse, with powerful neck muscles and strong teeth, to tear out mouthfuls of food from the top. As it is eaten, the bale's structure becomes weaker and it's easier for a human, with spindly weak arms, to pull haylage from it; but when it is new, it is nearly impossible.

That's why I had given Havana haylage from the third bale, which, having been two-thirds consumed by Toffee and Freddy, was no longer in any fit state to stop me tearing great wads from its core. Actually, I knew this was not Havana's 'haylage of choice'. In fact, with the exception of Toffee and Freddy (who are a law unto themselves anyway) it was no one's 'haylage of choice'.

With the same inevitable shame I would have felt if I'd been caught handing-in plagiarised homework – I was rumbled!

What made it worse was the magnanimous, polite way in which Havana let me know that I had let him down. Having enthusiastically devoured a big feed of 'mix' and 'Alfa', as usual Havana took a long drink from the water bucket by the door, before turning his attention to the heap of haylage in the corner of the stable.

In just three seconds I knew I had done the wrong thing. That was all it took for Havana to paw the third-rate fodder, dismiss it as inedible without even tasting it and step back onto his bed with an air of resigned pity that a human could be such a poor judge of haylage.

What else could I do but apologise? Then I pushed the offending heap to one side, whilst assuring Havana that he needn't eat it – and I would get him some better haylage.

Off I trudged down the field, with an empty hay net.

It was dark, but the snow on the field reflected bright moonlight. The big mares standing around the bale seemed slightly surprised when I joined them, tearing at their fodder.

The bale was looser now so, even with my puny, human arms I could pull out all the haylage I needed.

As I emptied the contents of the net onto Havana's stable floor, he walked forward. Without needing to sniff it first, he started methodically and contentedly chewing mouthfuls of the aromatic, golden haylage.

Even I could tell this was very tasty stuff.

I discreetly bundled up the original heap and returned it whence it came.

Toffee and Freddy, still stoically munching on bale three, seemed unsurprised; as if they had always known this inadequate human had got it all wrong!

CAUGHT
Monday, 9 February 2009

*A*ll day the weather has been bitterly cold.

At about 3 p.m., sleet began falling from the sodden sky. It was getting dark when I went into the field looking for Havana.

Their size told me the two shapes eating the soggy remains of the haylage bale nearest the gate were Toffee and Freddy.

Two other larger shapes, which I decided were probably the genteel, appropriately-named mares, Faith and Grace, were by the other haylage bale in the corner.

Under the shelter of one of the big oak trees, and pressed into the hedge which separates the field from the muddy paddock, was a morass of rumps. Assorted withers, necks and ears all seemed to float in the ethereal murkiness.

I assumed that Havana was there somewhere and was making my way towards the group, when the fact that my entire right buttock felt as if it had been grasped by forceful jaws, halted me in my tracks.

As I wheeled round, I was surprised to find myself face-to-face with Havana, whose quizzical expression told me he could not understand why his – usually reliable – person was going in totally the wrong direction, so he had intervened to curtail her folly.

I was unnerved. When humans go misguidedly wandering around horses' fields looking for them, the horses usually either stand and watch their apparently irrational behaviour with an air of mild amusement at our deficient human senses, or simply take advantage of the opportunity to continue grazing until they are caught.

I must have gone to fields to get a horse in on thousands of occasions over the years, but I have never been so unexpectedly, and decisively, *caught by a horse.*

If Havana is this bright at not-quite two years old, what will he be like at six, or at eight when he is psychologically mature?

I am slightly daunted, but really proud and excited, even with a bruised bottom!

HENNY PENNY
Thursday, 12 February 2009

Since Havana began spending every night in his stable six weeks ago, Henny Penny – the resident Rhode Island Red who probably regards all three stables as hers – has been moving ever closer.

To start with, she kept her distance; roosting on top of the redundant fridge freezer in the first stable, but maintaining her beady-eyed observation of the newcomer in the end stable.

After a couple of weeks, I was surprised and pleased to see Henny Penny roosting contentedly, her feathers all plumped-up around her, on a beam in the roof of the middle stable.

I thought her presence would be comforting for Havana. There are some adult horses who would object so strongly to being led away from their herd, that it would be impossible to stable them alone. Havana has been very good, especially for one so young, about being the only stabled horse.

However, I was glad he had the company of another living creature. So what if she was a hen and he was a horse?

Most nights last week, I found Henny Penny sitting on the horizontal rail between the middle stable and Havana's stable but, by the time I had fetched him from the field, she had returned to roost in the roof of the middle stable.

It was dark by the time I brought Havana in tonight. Agitated by 'a giant snake' – actually coils of thick rope, 'a slumbering monster' – a huge mechanical digger, and 'a lumpy monster' – a heap of recently-sawn logs, and temporarily blinded by the heat-seeking light on the newly-built house, Havana wheeled into the sanctuary of his stable at high speed.

As he made his customary one-hundred-and-eighty-degree turn to face the door, he was halted abruptly – at only ninety degrees – opposite the rail dividing the stables.

Havana and Henny Penny were face-to-face, only about ten inches apart. Havana's wide-eyed, ears-pricked, look of surprise was a picture; matched only by the spectacle of a hen doing something I have never seen a hen do before. Henny Penny was *leaning backwards* at a most improbable angle, trying to 'get out of Havana's face' whilst not ceding her position on her new perch.

Too bemused to fathom what was going on and with characteristic acceptance, Havana turned his attention to the heap of hay in the corner by the door.

It was clear that Henny Penny had moved in.

"… Henny Penny had moved in."

NEARLY TWO and THE DENTIST

Friday, 13 February 2009

*M*y email to Sharon – Havana's sire Falconwood's owner.

"Hi Sharon,

Havana gets more angelic, polite and well mannered by the day. He had the dentist (Geraint Hughes – Llangurig, Powys – *very kind)* last Friday, and endured a gag and drilling to wear off the sharp edges of his molars.

His enormous eyes showed that he was absolutely terrified, but he put up no fight whatsoever. A bucket of apples and carrots, and a lot of love and reassurance later, he was fine. He did far better than some adult horses who need sedating, just for an examination.

He does have to have tiny 'wolf' teeth extracted, but Geraint says that our vet can 'pop' them out, under sedation, when she comes to give him his next flu and tetanus injection in April.

I can hardly believe that Havana will be two on Tuesday – the time has flown, and I've enjoyed every minute of it. Well, only another 368 days, and counting, before we can go for rides … we're both looking forward to that. Not for me these ready-made horses, I have a lot of patience.

Love from Liz X and Havana x"

BANSHEE
Saturday, 14 February 2009

*T*he screaming sound of a chainsaw, which assaulted me the second I opened the car door, was alarming. What was even more alarming was that I was fifty yards away from its source, immediately behind Havana's stable.

Why had I been stupid enough to assume the men who had been felling trees and sawing logs in the wood behind the row of stables would not work on Saturday mornings?

Sawing had taken place in the week, after I had put Havana out in the field, but it had never sounded like this before.

I hurried to Havana's stable and, over the half-door, was very surprised to see him right at the back, looking out of the window nearest to the screaming, mechanical banshee. As soon as he realised I was there, he darted forwards – highly agitated – tore my woolly hat off my head with his teeth, rushed to the back of the stable again, deposited my hat on his wood shavings bed and resumed his brave vigil of the excruciatingly loud goings-on outside.

I had to get him out and away from the noise but, as he was so volatile, I needed to distract his attention.

I threw his breakfast into a bucket: a scoop of mix and a big double-handful of Alfa, diluted with a bottle of water brought from home in case the taps were all frozen. There was no time for his usual mineral supplement; the lid was difficult to prise off and it needed to be measured. He could have that this evening.

I grabbed the head collar, and 'hid' the breakfast by the newly-built house in front of the stables.

With his head collar on, we went out, pausing only to collect the secret bucket of breakfast as we made our escape during a lull in the sawing.

Immediately his nose was in the bucket, I whisked Havana to the relative safety of the gateway to his field. He grabbed huge mouthfuls of food, a lot of it spilling out of the corners of his mouth. He was not concentrating on eating at all.

Instinct in overdrive, his mind was on fleeing away from the terrible noise that he could not possibly understand.

As he ate and settled a little, I looped Havana's long lead rope over his back as usual; this meant that I held the bucket in both hands and did not hold the rope at all.

From nowhere, the awful sound screamed back into life. Havana fled to the metal-barred gate. For a heart-stopping moment, I feared that he was going to jump it; then he veered to the right in front of the wooden stile leading to the footpath. Again, he looked as if he was about to jump.

"HAVANA!" The panic in my voice caught his attention and, as he shot towards me, I grabbed the lead rope near to his head, so he propelled himself around me. After one revolution, he halted. I have never seen him look so tall and so muscular. He appeared to have grown to 16hh and developed a stallion's neck. He was a ticking time bomb, about to explode. I knew that he could detonate in any direction and that upwards – probably accompanied by flailing front hooves – was highly likely. I was scared.

In my haste to save Havana, I had forgotten my own safety. Yes, I was wearing steel toe-capped boots, but my riding hat, body protector and gloves were all still in the car. What good were they there? Without my 'riot gear', I'm not half as brave at handling Havana in a sticky situation; the fact that I was also in danger of communicating my fear to him made me even more frightened.

All I could think of was being felled by what must, by now, be nearly half-a-ton of horse, crashing down on to my unprotected skull. Steel toecaps would not protect me from that, would they?

I kept Havana walking in small circles around me and attempted to sooth him by stroking his taut, arched neck.

The sound ceased as quickly as it had started, but I didn't know how long the silence would last. I had no alternative but to place myself between the gate and Havana, whilst I fiddled with the gate fastening;

actually a chain with a short metal bar at one end, which has to be threaded vertically through several metal rings on the other end. The power of positive thought could not have been more urgently put to the test. I willed the metal bar to slide obligingly through the rings at the first attempt and, mercifully, it did. One shove, and the gate was open. Thankfully, Havana had calmed down enough to remember our 'gate routine'; he sashayed through the gap with me, turned to face the gate as I closed it and stood whilst I took off his head collar. Then he did exactly as I said:

"Go on boy – RUN!" and belted-off down the bank to join the rest of the herd.

As I stood on the top rail of the stile to get a better view, the choppy sea of bobbing heads and cavorting bodies indicated that 'Hurricane Havana' had just swept up Rollo, Flower and Prince and even the young piebald horse in the field on the other side of the footpath; all were now at category five.

The lessons you teach yourself are the most effective.

In our next emergency – and I am sure there will be many – I shall definitely make sure I deal with my own safety first; human beings are far more breakable than horses.

As for Havana, the sawing had stopped and, within half-an-hour, he was back up at the top of the field eating haylage with Rollo.

He was so settled and content that he was quite happy for me to spend twenty minutes silently leaning against him, with my cheek on his withers, one arm over his back and the other across his chest. I would tell anyone watching this that I was getting Havana used to my weight in preparation for being ridden; but really, I just love hugging him and I am certain his calm acceptance means he is happy to be hugged.

Also, I needed to hug Havana. The fear I had just experienced had left me drained and Havana restored my equilibrium. As he quietly munched haylage, I plugged myself into him and was, quite simply, recharged.

I discovered from the chainsaw operator that today, for the first time, he had used the optimum fuel in his saw and that, for the first time, he had needed to wear ear defenders.

The only defence poor Havana has in *his* ears is tufts of soft golden-brown fur.

When I told my sister-in-law Lisa what had happened today, she asked me a very logical question:

"*Why didn't you just ask the chainsaw operator to turn off the saw?*"

TWO

Tuesday, 17 February 2009

Havana's Second Birthday – 17 February 2009, with Mr and Mrs B.

THAT BIRD!
Monday, 23 February 2009

*T*hat bird is a liability!

Last night, as Havana ate eagerly from his feed bucket, which I was holding, I could see Henny Penny perched on a diagonal beam in the roof to my left, directly above Havana's rump. Even I could see, from the unusual splay of her talons and their apparently manic grip, that Henny Penny was having trouble holding on.

Sure enough, it wasn't long before she started to slide, in slow motion, down the beam; as if being transported on an ingenious, unseen, stage mechanism. Confused into petrifaction, she just floated effortlessly away from Havana and me.

Then, finding herself wedged into the apex of the descending diagonal beam and the vertical beam joined to it – and having taken a moment to recover her composure – Henny Penny alighted, amidst much flapping, onto the new, deep straw of Havana's bed.

Alerted to the obviously impending fracas, I had warned Havana:

"Hey Boo, Henny Penny's on her way down!" So when she landed behind him, Havana was so unfazed that, apart from momentarily stopping chewing, he didn't react.

Until yesterday, Havana's bed had been wood shavings; a firmer, more compact launch pad for anyone wishing to fly from it. Henny Penny's attempts to become airborne were now thwarted by the straw, which was caught in her feathers.

After a few failed attempts she sat in the fluffy straw, looking up at her elusive perch – the horizontal rail dividing the two stables. She sat for quite a long time; so long, in fact, that Havana and I both assumed she had settled in the straw and ignored her, at our peril.

The flapping and squawking with which Henny Penny launched herself onto the horizontal rail, resulted in Havana and I clashing skulls, as his head involuntarily shot up from his bucket and met my right brow bone.

I think I was briefly unconscious, although still standing, and it certainly hurt Havana who, as I 'came to', was shaking his head.

Tonight, I found an egg sitting cosily in a shallow nest in Havana's mound of evening hay. If Henny Penny thinks one egg is adequate reparation for the mayhem she caused last night, she is *wrong!* Neither Havana nor I like eggs.

A DISTINGUISHED VISITOR
Monday, 9 March 2009

A very historic day.

Corris came to meet Havana. It wasn't the first time they'd met; that was when Havana was about eight months old. But then Havana, who was in the muddy paddock with Ben and Flower, scarcely noticed Corris's appearance on the yard in front of the stables and Corris certainly didn't give a second thought to three inconsequential foals in the paddock.

This occasion was different. I had told Havana that Corris was coming to see him so they could get used to each other, eventually go for walks together and, later, when Havana is three, rides. I told him:

"Corris is very wise, it will be good for you to learn from him. When you see new things, you will be more confident because Corris will be with you."

I had intended to get Havana into his stable before Corris and Mrs B. arrived, but they were early. As I led Havana towards the field gate, we could see them approaching down the farm lane. Havana was very interested and very excited by the appearance of such a distinguished visitor. With head high, pricked ears, wide eyes and flared nostrils, he stopped – rooted to the spot. Corris continued walking on with majestic composure; alert, but unconcerned by his new surroundings.

With immature eagerness and his investigative instinct in overdrive, Havana tried to get as close to Corris as possible by rushing towards the gate. However, I curtailed his rather rude approach by insisting that he halted about three paces away from the gate, maintaining a respectful distance from Corris. It was like waiting to be spoken to by a dignitary rather than bowling up to him and slapping him on the back. Also, if there were to be any squealing and assertive pawing of the ground, which horses sometimes do when they meet for the first time, I didn't want either of them to risk getting a front foot caught between the horizontal bars of the metal gate.

Mrs B. chatted with me from Corris's back. He stood quietly enough, but after about ten minutes indicated that he was getting bored with standing still, by thrusting his neck out, snatching the reins from her hand and moving his weight from one hind leg to the other, and back again. This is a horse's way of saying:

"Come on, can't we get going? We've been standing here long enough."

Mrs B. and I agreed that it would be best if she led the way towards Havana's stable and he followed.

It didn't quite work out like that though. Havana was so desperate to get close enough to his new mentor to sniff his rump (also inappropriately familiar) that, despite leaving about four horse's lengths between them, as Havana escaped his field – his eager pace very quickly closed the gap. As a result, Havana's investigative muzzle made contact: first with Corris's rump, and then with his flank, before they were halfway to the stable.

With the imperious disdain of a royal equerry, Corris's expression suggested this had been a complete breach of protocol, but – especially with Mrs B. on his back – he was far too well-mannered to inflict a punishing nip on the transgressor.

I decided the best way to deal with Havana was to get him past Corris and bundle him into his stable, out of the way.

With his chest pressed hard against his stable door and his head and neck impossibly stretched over it, Havana continued to investigate his visitor; nostrils sensing every airborne clue, flicking ears capturing every sound. Havana could not have been more fascinated by Corris.

Eventually, Corris deigned to approach the door and the introduction continued in a more conversational, face-to-face way, with each horse's nostrils receiving the warm, exhaled breath of the other and the myriad information relayed by this – but not for long. It was plain that Corris really wasn't very interested in Havana. After all, what had an over-eager little upstart to offer such a seasoned elder statesman?

Mrs B. and I agreed that another introduction would be a good idea. We need to get Corris and Havana sufficiently familiar with each other, so that being with Corris will give Havana confidence in the unfamiliar situations he will inevitably encounter in 'the outside world' beyond the end of the farm lane.

As Havana watched Corris and Mrs B. ride away, I sensed he felt deflated after the excitement of having such an esteemed visitor. I praised him for being a good boy and reassured him:

"Corris will come back to see you again."

DRAGON
Thursday, 12 March 2009

*A*nother very historic day!

Corris came to take Havana for their first walk together.

Having had his breakfast early and having been turned out in the field for a few hours' grazing to settle him, Havana was back in his stable, groomed and eagerly anticipating … something.

He could tell by the brisk way in which I handled him this morning that we had an appointment. Usually, time stands still when I'm with him; we take whatever time we need and do things at Havana's pace – he's rarely rushed. So today he probably thought that either Sue, the vet, or

Stuart, the farrier, was coming to see him as their arrival is usually preceded by some preparatory 'sprucing up'.

Havana's surprised, alert expression indicated that he could hardly believe his eyes as Corris – with Mrs B. mounted – strode regally along the path leading to the stable. Very clearly a horse with vast experience and knowledge, Corris surveyed his surroundings.

At the sight of his visitor, Havana was full of uncontrollable, youthful excitement.

Mrs B. halted Corris opposite the stable, about three yards away. We wanted the two horses to become re-acquainted from a safe distance. Thankfully, Havana's impulse to barge up to Corris and get to know more about him by smelling his head, neck and shoulders was thwarted by the stable door.

While every sensor in Havana's body was locked onto Corris, Corris obviously didn't consider Havana worthy of very much attention at all.

Corris looked first to his right – taking in the muddy paddock with its open-fronted barn and big, old oak trees – and then to his left – along the back of the new house, the row of wooden stables and out to the front field.

Mrs B. and I agreed our strategy. She would ride Corris a little way ahead and I would follow, leading Havana. We would go up the farm lane like this, with Havana gaining confidence from Corris.

Again, we had failed to anticipate just how exciting this encounter with a role model was for Havana, whose floating strides, on elastic legs, quickly caught up with Corris's measured walk.

By the time we got to the beginning of the farm lane, Havana was close enough to Corris to stretch out his neck and rudely attempt to nip Corris's rump. Holding Havana back seemed unfair – he wanted to walk with Corris.

I thought that if I allowed them to walk side-by-side, this might settle Havana. How wrong I was! Once alongside, the rude little dragon made a lunge for Corris's flank and gave him a sharp nip with his teeth.

Thankfully, Corris's remarkable decorum under saddle meant that he did not react.

Ashamed of Havana's discourteous behaviour, I shortened the lead rope, determined to march him on so he was shoulder-to-shoulder with Corris. Once he was where Corris could see him properly, I hoped he would be cowed into behaving himself. But as we progressed, Havana was, once again, overcome by the desire to nip Corris. His next lunge did not connect with Corris at all, but with Mrs B.'s leg. Fortunately she was wearing sturdy leather boots, so hardly felt the bite.

I knew what Havana's problem was; this attempt at a stately procession was actually rather boring for him. In his baby-horse way, he was just trying to liven things up. This was what he would have done in the field if he were walking behind Rollo or Flower. A nip on the rump or flank could start a game – *far more* exciting than just walking! How could I blame him?

To protect Corris and Mrs B. from further assault, I urged Havana on so we were in front. He happily and confidently led the way along the farm lane to the road and 'the outside world'.

Mrs B. and Corris then went off for a ride. As they left, Corris seemed relieved to be dissociating himself from such a tiresome, immature creature, so he could get on with the responsible job of taking his person for a ride.

Havana was perfectly content to watch Corris and Mrs B. walk, and then trot off into the distance. He thinks I'm joking when I tell him:

"Havana, that's what we'll do when you're three – we'll go for rides!" For now, rides are what 'big horses' do and Havana's priorities are eating and playing – in that order.

PARTITION
Saturday, 14 March 2009

*T*onight Havana had a big surprise.

The partition between his own stable and the stable next door had grown taller since this morning.

In preparation for Corris moving in, and to stop Havana attempting to climb over or through it, large wooden boards have been added on what will be Corris's side, so the gaps between the parallel planks have been filled in and the partition is about a foot taller.

Havana clearly did not trust the new structure. With an expression which was a curious mixture of apprehension and indignation, he managed to stay as far away as possible from the partition, even though his stable is long but not very wide.

It was not until I had done my usual 'reassuring routine' of stroking the offending partition and praising it for being a "nice partition", and a "lovely partition", that Havana warily stretched out his neck and sniffed the newly-added board.

As his confidence returned, he lifted his chin over the top of the partition and seemed surprised that his view of the other side was just as it had always been!

When I encouraged him to look over from the back part of the stable, where his bed is, the extra height gained by standing on the thick straw made looking over the partition easier. This must have pleased him, because Havana's observation from this elevated vantage point lasted a very long time.

CORRIS'S ARRIVAL
Sunday, 15 March 2009

*C*orris arrived this afternoon.

Mrs B. rode him from Gunstone Hall like a cowboy, carrying his rolled-up turnout rug across the front of the saddle.

When Corris came into the stable next to his, Havana demonstrated his excitement at having a companion – this time a horse, not a hen – by continually sticking his head over the partition to check, and re-check, that Corris really was there.

Corris reacted characteristically to the unwelcome intrusion of Havana's inquisitive nose protruding into his new domain, by snapping at it with lightning-fast teeth. Undaunted, and like a demented glove puppet, Havana just kept popping up at another point along the partition. For him, the excitement of at last having a stable-mate far outweighed the threat to his muzzle from Corris's incisors.

Only a bucket of feed could distract this excited baby tonight. As Havana ate, I reassured him that:

"When you go to sleep Corris will be there, and when you wake up in the morning, he will *still* be there."

I am certain that Havana is very, very happy that Corris is next door.

FAITH
Monday, 16 March 2009

I really do believe in miracles!

The sight of Havana in the early morning mist, grazing shoulder-to-shoulder with Cayman's former stable-mate, Corris, just fifteen minutes after they were turned-out together is, quite simply, a miracle for which I am very thankful.

* * *

Havana had an air about him of one who is bathing in reflected glory. It was as if he thought his allegiance to Corris now accorded him greater importance in the field.

However, by fetching-in time Corris had formed what looks like a serious attachment to Faith, the eighteen-year-old Hackney mare.

Faith is genteel and determinedly solitary as a rule.

The fact that she and Corris were splendidly alone, either side of one of the huge bales of haylage – like an aristocratic couple at opposite ends of a grand dining table – whilst the remaining seven horses crowded round the other bale, indicates there could well be a 'special relationship'.

I am so pleased for Corris, because he has lived, quite unnaturally, for the past fifteen years in a herd comprising only geldings; and for Faith, because her life has been a hard one: a foal every year from the age of four, so continuously both in-foal *and* suckling a foal until she was rescued, in very poor condition, aged sixteen.

Faith deserves a 'gentleman companion'.

I must say though, that the speed of Corris's seduction is breathtaking! I suspect that switching his allegiance to a new grazing partner – from morning to afternoon – means that poor Havana has been demoted back to being the *least* important horse in the field.

"… reflected glory."

HERO

Tuesday, 17 March 2009

*E*vidently, Havana is still totally smitten by Corris.

As I let him out of his stable this morning, I offered him the choice of what he wanted to do. Corris had already gone out to the field as he has less breakfast than Havana and eats it quickly. Corris's stable door was open and Mrs B. was mucking-out.

Havana's choice was instant; straight into Corris's stable.

First, Havana checked that Corris had not left any breakfast. No – his feed bowl was empty. Next, he explored Corris's bed, tramping round in circles, sniffing and messing-up the wood shavings that Mrs B. had just made clean and tidy. Finally, Havana investigated Corris's night rug, which was hanging over the partition separating Corris's stable from the third, unused, stable. Eagerly he sniffed it all over, his intent expression indicating that his nostrils were relaying some fascinating information.

If I had not decided that was enough hero worship for one day and urged Havana out, I suspect he would still have been sniffing about in Corris's stable when it was time for Corris to return.

Havana's juvenile excitement and happiness at Corris's arrival are so genuine; it's really sweet.

MORE Mr B.

Wednesday, 18 March 2009

*W*hat a lovely sight.

Mr and Mrs B. had arrived before me this evening and had already put Corris into his stable.

In case Corris became unsettled, Mr B. had gone to get Havana in and they were coming up the gentle gradient towards the top of the field just as I arrived.

Mr B. had Havana firmly under control!

It might not have been really necessary for him to have such a firm grip on Havana's head collar but – with his huge, farmer's fist wrapped tightly around the back of the nose band – Mr B. was taking *no* chances with this lithe little flight animal.

Havana's alert, slightly anxious, but totally angelic expression said it all; he was unused to being handled so decisively by such a big person.

Sensing this was an occasion when his very best behaviour was expected, he was walking with Mr B. with the aching politeness and deference of a seven-year-old school boy who had been summoned to accompany the headmaster.

He looked heartbreakingly adorable.

I felt a surge of pride that all of my lessons in manners – some of which I thought Havana had disregarded totally – were now distilled into one, exemplary, demonstration.

SPRING

Saturday, 21 March 2009

Mrs B. decided it was time Corris went for a ride.

So that he was not unsettled, she took him off in the opposite direction from Gunstone.

Havana was also overdue for some education so, after breakfast, feet, and grooming, we went for a walk down the farm lane.

It really felt as if spring had arrived; blue sky, light fresh air, birds singing, tiny green leaves on the hedge – and much warmer.

Havana was feeling good; his high head, pricked ears and flared nostrils all indicated that he too was absorbing the beautiful morning. We strode along the lane together, both relishing being part of the nature that was all around us.

At the end of the lane, we stopped for some grass in the gateway. The last time we did this the grass was dry and burned by frost, but now it was fresh and green. After five minutes' grazing, Havana's attention was quite clearly on the other side of the road; he wanted to continue our walk down the footpath opposite.

The high hedge on one side and fence on the other make this a good place for some 'Halt! – Walk-on!' practice.

Using voice commands which I thought could prepare Havana for being lunged when he is older, we 'stop-started' our way along the path to the metal gate across it, then back to the road. Havana was quite good at this, if a little distracted by trying to look over the hedge at the fishing lake and caravans across the field.

Once we were back on our own farm lane, I had an idea. What if I simply stopped then walked on again, without saying anything to Havana? Would he notice? Would he mirror my behaviour or just carry on walking? After all, he was now on his way back to his field.

When I put all of my concentration into stopping abruptly, I could scarcely believe it when – with military precision – Havana did the same.

We stood shoulder-to-shoulder and, when I walked again, Havana did too. I was amazed. I hardly dared repeat the exercise in case it had just been a fluke and Havana wasn't really tuned-in to my behaviour. But once again, the instant I stopped, Havana came to a smart halt!

We did this several more times. Then I decided really to put this little horse to the test; I walked just *one* pace forwards and stopped – my little horse-shadow did the same. Another single step – the same again. Another, then another.

Joy, relief and amazement all swelled in my chest. Havana and I could have *waltzed* together! As I rubbed his forehead, I'm sure he knew why my beaming smile was directed at him.

I was delighted by all that concentration, attention and control given so willingly, by one so young. The significance of this was brought into sharp focus when I turned Havana out into the field a few minutes later.

The second his head collar was off, he turned and *galloped* towards his friends, bucking with joy at being young and free on such a beautiful spring morning.

LISTEN AGAIN!

Monday, 23 March 2009

*H*istoric day number three!

From the safety of the gateway at the end of the farm lane, Havana has shown little inclination to go either left or right along the quiet, narrow road which, for him, constitutes 'the outside world'.

Why would he need to go any further when there's plenty of grass in the gateway?

Now that Corris lives with Havana, I hoped his presence would give Havana the confidence to explore just a few yards into 'the outside world' to the left – where there are wide grassy verges and good visibility, so any approaching cars would not startle him.

As usual, Havana bowled along the farm lane, confidently leading the way. Mrs B. rode Corris behind us. After a break for Havana to be rewarded with some grass in the gateway, we agreed that our strategy would be for Corris and Mrs B. to ride a little way down the road, to the left, and then to halt in the wide entrance to the fishing farm.

That way Havana would see that, as Corris was perfectly safe and settled, there was certainly no danger for horses in that part of 'the outside world' and, being a herd animal, we hoped he would feel the need to follow Corris. Once that part was accomplished, Havana would again be rewarded with some grass on the wide verge, before being escorted safely back to the familiar territory of his own gateway at the end of the farm lane.

Well, that *was* the plan.

In reality, contentedly munching tasty grass, Havana watched unconcerned as Corris and Mrs B. rode off to the left. I had quite a job persuading him to lift his head from the grass and look down the road to observe that Corris and Mrs B. were now standing safely in the entrance to the fishing farm. As Havana stood by my right shoulder, he seemed to be thinking:

"So what?" and then, as I urged him forward out onto the road and into 'the outside world':

"No; I don't think horses are meant to do this." By the time we had 'stop-started' ten or so paces towards Corris and Mrs B., it was obvious that Havana had decided:

"Horses definitely *don't* do this!" Every atom of his tense, agitated body was signalling total psychological overload.

Attempting to look in all directions at the same time, his panicked vigilance necessitated a very high head carriage. Somehow, Havana's frame seemed to have compacted lengthways, but become much, much taller; he was *at least* 17hh, and alarmingly light on his feet. My trump card – the reassuring presence of Corris – was, to Havana, an irrelevance, as was having his person by his side. For him, it was 'every horse for himself!' My gloves, riding hat, body protector and steel toecap boots might as well have been made from tissue paper for the comfort they gave me. I was alarmed by the potential power of the 'bomb' on the end of Havana's lead rope.

Ten hurried paces later, we were back in our own gateway and the 17hh 'bomb' had calmed back into a gentle, relaxed 14.2hh baby horse.

I have learned another valuable lesson – a reminder:

"Lay off the human agenda, the targets, the developmental milestones, the strategies. *Listen to your horse – he'll* tell you what *he's* ready to do!"

CARROTS
Friday, 27 March 2009

*H*avana really was behaving very strangely this evening when I got him in from the field and I think I know why ... carrots.

Yesterday, when he was in his stable for worming, I kept my promise (admittedly made a couple of months ago) that I would buy him a whole net of 'horse carrots'.

Horse carrots are sold by greengrocers in nets weighing about ten kilograms. They are inexpensive because they are usually unconventional sizes – ranging from giant to minuscule – and very nearly at the end of their shelf-life.

None of this concerns horses and, for Havana, Friday's lunchtime carrot feast was the most glorious gift from heaven imaginable.

The finely-chopped carrots in his evening feed were another very welcome surprise, as were those in his breakfast this morning. You see, you do have to get rid of these carrots pretty quickly as, in no time, they start to go bendy, then black, then mushy and need to be thrown away.

By now, Havana was probably beginning to view carrots with every meal as a fact of life rather than a wonderful surprise.

When Mrs B. and I went into the field this evening to get Corris and Havana, it was becoming dusk. We could easily see Corris's brilliant-white head, neck and legs protruding from his turnout rug. He was grazing a little way down the field and took his time to look up and start walking towards us.

Sylph-like, the dark shape of Havana was nearly on top of us before we even noticed him eagerly making his way up one of the rutted tracks towards the gate.

As Havana is so good at our gate routine, he and I went through and then politely held the gate open for Mrs B. and Corris, before chaining it closed.

It was whilst I was fastening the chain that I noticed how agitated Havana had become. Usually he stands patiently, but tonight he was so keen to dart off that I had to keep him on a very short rope and keep my eye on him whilst I secured the gate, which was not easy.

Corris and Mrs B. were probably already in their stable.

The minute we turned up the path to the stables, Havana was so light on his feet that he was nearly airborne. His neck was vertical, making him suddenly very, very tall. Circling slowed him down for a couple of paces, but he quickly gathered momentum and reverted to 'over-excited racehorse pace'.

I circled him most of the way to the stable and, as we approached the doorway, threw the lead rope over his back as he surged inside. Thankful that he was now contained, I closed the door.

"You can sort yourself out Havana, I'm not coming in until you've calmed down!" I went into the tack room to make his feed.

Corris was already eating when, having taken off Havana's head collar, I held out his feed bucket as he virtually dived into it head first. Havana's excitement at being presented with a feed containing so many carrots was too great for him to remember his manners.

With lengthways-sliced carrots cascading from the corners of his mouth as he chewed, it was alarming to consider how many carrot pieces must still be inside Havana's delicate little mouth. Seeing him so evidently relishing his food did make me smile with satisfaction that, according to him, I was at least doing *something* right.

It is normally at this point that, standing in front of Havana, I would put an arm over his mane and stroke his neck, whilst balancing the large, heavy feed bucket on one raised knee and steadying it with my other hand. (This *is* as difficult as it sounds.)

When I attempted to do this, however, Havana's reaction was unexpected. With his muzzle still in the feed bucket, he instantly rotated his back end a quarter turn towards the door, as if sweeping away imaginary intruders from that part of the stable.

Havana doesn't bolt his food, but always chews it methodically and thoroughly. He usually takes a long time, but the addition of so many carrots meant that, tonight, it was taking Havana *forever* to eat his tea.

I decided to put the feed bucket, carefully, on the floor.

Not a good idea. Havana's enjoyment quickly translated to front leg waving – resulting in the bucket being tipped-up and food spilling over the floor.

Once he, apparently, had got the hang of finishing his feed in a more adult way – without me holding the bucket – I took the opportunity to check him over for injuries, as I usually do.

As soon as I started running my hand gently along his offside flank, he bunched-up his rump and 'cow-kicked'. Fortunately, he didn't do this with his offside back leg, but with the back leg on the *opposite* side from me. This apparently irrational action (as there was no intruder or predator on that side) was definitely a defensive one.

I was not going to remain in the stable with a little horse who was, unusually but obviously, on defensive autopilot. I said: "Goodnight Havana", although he probably didn't hear me over the noise of his own jaws.

As Mrs B. and I walked away from the stables, I tried to rationalise Havana's behaviour

"He's not usually so rude and threatening when he's eating – Corris has been here a week now and he hasn't been like this before."

"Something must have changed." Mrs B. prompted. Then it dawned on me; carrots!

Havana has finally been granted his greatest wish – carrots at every meal. He clearly felt threatened because Corris was in the next stable, so he was acting entirely logically in guarding his carrots from potential carrot thieves; whether equine, human or imaginary, he draws no distinction. A carrot thief is a carrot thief and a horse is simply programmed to guard his carrots.

SPRINGBOK
Friday, 3 April 2009

It's quite obvious that Havana really wants to be a springbok gazelle.

Never before have I seen a little creature 'boing' so impressively off all four feet, straight into the air.

He must be getting some spring grass.

When I went into the field with Mrs B., Corris saw us and obligingly walked up from the bottom of the field straight to the gate.

Havana, on the other hand, just kept on grazing.

Determined *not* to walk all the way to him, I walked halfway down the field, stood looking hard at Havana's back end as I counted to ten, then turned and walked away.

Miraculously, given the fresh green circumstances, Havana lifted his head and began meandering up the field towards me – but he was very soon distracted by more succulent shoots of new grass.

I repeated my predatory technique and, sure enough, up came Havana's head and he meandered a bit further up the field, but with no real sense of urgency. Inevitably, his concentration soon faltered and, once again, he was tearing at the tasty pasture.

Another ten-second stare produced relatively spectacular results. As I looked over my shoulder, Havana was trotting eagerly to catch up with me.

"That's it," I thought, "home and dry."

Havana actually beat me to the top of the field but, once there, he was instantly overtaken by playfulness.

From standing stock-still, he launched himself into a perfect vertical take-off, flinging out one front leg as he did so. It was alarming … but very impressive.

As he landed, he turned and careered back down the field, bucking for all he was worth and at such a thunderous gallop that the sound of his hooves brought Mrs B. out of Corris's stable to see what was going on.

Havana galloped in a big arc around his herd, before almost crashing into Prince. He nipped the big dapple grey Cob's shoulder:

"Come on Prince – let's play galloping!" No go; Prince preferred to graze in the late evening sunshine.

This ballistic baby tried the same energetic tactic with his friend Rollo … with the same result.

I strode purposefully down the field.

By the time I reached the bottom, Havana had resumed grazing, apparently now quite oblivious to what had, only a few seconds earlier, been the dire need for a galloping game.

Wary of the explosive energy of his previous antics, I put on

Havana's head collar and led him assertively, 'Mr B. style', with my hand firmly holding the back of his noseband to pre-empt any reignition of his game.

Havana walked up the field with me like a lamb although, as he was still wearing his winter-fur coat, a rather sweaty one.

CYCLISTS
Sunday, 5 April 2009

*I*t was like holding the string of a helium balloon, except this one must have weighed nearly half-a-ton.

In fact, it was Havana – in the sky, somewhere above me. Momentarily, he had landed but become airborne again in an instant.

The cause?

Two surprised gentlemen, out for a bicycle ride yesterday morning; one in a yellow cycling cape.

Out of consideration, fear, or confusion at the little horse's reaction to their movements, they had both halted a few feet from us.

Havana's perception: '*unfathomably terrible monsters – hunting in a pair – positioning themselves to pounce.*'

Once the cyclists had continued on their way, Havana quickly regained his composure. We were in the gateway at the end of the lane, where his attention was diverted by the tasty new grass.

As Havana's reaction had been so extreme, I knew that I needed to do all I could to help him feel less threatened by yellow-clad cyclists and their bicycles.

Havana, bless him, is so used to me doing strange things, that when I gave him his evening feed he didn't seem to notice I was wearing a voluminous, ankle-length, bright yellow riding coat made of stiff plastic – which made cracking sounds when I moved.

And this morning, although he had never seen *his* person on a bicycle before, Havana looked only mildly surprised when – dressed in a high visibility yellow "Caution Horse and Rider" tabard – I wobbled my bicycle back and forth over the gravel and the muddy path outside his stable.

As I led him out to the field, past the bicycle, his interest in it peaked when he thought he could nibble the front brake cable – which looped up above the handle bar at about the same height as his mouth. When I *didn't* allow him to supplement his breakfast with bits of bicycle, he lost interest in it altogether.

It will be fascinating to see how my attempts at desensitisation affect our next encounter with a cyclist.

PRIDE
Monday, 6 April 2009

*T*oday I am overflowing with pride.

Havana has had two visitors: 'Auntie Alison' and her good friend, Alison Number Two. Both former horse dealers and showjumpers, there isn't much they don't know about horses – and they're certainly not easily impressed.

When I gave Havana his breakfast, I told him that we were having visitors so he must be on his very best behaviour. But I wasn't certain I could trust him not to do something cheeky and boisterous – like inviting his visitors to play with him by nipping their arms or legs.

As I walked down the field after lunch with Alison and Alison, Havana was grazing peacefully. Rollo noticed us first and came to greet us. When Havana noticed us, his expression was one of total bewilderment … what was I doing in his field at this time?

I slipped on his head collar and that is when the surprise started; I could not have asked for him to stand more courteously!

His fine, intelligent head was high; perceptive nostrils relaying information about his visitors; dark, liquid eyes engaged; ears mobile and alert as he listened to the knowledgeable comments drifting in the air around him.

"Certainly takes after the Thoroughbred side." "So fine." "Beautiful conformation." "What a kind eye." "He's got a lovely stamp on him."

Havana stood, poised and elegant, with not a thought of a nip or a cheeky game. I could hardly believe it!

If a horse knows how to propel himself straight into a person's heart, it's Havana.

His effortless charm offensive continued in the stable, with abundant quantities of what Alison Number Two described as 'necky love'; when Havana simply rested his delicate, velvet muzzle gently against the side of her neck and let his warm breath envelop her.

So much affection freely given by a young horse who is sure people love him – which they quite obviously do – is a far better strategy for making friends than nipping people.

Perhaps Havana is growing up ....

WOLF TEETH
Thursday, 16 April 2009

*P*hew, I'm exhausted!

Today Havana *didn't* have his wolf teeth out.

It started yesterday when I went to see Alison W. and just happened to mention today's appointment as I was leaving her yard.

"Why are you having his wolf teeth out – are they hurting him?" I answered that they didn't seem to be.

"Well why can't they stay in? Some babies have wolf teeth so, why can't you just let him be a baby? Poor little Havana!" I was confused. I protested about it being better for Havana to have them out now, rather than later when the teeth were bigger and with more root.

"They don't get more root!" Alison was decisive; an experienced horsewoman, and former RSPCA inspector, I respected her opinion.

"Applying your logic, I would have had all my son's teeth taken out as soon as they grew, just in case they caused him problems when he was older!"

I had just had the rationale for my decision 'blown out of the water'. Alison's opposition to my plan was so vehement, that I was only able to placate her by promising faithfully to reconsider.

Confused about what to do for the best and running out of time to make my decision, I rang one of my other professional equestrian friends. Lisa ran through some general reasons for removing wolf teeth:

"If they become painful later, when Havana starts to wear a bridle, he could mistakenly associate the pain with his bit, which could then make him reluctant to have his bridle on. If he has to have his wolf teeth removed later, then he can't be ridden whilst his gums heal, as his bit may cause irritation. Or he could develop problems at a really inconvenient time, like just before an important competition." I protested that I didn't want to take advantage of Havana's good nature. When he had had his teeth drilled only a couple of months ago, he had been remarkably brave and tolerant in a really frightening situation, but I didn't want him to be frightened again unnecessarily. Lisa reminded me that, this time, he would be sedated so should not be frightened.

"I think I would probably have them out ..." was Lisa's conclusion, "... but it's your decision."

I rang 'Auntie Alison':

"I thought you were going to have them out?"

"Yes, I was, but now I'm not sure. I don't want to upset him as he's so good. I don't want to put him through something which might not be necessary."

Alison understood my dilemma and very helpfully ran through the pros and cons – except the pros were the same as Lisa's and there didn't really seem to be any cons.

So, two for wolf tooth extraction and one against. I was still 'on the fence', unable to cast my vote. My head said 'yes', but my heart screamed 'NO'.

Mrs B. reminded me that Cayman had wolf teeth that caused no problems. Genetically, Havana is Cayman's half-brother, so perhaps *his* wolf teeth would be trouble-free too.

I am so grateful to my friend Gill – an experienced riding instructor *and* psychologist – for her lateral thinking.

"What would Terry do?"

Terry is the North Wales horse breeder, with a lifetime's experience, who had bred Havana. Gill had accompanied me on one of my many visits to Terry's farm to see Havana before he was weaned.

Genius! This was the sword that slashed through my dilemma. I knew exactly what Terry would do. I could easily imagine his kindly, yet incredulous expression at the idea of paying good money to have a horse's teeth taken out when you didn't have to.

It was a 'no brainer'. My decision was made. Unless Sue, Havana's vet, came up with something that no one else had thought of, Havana would keep his wolf teeth.

I rang the surgery to give advance warning that the visit, which had been booked as 'injection and wolf tooth extraction', was now – subject to Sue's advice – likely to become just 'injection'.

I was starting to feel relieved that by protecting Havana from possible further psychological upset concerning his mouth, I was doing the right thing. After all, it will only be a few months before I introduce him to the reality of having a bit in his mouth, so I don't want to do anything to upset his trust that I will not hurt him.

"Is he three now?" Sue was sheltering from the pouring rain under the tailgate of her car as she got out the flu and tetanus vaccine and what looked like a big metal toolbox but was, in fact, her dentistry kit.

"No, he's only two, his birthday was the seventeenth of February."

"Ah yes, you had him so young – it seems as if you've had him for a long time."

Havana was snug and dry in his stable with Mrs B., whom I had asked to come, probably more for *my* wellbeing than Havana's.

I explained my reluctance to have his wolf teeth taken out if it was not necessary.

"Hello Havana!" Sue stroked his neck, as Havana smelled her hair. Greetings exchanged, Sue felt inside Havana's upper jaw.

"They're fine; they're perfectly in line with the other teeth. They'd only really need to come out if they were somewhere strange, sticking out where they'd cause a problem." Thank goodness … what a relief!

The injection in his neck was no more painful for Havana than a midge bite, and that was all he had to endure today.

The rest of Sue's visit was spent with Sue, Mrs B. and I 'talking horses' in Havana's stable whilst Havana, unaware of the dental assault he had nearly suffered, dozed, lulled into relaxation by the sound of our voices.

Havana might eventually have to have his wolf teeth out, but that's a chance I'm willing to take. For now I'm happy that I've made the right decision, but the psychological contortions I've gone through have worn me out.

RUN!
Friday, 17 April 2009

*T*he little wild rabbit-coloured terrier from the neighbouring farm was energetically rooting about in the bottom of the hedge, about twenty feet away from where Mrs B. and I were standing chatting, outside the field.

His foraging transported him systematically along the hedge bottom towards us so that, by the time I was ready to walk down the field to find Havana, the little dog was level with the gate but still on his owner's side of the hedge.

My mistake was to look at him and, in a soft voice, say: "Hello little dog!"

In a rustle of dry leaves, he had squeezed through the roots of the hedge bottom and was accompanying me through the gate. Seized by a scent, he scampered, in loops, down the field, nose in overdrive and oblivious to the herd of horses grazing on the fresh grass at the bottom.

Flower noticed me first as she was facing me, straight ahead, but her attention was very quickly diverted by the tiny creature to my left, scenting its way towards her.

For a moment this bright, pretty filly, with her charmingly askew white blaze – not quite down the centre of her nose – and alluring giraffe-like eyes, watched the blissfully ignorant terrier cascading towards her. But then, I was shocked to see a malevolent transformation of her beguiling face. As she walked, then trotted, with arched neck, in short, elevated steps towards the furry trespasser, a completely demonic expression spread across her forehead. She was a horse possessed.

With synchronization to which ice dancers might aspire, Havana – who had been grazing to Flower's right – drifted effortlessly into the fray, as Rollo joined in from the left.

The little dog sensed that he was suddenly the object of a lot of unwanted attention and made a dash for the fence that runs up the side of the field. He was only halfway there when the now *galloping* trio of excited and playful young horses caught up with him.

Why do people stand stock-still, open their mouths, widen their eyes and put one hand on top of their heads when they witness – or think they are about to witness – a disaster?

I don't know; but it's what I did as Flower galloped *right over* the tiny dog.

He would surely have met an agonising, traumatic death and it was entirely my fault for encouraging him into the field.

I could hardly believe my eyes when the little creature bolted to the left and – unable to get through the square mesh of the sheep netting – fled up the fence line. *He was still alive!*

The awesome sound of twelve thundering hooves was dramatically amplified when two heavyweights, Prince and one of the usually sedate Beauties, joined in the final charge to the finishing line.

How had a terrified little dog, with legs only about four inches long, managed to out-gallop five tyrannous horses to squeeze under the gate to safety?

I'll never know; but the answer may have something to do with the fact that he was terrified – literally running for his life. For the horses, it was just a good game – a momentary diversion from grazing which they all quickly resumed.

All, that is, except Havana, whose innate over-exuberance fuelled another *two* delirious laps of the perimeter of the field at a flat-out gallop, before he settled once more to graze.

WONKY
Tuesday, 21 April 2009

I was intrigued by 'Auntie Alison's' observation a couple of weeks ago, that – even when Havana was standing facing us on the part of the field which slopes away downhill – his back end was still higher than his front end.

So today, I decided to 'get scientific', using my retractable steel ruler and straight, flat wooden baton which looks as if it might, at one time, have been part of a piece of furniture.

Havana is used to me measuring the height of his withers with monotonous regularity, to see whether he has grown.

When I placed the wooden baton horizontally across the highest point of his rump, my matter-of-fact manner must have reassured him that it is also quite normal to measure a horse's height from this point. It isn't – but Havana doesn't know this!

His long, lanky hind legs do seem to thrust Havana's rump well up above the rest of his back, but the actual measurements made me laugh:

Withers: 14.2½hh, rump: 15.1hh.

I really had not anticipated a discrepancy of two-and-a-half inches between the front and back end of this wonky little creature.

It will be interesting to see what happens when he has his next growth spurt. Last year's was between April and June, so not long to go ….

14.2 ½ h.h   15.1 h.h

"… a discrepancy of 2½ inches"

DINOSAURS
Friday, 24 April 2009

*D*on't tangle with dinosaurs!"

Mrs B.'s advice was right, but it came too late for Havana and me.

Whilst Havana eats his breakfast, I still need to hold his big feed bucket to stop him sending its contents flying with his pawing front feet.

Occasionally, Havana is distracted; needing to look out over his door, or through one of the four windows. As he moves his head I try to follow with the bucket, to catch the grain which inevitably spills from the corners of his mouth. I don't always succeed and, when it suddenly 'rains grain', Henny Penny is quick to pick it up.

In fact, this manna from Heaven is so guaranteed that when Havana is having his breakfast, Henny Penny is usually scratching around vigilantly amongst the bits of straw and hay on the stable floor, perilously close to his hooves.

Havana doesn't seem to mind that Henny Penny always takes the shortest route to the next grain, even when that route is directly under his belly.

A horse does have 'blind spots', one of which is the ground directly under his jaw.

To look at this he needs to tilt his head slightly to one side, arch his neck and draw his head in towards his chest. To investigate closer he also needs to lower his head.

That is exactly what Havana was doing; he was evidently aware that there was something down there.

As he gently lowered his muzzle towards her, Henny Penny puffed-up – instantly becoming a spherical, feathery pompom – launched herself into the air and lanced the side of Havana's descending nose with a ferocious beak jab.

The poor unsuspecting little horse was so startled.

He shook his head, instinctively returned his muzzle to the safety of his breakfast bucket and – with an air of total incomprehension – resumed eating, his eyes still wide with surprise.

I really can sympathise with Havana because yesterday, when I was inside the stable replacing the 'hen brick' under the door (to stop the hens walking in), my finger curled around the brick must have looked – to Henny Penny, who was outside – like a *juicy pink worm*.

The speed of her peck was frightening.

The pain made me shriek and the accuracy of her aim – midway between the first and second joints of my right index finger – was impressive.

Whilst Havana finished his breakfast, Mrs B. and I were discussing the evolutionary link between birds and dinosaurs:

Could dinosaurs' ferocity have been inherited by hens, *and by one hen in particular?*

WHERE TIME IS SUSPENDED
Friday, 1 May 2009

*T*his morning, after a fairly chilly night, the whole herd were recharging themselves in the warm sunshine.

One of the Beauties and Grace, were standing on sentry duty; everyone else was sitting down – evenly spread and an equal distance from each other – in the sunniest corner at the bottom of the field.

Havana was very, very drowsy, with his muzzle resting on the grass and his eyes closed.

Careful not to disturb the sleepy group, I approached quietly, looping round the outside and making my way, gently, to Havana.

I spoke soothingly; my words soporifically stretched into each other:

"H-e-l-l-o-b-o-y."

His heavy lids half opened.

There was only one thing to do. I sank to the ground, in between Havana's curled-up front and back legs, having first put his leather head collar there to sit on to keep me very slightly off the dewy grass. But a wet bottom is a small price to pay for the privilege of an innately over-reactive flight animal allowing you to sit down with him.

The hair on Havana's side was almost too hot to touch; in fact the heat radiating from the flat expanse of his ribcage reminded me of a barbecue. You could have fried eggs on him and he was so relaxed that he probably wouldn't have minded!

I slipped my right arm over Havana's back and my left arm across his chest.

I was shocked when he lifted his head a little, wrapped his neck around my left shoulder and pressed his jaw against my back, very effectively pulling my upper body close to him so my weight was against his side.

To my amazement, he continued to doze in this position, with his head and neck curled around me.

Enveloped in the comfort of that big, horsey hug, time slowed to the rhythm of Havana's peaceful breathing. As his relaxation deepened, my mind stilled and drifted to where time is suspended; a place that horses seem to know so well.

FIRST MOTORBIKE
Sunday, 10 May 2009

*T*his is a new feeling – and it feels wonderful!

It's as if Havana and I have been for a really enjoyable ride together; a ride that has bonded us.

What we actually did was simply walk down the farm lane – and Havana grazed in the gateway at the end, as usual.

What *is* different, is that we were by ourselves and we overcame something scary but, for the first time, I was totally relaxed; no adrenaline at all.

The 'something scary' was Havana's first motorbike. It was a fine specimen: big, shiny burgundy tank; throbbing engine; radiant, halogen headlight.

For a little horse, this could all have added up to being quite a 'monster'.

As it approached, Havana threw up his head.

From being by my side, quietly grazing, he leapt to safety right behind me!

As the motorbike considerately purred … very slowly … past us, I glanced over my right shoulder to see Havana giving it a hard stare.

As soon as it had gone off round the bend in the narrow road, he emerged from behind me and resumed grazing as if nothing had happened.

Although Havana had obviously been frightened – and this was certainly a situation where *I* could have been – it makes me happy that I understand him enough to feel, not fear, but compassion, love and a very strong bond between us. I know this bond will develop and strengthen as we enjoy our future together.

What a wonderful prospect! I feel so excited about it already.

YOGA
Tuesday, 12 May 2009

*A*ll I wanted was a current picture of Havana to email to Ricky in the Middle East, so he could see how he's growing and to remind him of home.

Well, they do say: 'never work with children or animals'.

At the exact moment when Havana was nicely framed through the viewfinder of my camera, he had the most irritating itch halfway along his mane.

As any horse knows, the way you deal satisfactorily with an itch there is to bring your head round towards your back end, and your back hoof (on the same side) round towards your head. Your other three legs form a steady tripod so you can scratch your neck with your foot and not fall over.

The resulting photograph certainly demonstrated Havana's athleticism, suppleness, co-ordination and balance.

In a nanosecond it was emailed six thousand miles to Ricky, who was amazed and amused by our pet contortionist.

Then I sent the photograph to Mrs B. who, in turn, sent it on to her yoga teacher.

Oh dear … might 'The Havana' become the newest exercise?

I wouldn't like to be in Mrs B.'s next yoga class!

'The Havana'

REPEL ALL MIDGES!

Friday, 15 May 2009

*I*t's so good to feel needed and today Havana let me know, in no uncertain terms, that he *did* need me.

This morning, he must just have been feeling greedy because, as soon as he saw me, he came trotting up the field, head high, all eager and excited at the prospect of having his breakfast, despite the fact that he had probably been eating grass all night long.

Mr and Mrs B. are on holiday, so I am looking after Corris.

To avoid upsetting Havana, I got him in first and settled him down with his bucket of feed before I fetched Corris in. But, because I don't want Corris to feel deprived, he does also get some fuss and stroking.

When I'm in Corris's stable, Havana keeps an eye on me. Now that he's getting taller, it's easy enough for him to put his head over the wooden dividing partition. Resting his jaw on the top, he peers over like a nosey neighbour; he looks very sweet. I'm sure he's checking that *his* human isn't giving Corris too much fuss, or worse, extra food.

It does Havana good to see how a horse as exemplary as Corris behaves in the stable; he can learn by example.

So, when Corris stood, rock-solid, whilst I sprayed him all over with fly spray, I was glad that our nosey little neighbour had his head over the partition – his surprised expression was a picture!

After spraying Corris, I gently sprayed a little of the pungent fly repellent, in short bursts, directly at Havana's forelock and then some more onto either side of his neck.

His innate reaction – to move away from the source of the hissing noise – was now balanced by his knowledge that Corris had not moved a muscle when he was sprayed. So, despite the surprising sound and the strange smell, Havana didn't retreat – perhaps concluding that being sprayed 'isn't anything for a horse to be too bothered about'.

This evening, Havana needed me desperately. His gangly, careering canter towards the gate told me that he wanted my help *now*!

The sharp sting which I felt on my scalp enabled me to understand Havana's problem. A storm had just finished and the midges were lethal. I could see by the agitated way in which the other horses were swishing their tails that everyone was being troubled, but only Havana was reacting so dramatically. In fairness though, with his fine coat and skin, he would feel the bites more than they would. I really was very touched that he saw me as someone who would sort out his midge problem.

After reassuring him that I understood what he was telling me, by giving him a good scratch on his rump, I decided that I needed to get him into the stable to apply more fly repellent.

"Stay by the gate Boo; I'll get your head collar."

I half expected him to go galloping off down the field, tormented by the incessant stings, but as I rushed back with the head collar I was pleased to see him standing by the fence, still at the top of the field; he looked glad to see me too.

Once horses are in stables, midges leave them alone. Havana's salvation was instant and his return to his usual calmness told me that he was so relieved.

This morning I had used up all of Mrs B.'s insect repellent on Corris. In our medical chest I had some roll-on insect repellent lotion for people. It was from last year and there was hardly any of that left either.

The faint trundling noise of a roll-on applicator seems to worry horses less than the hiss of a spray. To make the most of what was left, I rolled it onto my hands and wiped them all over Havana's body, starting with his head and ears. After that, for good measure – and to let Havana know that I really was trying my hardest to help him – I combed the top of his tickly tail with the metal comb and applied a good dusting of louse powder. I hoped that, to a midge's scent receptors, the smell of the fine anti-louse dust would also be a repellent.

Havana seemed satisfied with my efforts. I promised to get him some more anti-midge roll-on, then gave him the choice of staying in the stable a while longer or going back out in the field.

The decision was made for us by Henny Penny, the mad hen.

Whilst I had been administering fly repellent, she had been sitting on the floor of the stable, eyeing-up the partition. When she became airborne – in a ridiculous whir of inadequate, short wings – it was a miracle that Havana didn't crush me in the corner as he involuntarily shot forward in surprise.

From the partition, Henny Penny was considering the next stage of her feat of aviation; the beam in the roof. It was time for us to leave her to it.

Havana strode off happily down the field, in a cloud of chemicals.

Around him, as if rebounding from a force field, I could see midges making last minute changes in their flight paths; a victory for us!

MORE GAMES
Saturday, 16 May 2009

*N*ever would I have imagined that, for £1.25, Havana and I could have so much fun!

That was the cost of the latest addition to our grooming kit – an almost-square glove from 'Auntie Alison's' saddlery, with spiky woven cactus on one side and soft towelling on the other.

Originally the glove was a source of great disappointment to Havana. Often, when I want to introduce a new object, I put it on the floor of the stable for him to investigate – provided it is too big for him to swallow, so there is no risk of him choking.

A thorough investigation involves him first looking carefully to make sure it isn't a predator of any sort, then sniffing for more clues, finally pawing at it with a front foot and possibly biting it.

A couple of weeks ago, I had thrown the new glove onto the concrete floor at the front of the stable; it landed white towelling side up. With no hesitation at all, Havana walked urgently to it and, dispensing with the usual preliminary stages of investigation, proceeded to eat it – or at least that was what he intended to do.

But, with half of it in his mouth, he discovered it was not soft, chewy and tasty, but firm and spiky. It was not the same as the slices of delicious, soft white bread which were sometimes thrown over the fence onto his field, causing an equine feeding frenzy; in fact, it hardly seemed edible.

Being innately cautious of poisoning, horses are adept at ejecting anything offensive from their mouths. The way in which Havana not only ejected, but then stamped on, the glove indicated his disgust at discovering just how inedible it was.

However, when I decided to groom Havana's face today, the sight of the glove once again provoked a strong urge in Havana to get it into his mouth. So, standing in front of him, holding the bottom edge of the glove tightly, and with his front teeth clamped firmly onto the top edge, we started the sort of game I would expect to play with a dog, not a horse. As I tugged my end of the glove, Havana tugged his end. His wide eyes indicated that he was particularly amused when I tugged in short, sharp bursts, accompanied by "Grrrrrrrr", "Grrrrrrrr", growling noises.

It wasn't actually too difficult to extract the glove from Havana's manic grasp; a finger and thumb inserted into the corner of his mouth has the almost magical effect of taking the pressure off his incisors.

Having regained control of it, I slipped the glove onto my right hand. Havana remained engaged, watching me and anticipating another game. I stroked his left cheek with the coarse side of the glove. He liked that and so leaned his face into my hand … but then it was gone! … to his right cheek … where the same thing happened. Havana showed his enjoyment at having his right cheek stroked, by tilting his head to the right; but no glove! It had gone … back to his left cheek. Then right … then left … alternately.

Havana, by now anticipating and – like a Balinese dancer – tilting his head beguilingly, was completely in synchronisation with my actions. Encouraged by my helpless laughter, he was very good at this game.

Relaxing forehead stroking, with the soft side of the glove, was my attempt to settle him, as it involved no corresponding activity on his part, but when I stroked the glove all the way down his nose, Havana was quick to grasp its edge in his playful teeth once again. So, with his head firmly attached to my hand in this way, I decided to test the flexibility of Havana's neck.

As my hand went to his ribs, where the girth would be if he wore a saddle, so did Havana's head. Then, round one-hundred-and-eighty degrees, and Havana's nose was touching the corresponding ribs on the other side. I was impressed. Havana's grip on the glove was as firm as ever, so I decided we should try the ultimate challenge! I guided his head down between his front legs and his neck flexed into a beautiful compact arc.

Back in a normal position, with the glove once again under my control, I stroked Havana's neck and gave him a lot of praise. When I had attempted this exercise with a carrot as a lure (I call it 'bendy carrots') a few months ago, Havana had not 'got it' at all, and was quite cross that, by walking backwards, he still could not reach the carrot which I held by his side, let alone the one between his front legs.

Today's game showed me that Havana's flexibility is wonderful; he just needs to understand what I want him to do – which is *my* responsibility, not his.

Finally, I found another use for the glove which Havana really enjoyed – a rump massage, in a firm, circular motion, got rid of all his remaining tickles *very* satisfactorily.

VISITORS
Saturday, 23 May 2009

*T*oday we had a lovely surprise – visitors!

Havana enjoys having visitors any time, but Claire and her grey Anglo Arab mare, Bella, could not have timed their impromptu visit better. Havana had had his breakfast, I had groomed him and, for the first time ever, trimmed the bottom of his tail.

I can hardly believe that the little orange caterpillar of a tail, which I first encountered, has turned itself into a fetlock-length horse-tail. I cut off the last two wispy inches, which I ceremonially tucked into my jeans pocket to keep. This made so little difference that I then hacked off another three inches, wishing I'd done it all in one go in the first place, which would have made my keepsake easier to handle. Havana's lustrous, thick black tail looked magnificent, every hair rippled from top to bottom. Now that it's trimmed, it's very swishy, so he'll find it more effective for keeping flies away.

Claire rode up in front of the stables and, not knowing how Havana would react to Bella, halted about twenty yards away. I reassured her:

"It's OK he's fine, you can come closer."

Obediently Bella walked forwards a few paces, so that she and Claire were only a couple of horse's lengths from Havana's stable door.

For ten minutes or so I stood in the stable, close to Havana's left shoulder, chatting to Claire over the half-door. Havana was contentedly alert, taking in the appearance and smell of this new horse and the sound of human chatter.

Then it occurred to me that it would be easier, and rather more polite, if I went outside to talk to Claire. As usual, I asked Havana to take a step back, away from the door, whilst I made my exit. As soon as I was out, Havana repositioned himself, with his chest pressed against the door, not wanting to miss a thing. In preparation for a walk I had already draped the numnah, surcingle and twelve-foot rope over the door.

Claire and I were soon engrossed in conversation. As I stood by Bella's shoulder, my vision angled-up to Claire's eye level, my back was inevitably turned to Havana. Just as I was learning about Claire's recent trip to The Royal Windsor Horse Show, our dialogue was interrupted by the dull sound of leather and webbing landing on the concrete outside Havana's door – having been propelled there by his teeth. I glanced over my shoulder to see the surcingle on the ground and Havana looking at me with an engaging expression. I was *not* going to have my conversation with my friend interrupted by a demanding little horse, so I ignored him.

Intrigued to hear about the intricate tooling on the pair of Spanish riding boots Claire had bought at the show, I was just conjuring-up their exotic image in my mind, when it vanished … due to the flopping sound of Havana's long rope landing near the surcingle. I ignored that too.

I was querying whether Claire – my most stunningly attractive, single friend – had noticed any eligible bachelors at Windsor, when what sounded like a pillow fight in the stable could not be ignored. Havana had his large black quilted numnah in his front teeth and was determinedly shaking it so it repeatedly hit the door. When he released it, it fell on his side, where he trampled it with his front feet, before picking it up in his teeth again and ejecting it over the door.

As I picked up the numnah, Havana's bright expectant expression indicated that, as far as he was concerned, his game now had two players. I had a slightly wicked idea, but I felt confident that I knew how Havana would react to it. Holding opposite sides of the numnah, and taking very careful aim, I lobbed it onto Havana's head.

I hadn't thrown it quite hard enough, it fell short, but Havana hadn't moved a muscle.

My second throw was perfect, the numnah sat like a floppy hat over Havana's ears. Again, he didn't move; he was obviously content to feel included, once again, in the interaction – even if he was unable to fathom his person's curious behaviour.

As I gently bunched the numnah together under his jaw, so it looked like an Edwardian lady's bonnet, the incongruity of Havana's appearance made me laugh; he reminded me of a very friendly version of the wolf in Little Red Riding Hood. His horizontal neck indicated that he was calm and settled, enjoying the game.

Deciding that Havana's beautiful, relaxed temperament had totally surpassed itself, I let go of the numnah, expecting him to shake it off his head, but all he did was walk backwards a couple of paces, presumably applying the same principle as if he were backing out of a tunnel. When he found that the tunnel went with him, he just stood still, his head and neck remaining contentedly horizontal.

I was starting to think that he really liked the cosy feeling of this soft, dark hat which, after all, would smell comfortingly of him. As I looked at his kind, trusting eyes in the 'numnah tunnel', gravity got the better of it and it finally slipped off his head.

There was no way that I could *not* give this remarkable little horse a lot of praise for simply trusting me and for the entertainingly ingenious ways in which he had recaptured my attention.

"… in the numnah tunnel"

THE GREAT ESCAPE
Sunday, 31 May 2009

*H*avana's innate good manners enable him to slip between the exacting protocols of interaction with his own species and what must, for a horse, sometimes be the baffling etiquette of interacting with people. For Havana, the result really is the best of both worlds.

'Best', by equine definition, often means 'resulting in the most food', and that's exactly the reward his social skills brought Havana this evening.

Mrs B. had already telephoned me to say that she and Rollo's owner had succeeded in herding all of the horses off the bog *except* Beauty, the lead mare, and had re-erected the fence post which the horses had pushed over.

I was unsurprised, when I walked down the field an hour later, to find the whole herd – except Faith and Grace – on the bog. Faith and Grace are the two most solitary and genteel mares, who may not have felt safe walking on this uncertain, oozing part of their pasture, to which they were unaccustomed as access is usually prevented.

The electric fence had been broken; quite likely by Beauty (number two), who suffers from sweet itch, so wears a midge-proof rug with a neck cover. She would simply have put her head down and forced her half-ton body – clad in 'shock-proof armour' – under the fence, so the fine conductive wire, interwoven with thin string, obligingly snapped.

What an asset Beauty (number two) is for a herd of would-be equine escapees, seeking yet more fresh forage!

The variety of grass and plants on the bog is very appetising. I knew that to get everyone off the bog I needed to employ tactics; I would catch the lead mare. I walked back up the field, ducked through the fence into the muddy paddock (which had now dried up) and went past the stables to the tack room, where I collected Havana's head collar. It was Cayman's and so is adjustable to fit heads much bigger than Havana's.

Beauty isn't lead mare for nothing. She saw me coming and simply sashayed onto a part of the bog so squelchily similar to uncooked chocolate pudding, that my inability to move my feet quickly would have made it dangerous for me to follow her.

Score: Beauty – 1, Liz – 0.

I retraced my steps all the way back to the tack room, where I collected six red buckets and put a tiny amount of feed in each. Two-thirds of the way down the field, I carefully positioned the buckets well spaced out, to avoid kicking when, as I hoped, the horses came to investigate their contents.

Although they would have recognised these buckets, there was no reaction from the horses. It then dawned on me that they actually couldn't see them. The evening sun behind me was so strong that, even if the horses took their attention off the grass for a second, all they would see were black silhouettes; certainly nothing which would entice them to move from the bog.

Feeling like a very inept scientist attempting to carry out an equally bumbling animal behaviour experiment, I gathered up the six red buckets and repositioned them far lower down the field, so the horses would surely recognise them.

Still nothing. In desperation, I picked up a bucket and slapped my hand against its side whilst calling:

"Come *o-o-o-n!* Come *o-o-o-n!* Come *o-o-o-n!*"

Like a startled gazelle, Havana put up his beautiful, fine head; urgently he made his way through the wide gap in the electric fence and straight to the bucket I was holding. This, after all, is how I feed him every day in his stable. For him it's entirely normal to eat out of a bucket which a person is holding for you. The little star was on 'breakfast routine' autopilot.

The remaining horses on the bog continued to graze greedily, with not a thought of moving from their deliciously-varied buffet table. They included Corris who, whilst old enough to know better, was also wily enough to act as if he hadn't even heard my bucket-slapping commotion.

From Havana's perspective, and as he had no competition at all, it was perfectly natural to progress along the row of six buckets, devouring the tasty morsels from each. Then, at the far end of the row – with his horse-human etiquette outweighed by equine herd instinct, or just greediness – he very sweetly skipped off back down the field to rejoin his trespassing herd and resume grazing, as if he *hadn't* just eaten everyone else's bucket of feed.

I didn't really have much conviction that my third strategy would work, but by now I was running out of ideas.

I collected Havana from the bog, smiling to myself at what a beautifully mannered little creature he is. His resistance at being led away from the luscious picnic by his person was token, and in no time we were walking together up the field, with me carrying a stack of six red feed buckets.

My hope was that the other horses, seeing us vanishing with the buckets, might think that Havana was about to receive even more food and become envious, so decide to follow us.

We got right up to the water trough at the top of the field, without another horse even lifting their head from the grass. No sooner had I thanked Havana for his co-operation, and slipped the nose band of the head collar from his muzzle, than he turned on his haunches and tore back down the field – as if pulled by an irresistible force.

Eventually, I concluded, the herd would need to drink, so they would all march up in 'elephant-file' to the trough; then the electric string fence could be tied and they *should* be unable to get back onto the bog.

I left a note to this effect for the farm owners, who were out, but whose kitchen window is very nearly opposite the water trough.

Final score: Horses – 1, Liz – 0, Havana – A*.

HENNY PENNY R.I.P.
Monday, 1 June 2009

*J*an told us this morning that Henny Penny is "missing".
Her resigned tone implied "missing, presumed dead".

The week before last, a fox killed four of Jan's hens and a cockerel.

Then the neighbouring farmer had reported that all of the baby rabbits in his fields at the end of the lane had gone; certainly devoured by a fox.

Evidently – for a fox with no rabbit left – chicken became, once again, the next dish on his menu.

Poor Henny Penny – it doesn't bear thinking about.

I know that she was a bit of a nuisance, but Havana and I had got used to her and, in winter, it was comforting to go into the stable in the evening to find her already settled-in for the night, roosting on a beam. It was like not going home to an empty house.

We will miss her.

MARILYN
Tuesday, 2 June 2009

I'm a speed-freak adrenalin junkie on the back of a horse.

The new bridle paths around the edges of field after field, where 'Auntie Alison' lives, mean that when I have ridden her big, seven-year-old Cob, Banks, it would be a waste of such an idyllic environment *not* to gallop … and gallop … and gallop.

Since sitting still for most of twenty-three hours when we flew to New Zealand last December, I have had a 'funny feeling' in my back. After so much galloping, the 'funny feeling' became painful and not 'funny' at all.

"You need to see Marilyn!" was Alison's advice. "She's a witch! She always sorts me out. I've gone to her doubled-up and come out walking straight. She does Reiki and healing, as well as all sorts of beauty treatments."

Marilyn's treatment rooms are in the gardener's cottage of a grand Georgian mansion, which is now used for business conferences.

From the imposing wrought iron entrance gates, hung on statuesque columns, the drive leads through a dense shrubbery of rhododendrons, blooming exotically with deep purple-pink flowers. I drove on into the walled garden, where Marilyn said we would meet so she could guide me to the hidden-away gardener's cottage.

I felt as if I was in the Garden of Eden. Abundant vegetation shone with life in the intense mid-morning sunlight; the temperature was sweltering.

An immaculate lady with stunning auburn hair, wearing a smart brown tunic and trousers, stepped out from the shade of the garden wall. With my new guide, I continued driving slowly through ornamental woods.

"On the next bend, have a look to your right."

I did as Marilyn suggested. It was like looking into a fairy tale. There, in an overgrown clearing, was the most enchanting domed, glass forcing house. Semi-derelict, most of its small square panes of glass had long since shattered, but enough remained to create a reflective aura of pure magic.

We parked the car and walked to the gardener's cottage, chatting.

Marilyn told me that she was looking forward to going to the races on Saturday, but that rain was forecast. My comment that rain should make the going better for the horses' legs told Marilyn that I knew something about horses and cared about their legs.

This led Marilyn to ask me whether I had a horse. When I said I had, her enquiry about how long I had had him, was met with:

"Well ... he's two – but I have had him for *twelve* years!" Marilyn was a Reiki Master and healer; I knew that I could tell her our story.

I was so busy telling Marilyn the story of how Cayman had died tragically and how, miraculously and as predicted, I had been led to his half-brother Havana, that I was still telling her as she began reflexology; by examining the soles of my feet to find out what was wrong with my body.

Marilyn confirmed that what she had learned from examining my right foot definitely accorded with the pain I was experiencing on the right side of my back. "… and there is that pain down the right side of your neck and in your right shoulder."

I was stunned. Marilyn was certainly 'the real deal'. I had been so busy talking about horses that I had completely forgotten to tell her about the pain in my neck and shoulder. Obviously, I had not needed to.

During the Reiki, Marilyn encouraged me to relax by asking me to imagine walking in beautiful pasture, by a clear stream. Her calm, healing presence, the scent of therapeutic essential oils, the tranquil music and comfortable treatment bed all made this easy to do.

In my mind I was standing on high ground, by a majestic mature tree, looking out over a patchwork of lush, rolling green fields; I could feel the breeze on my cheeks.

I was aware that I was not alone. There, standing by my left shoulder, was Cayman – tall and strong, dapple grey and so beautiful. But, for the first time, I did not feel his love or his reassurance. I did not feel anything. A feeling that something was missing made tears fall slowly from the outer corners of my eyes.

When Marilyn roused me from my meditative state, I felt the need to explain why I had been crying when I was supposed to be relaxing:

"Cayman was with me." I told her.

"Yes, I know, I saw him. I didn't notice him at first he was at the side, but then he caught my attention because he was pawing the ground with his front foot."

I realized that, now, I receive love and reassurance in bucketfuls; it's the same love – it just comes via *Havana*. I really could not ask for more.

It was not until after Marilyn had accepted my invitation to visit Havana, that she let me know that not only does she specialise in equine Reiki, but she is also an animal communicator. I insisted that she should turn our social visit into a professional consultation, but Marilyn would hear none of it, saying that she really wanted to meet Havana.

When I checked Havana this evening, I told him that he would be having a visitor next Tuesday – a special lady who can communicate with horses. I wanted to prepare him.

Havana was intrigued by the 'pink sticks' that I stand on; he had not seen my bare legs since last year and had probably forgotten them anyway. I could tell that he was particularly fascinated by the smell of the massage oil on the backs of my ankles, because he repeatedly, and very deliberately, pressed the side of his nose into them, drawing long draughts of aromatherapy. It's a curious but lovely feeling to have the soft, warm velvet of a little horse's nose pressed into your ankle; a therapy in itself.

TROT ON!
Saturday, 6 June 2009

*H*aving set myself the task, a couple of weeks ago, of teaching Havana how to trot 'in-hand' (by my side), I had attempted to do so by energetically, and excitedly, jogging along by his shoulder encouraging him:

"Come on Havana, *TROT ON!*"

When that had had no effect whatsoever, I had skipped, gambolled and cavorted my way ahead of him to the end of the twelve-foot lead rope, rallying him with a playground song:

"Come-on-Hav-ana! Come-on-Hav-ana!" Still nothing.

I had tried as we went from the field to the stable for breakfast – thinking the anticipation of a feed might produce some momentum. I tried again as we went from the stable to the field after breakfast – in case the promise of grass and a game with Rollo enlivened his pace.

Havana's reaction was simply to look at me with his sweet, surprised expression which, apart from making it plain that he believes his person is 'a few hay bales short of a stack', clearly says:

"No – that's *not* what horses are supposed to do!"

I had decided the time was not right and the exercise should be shelved, to let time catch up with it.

Although it is nearly mid-summer, this morning was so wet and cold that poor Havana was standing – one of a row of wet horses – by the hedge on the far side of the field, apparently in suspended animation.

His eyes were glazed and his rump was tucked under him. Large raindrops dripped ponderously from the bottom of his mane and from the little pointed triangles of hair which his coat so effectively forms all over his body.

Usually he sees me and either walks briskly or trots in my direction, eagerly anticipating breakfast in his stable.

Today, after a wet night, he was soggy and forlorn, reluctant to walk forwards because this meant the rain would sting his face. Horses particularly hate rain in their ears or their eyes.

After some cajoling, reassuring words, Havana agreed to come with me.

I had on my long waterproof coat with the hood up, but I was still getting rain in my face – which *I* also disliked.

I decided that this could be an ideal opportunity to persuade Havana that horses really do trot along with people. Now he had an incentive. We both had the same incentive: to get out of the sharp, cold rain.

I began to trot and, before I had got to the end of the rope, sure enough Havana was trotting too. I had to turn my trot into a run, otherwise Havana would have overtaken me.

We reached the gate; in no time, we had opened and closed it and were continuing our dash to the yard and the sanctuary of the stable.

This time Havana understood what we were doing and, more importantly, *could see the point of it*. For once he endorsed his person's unusual behaviour. It's so good to have his approval!

Next, we'll have to try trotting together on a dry day.

REIKI
Tuesday, 9 June 2009

*T*oday Havana had Reiki by Marilyn, these are the notes I made during the session.

Havana's Head Chakra:
Cayman's soul is there, his life was cut short.
Cayman has the opportunity to teach Havana, to shore him up and, through Havana, to be with Liz. He's looking forward to being ridden.

[I asked Marilyn whether there are two souls in one body, like a 'split personality'.]

Both souls are merged together, Cayman and Havana, they are not distinct.

Havana is solidly equine.
A young horse with so much interaction with humans could become confused, but Havana is not at all confused, he knows he's a horse.

The ease with which he allowed Marilyn 'into his space', indicates Cayman's influence, a young horse would not behave like this.

The depth of the bond between Havana and Liz is very different from the bond created by simply providing a youngster with all his needs. It is far deeper as it was already established with Cayman.

Havana is very content and balanced. He is accepting of Liz 'in his space'. Liz's soul is merged with his.

At the end of the session Marilyn declared Havana's effect upon her: "He fills your head!"

[Yes, I know he does!]

REIKI HANGOVER
Wednesday, 10 June 2009

*A*fter yesterday's Reiki Havana was so relaxed that, when I gently groomed his face in the stable this morning, he simply sat down in the straw!

We do sit down together in the field, but this has only ever occurred when he has already been sitting down when I have arrived.

In forty years of being around equines, I have never before experienced such absolute trust.

Havana's siesta started at about 11a.m.

He's very sweet; as he's falling asleep he makes little whinnying sounds.

I sat with him until 1 p.m., then crept off home to do 'human things'.

When I returned at 3 p.m., I could see, by the imprint in the straw, that he had been lying flat out.

I know exactly how Havana felt.

The day after my Reiki, I was too exhausted even to go to my meditation class that evening!

COMPLETE TRUST
Tuesday, 30 June 2009

*H*e did it again! – this time with no 'Reiki hangover'.

All I was doing was grooming Havana's rump and the top of his tail with Corris's spiky, rubber currycomb. I'd only been doing it for two minutes when he sat down, sleepily, in the straw for an after-breakfast snooze; so relieved to be out of the heat and the annoying flies.

What else could I do but sit down too?

Various bits of me – the top of my head, my right shoulder, my legs – were used by Havana, alternately, as a nose or headrest.

There was a lot of sighing, snuffling and even a 'dream whinny'. Although his heavy-lidded eyes were open, they were glazed. Havana was definitely 'out of it'.

Eventually I needed to change my position, so I reclined, right back, resting on both elbows. At that elevation, I was even more useful.

Havana rested his outstretched neck across my hips, so his body was on one side of me and his head on the other side.

Then, when he decided to unfold his front legs and give them both a really good stretch, the uppermost leg ended up extended across *my* legs, just above my knees. As this was not uncomfortable for either of us, it stayed there.

After an hour, Havana sat bolt upright. By pulling his nose tight into his chest, he arched his neck magnificently, giving it a luxurious stretch. This was a sign that his mind was reconnecting with his body and that he would imminently be jumping to his feet.

Fortunately, we *both* jumped to our feet at the same time.

After a long 'call of nature', Havana started searching the stable for something – anything – to eat. It was time to take him back out to the field to graze.

To think that, this morning, I had planned grooming, followed by a walk!

Instead, I have received a priceless honour; yet another example of the complete trust of a beautiful young horse.

ENCHANTED
Sunday, 5 July 2009

*W*ow! This morning was *so hot* – about ninety degrees Fahrenheit.

After breakfast, Havana wanted to stay in the cool gloominess of the back of the stable but, like extracting a snail from its shell, I prised him out into the searing sun.

This was proof, for him, that people have no common sense at all!

Once in the field, Havana avoided the heat by joining the rest of the herd in the welcome shade of the old oak tree.

Everyone stood, wilting, heads low, tails automatically swishing away annoying flies.

On the other side of the wire fence, the half-dozen coloured horses who live on the neighbouring farm shared the shelter of the same tree. A more peaceful sight would be difficult to imagine.

I went back to the stable to rinse out Havana's breakfast bucket and sweep up.

When I next glanced over at the dozing horses I noticed that, unusually, Havana had his chest pressed hard into the wire netting, as if he was trying to push the fence back.

His head was high; he was obviously very interested in something on the other side of the fence.

It's usually Rollo who 'climbs up' the fence, trying to reach any new, fresh vegetation which takes his fancy, but it clearly wasn't food that was luring Havana.

I went into the field and into the herd and quietly made my way to Havana.

As we stood shoulder-to-shoulder, my gaze followed his to the *exquisite,* four-week-old filly standing at her mother's side.

Often, when Havana sees something new, his wide-eyed expression is quizzical, but this expression was different.

His huge, kind, liquid-dark eyes seemed to be drawing in the elegant beauty of the mysterious little creature while, at the same time, exuding gentle, accepting compassion.

Receiving … and giving … in perfect equilibrium.

Havana was enchanted.

GET UP!

Tuesday, 14 July 2009

*H*avana's after-breakfast snoozes are becoming a habit.

On Sunday morning, he soon settled down to sleeping droopily; legs locked, eyelids heavy and half-closed.

After a minute or so, the weight of slumber folded his legs and he sank heavily down into the straw, where sleep overcame him.

Unable to resist his soporific aura, I curled-up in between Havana's front and back legs, the muscle of his shoulder a warm pillow. Horses always get up front feet first, so one hand clutching Havana's knee acted as my early-warning system.

Our doze together was timeless; half-an-hour? an hour? I didn't know. But towards the end Havana's muffled, sporadic 'dream-whinnies' became louder and their frequency increased, until they were a continuous volley.

Then, all of a sudden, he jumped to his feet (thank goodness I did too!) and looked behind himself in alarm. Had he had a bad dream that he was being chased?

This morning I pre-empted Havana.

After his breakfast, I took up my position; sitting on the front corner of the straw bed, leaning against the wall. It wasn't long before Havana obviously decided that his person had the right idea and he sat down so sweetly, like a big dog, right in the middle of his bed. He remained alert though and sat with his head up, unable to relax properly because of the tiresome flies which kept biting him, so he needed to scratch the irritation regularly with his teeth. The wonderful ability that horses have, to 'shiver their skin', did not relieve Havana of his incessant pests.

Exasperated, he got to his feet again, which at least enabled him to swish his luxuriant tail properly. Havana's tail is an effective fly switch, reaching well along either side of his body, as well as between his back legs and under his belly.

If Havana wasn't going to snooze, neither was I. He made sure of that by walking over to where I was sitting with my legs stuck out in front of me and, carefully but very deliberately, clamping his jaw, softly, around my nearest ankle.

I've seen him do a rougher version of this in the field; biting Rollo's, Prince's, or Flower's fetlocks ('ankles') to make them stand up.

Knowing that Havana could become *very* insistent, I needed no further prompting to jump to my feet and lead him out of the stable to his field.

Once in the field we could see Rollo and Flower, both sitting down.

Havana immediately went to Rollo and, standing behind him, grabbed the skin on his hip in his teeth and lifted his head, as if trying to lift Rollo off the ground.

After several goes, this had not worked; in fact Rollo was so unconcerned by Havana's attempts to rouse him that he had keeled-over and was lying flat out.

Not deflected from his quest, Havana continued trying to lift Rollo by the hip with his teeth, whilst at the same time pawing at Rollo's ribcage with a front foot.

Eventually, this did provoke a response, of sorts, and Rollo sat up.

Eager to capitalise on this advantage, Havana released his grip on Rollo's hip, walked round to his chest and started nipping at it. At this point Rollo threw in the towel and hauled himself, laboriously, to his feet.

From Havana's insistence that he should get up, Rollo might well have anticipated that he wanted to play; chest nipping is, after all, often an invitation to a game. But no, the minute Rollo was on his feet, Havana moved away and started to graze.

What a rotten trick! Poor Rollo – could *you* imagine having a friend like Havana?

All this time Flower lay blissfully slumbering, flat out. Havana obviously considers other *geldings* fair game for his practical jokes – however, I'm glad that *I* stood up at the first time of asking!

CATCH ME IF YOU CAN!
Wednesday, 12 August 2009

*Y*ou *don't* just canter up the field!

I wondered what Havana was doing. He definitely knew I was there.

The herd was grazing right down at the bottom of the field and, as usual, I walked a little way down the bank then stood, looking hard at Havana's back end, counted slowly to ten and began walking away. This usually causes Havana to stop grazing, look up and eventually follow me.

Today, he didn't actually look up, but he did seem to have made a decision to walk deliberately along the bottom fence line, away from the herd, although not really towards me.

As I watched, he reached the mid-point in the fence; the point where, if a line were drawn up the field, it would be perfectly bisected. Here, he made an equally decisive right-angle turn, so he was looking up the field, and, at the same moment – as if shot from a cannon – careered into an earth-pounding canter.

This was obviously the starting post; the *right* place from which to canter up the field. Havana's intent expression, bright eyes and flying mane were breathtaking.

I could not resist it; his obvious enjoyment at speeding wildly, straight towards me, made me want to join in the fun. Mischievously, I bent my knees, crouching a little, hunched my shoulders and stared, eye-to-eye, challenging the equine meteorite accelerating towards me.

Perhaps Havana thought I was about to pounce! Looking surprised, he veered off to my left, looped round me and slowed to a trot, then walk, before halting a little way off, head and tail high, as if to say:

"*Well – do you want to catch me?*"

Again, the provocation was too much for me to resist; I wanted to share Havana's game. I started to sprint for the gate. For a split-second Havana looked startled by my behaviour, but then his expression became one of excitement as he realised that his person wanted to play his favourite game. It was now a race! Two exuberant bucks, with both back legs skewing out to the same side, confirmed Havana's excitement (and that he still has his cough).

Of course, the race was won before it started; Havana's ancestors are racehorses, mine are farmers!

At the gate, Havana was floating about, light on his feet, waiting for me to catch up.

Had I invited him to join me in another energetic game, I know this would have convinced him of my worth as a playmate. But now my job was to quieten him, get him to allow me to put on his head collar and lead him, calmly, to the stable for his cough medicine, in a tiny feed.

It wasn't difficult; some soothing words and deliberate neck stroking and, in no time, Havana's energy level had lowered to relative tranquillity.

That's one of the things I love about him; he is so full of joy – it ignites in an instant – but underneath there is a deep well of innate calmness, which belies his youth.

MY PERSON
Saturday, 5 September 2009

*S*ome days I give Havana his breakfast, other days it's Mr B.. Sometimes Havana shares Mrs B. with Corris so, on those days, as Mrs B. is *Corris's* person, Corris gets his breakfast first.

Havana must have thought that yesterday was one of those days; no sign of Liz, nor of Mr B., so Mrs B. would certainly lead him into his stable for breakfast.

It's hardly surprising that, as Mrs B. told me this morning, poor Havana came to the gate – as she put a smug and satiated Corris back into the field after his breakfast – to tell her plaintively:

"*I haven't had my breakfast!*"

I received a call from Mrs B., on her crackly mobile phone, just as she was leaving the stables; she wanted to check that she had not made a mistake and that I *was* going to be giving Havana his breakfast.

I was penitent. I had overslept but assured her that I would be there in a few minutes.

Propelled by guilt, I arrived in record time.

Looking down the field, I saw … no horses.

In the moment it took me to unchain the gate, I heard the sound of one set of galloping hooves and was startled to see Havana, by now only yards from me, whinnying the most shrill, most relieved whinny I have ever heard.

He was clearly beside himself with anticipation of his breakfast.

This evening the tables were turned. Mrs B. had deputised me to check Corris for her.

Corris must have worked out the arrangement. Mrs B. is punctual; Corris knows when she'll arrive. As she hadn't arrived, and as I was walking towards him – albeit a couple of hours later – he appeared to know that, tonight, he'd have to make do with me.

I was not surprised when – in character, as the dominant male of the herd – Corris, with his ears back, teeth bared and neck outstretched, lunged aggressively at Havana.

Much as, I am sure, he views me as a poor substitute for the impeccable Mrs B., as I was the only visiting person this evening Corris's superior status in the herd entitled him to my attention, before Havana.

Warned off by the flat ears and bared teeth, Havana floated away at a trot, as Corris continued walking imperiously towards me.

I greeted Corris, briefly ran my hands down his neck and shoulder and down his front leg, then along his belly and down his hind leg, before repeating my tactile inspection on the other side. He was fine.

As I straightened up, I was aware of a bright bay rump accelerating towards me.

Havana reversed straight into me; a signal to me that he wanted the top of his tail scratching. To Corris, it was an assertive and rather brave statement, from such a subordinate member of the herd, that:

"This is my person! Look – she's scratching *my* tail!"

FIRST SADDLE
Saturday, 19 September 2009

*T*oday is a momentous day!

For the first time, Havana has had a saddle on his back ... and he slept through the whole experience.

Mrs B. was intending to ride Corris but, for only about the fourth time in their twenty-one-year partnership, Corris had lost a shoe; so no ride.

It was too good an opportunity to miss, especially as it looked as if Corris's saddle would be just the right size for Havana.

Being ultra cautious, we took off the stirrups, in case having things dangling either side of his back frightened Havana. Also, although I was probably being ludicrously over-protective of his developing skeleton, I was worried the heavy stirrup irons might add too much weight.

I put on the thickly-cushioned numnah which Havana is already used to.

I have always told him that this was "a saddle" so, today, when I held the real saddle under his nose for him to smell, I did have to admit to him that, actually: "This is a real saddle."

Dozing after his breakfast, Havana was not even sufficiently interested in the real saddle to sniff it.

Quite unnecessarily I'm sure, I gently slapped the flaps and seat of the saddle, so Havana knew what noise it made.

As I couldn't think of any other preparatory exercises, and as Havana didn't seem in the least bit perturbed by the real saddle, I quietly moved to his left shoulder and settled it on top of the numnah on his back.

No reaction.

I rocked the saddle about a bit, locating it in just the right position, still no reaction. I stroked Havana's neck as he continued to doze.

Moving round to Havana's other side, I carefully lifted the girth from over the top of the saddle and allowed it to dangle straight down behind his front leg.

Moving back to his left side, I leaned under Havana's belly to retrieve the girth and gently pulled it towards me.

Lifting the large flat leather flap on the side of the saddle, I secured the girth by slipping its buckles onto the saddle's straps and shortened it so it was a comfortable, but not too tight, band around Havana's ribcage.

This was a feeling that he was already used to as we had practised with the surcingle; a thick webbing strap which I have used to hold the numnah in place.

Havana's lack of any reaction at all was confirmation that our 'numnah and surcingle preparation' had paid off.

To get Havana even more accustomed to the real saddle, I stood at his shoulder with my arm nonchalantly dangling over the saddle. I thought this might get him used to the idea of my leg eventually being there.

For effect, I again slapped the saddle flap a few times with my hand to see what Havana made of its leathery sound now it was on his back.

You've guessed it … No reaction!

Mrs B. and I stood in the stable, chatting, for another ten minutes or so.

As Havana was clearly not at all bothered by having a real saddle on his back, I decided the logical thing to do next was to take it off.

It was as I was easing the saddle's straps back out of the girth's buckles – which made a ratcheting sound – that Havana drew his jaw in towards his chest, arched his neck and stretched his entire body upwards, as if pulled by an invisible magnet in the roof of the stable.

I love his 'sea horse stretches'; he seems to grow by about three hands and looks so magnificent.

He started blinking, his glazed eyes re-focusing, then licking his lips and chewing. He was waking up, which means he must have been asleep.

Typical! Havana slept through what, for many horses, is one of the most traumatic experiences of their young lives; having something, which could be a predator, strapped onto their backs and being unable to get it off.

Havana is so brave, content and trusting. I don't think he would have minded if I had got onto his back on top of the saddle … but one thing at a time.

HAVANA'S THIRD TRIP
TO THE OUTSIDE WORLD
Sunday, 20 September 2009

*T*oday was Havana's third trip to 'the outside world'.

Mrs B. and I decided to organise it a bit differently from his second trip, which was on Wednesday – six months after his rather traumatic first trip in March.

On Wednesday, we had thought that to accompany Corris might give Havana confidence.

As if he needed it! Havana was thoroughly cheeky and disrespectful to Corris.

With Mrs B. mounted, Corris led the way down the farm lane, with me leading Havana behind. But Havana's excited, eager stride meant that, in no time, he was rudely trespassing in Corris's 'personal space' around his back end.

I thought it would settle Havana if he was allowed to walk a bit closer to Corris, so his nose was about halfway along Corris's side. That way, as 'pace setter', Corris would still have the superior role and dignity would be honoured.

As we moved up alongside Corris, I was horrified at my cheeky baby's exhibition of deliberate, provocative rudeness; first he nipped Corris's flank, then darted his neck, goose-like, to nip his belly as we passed.

Havana was definitely in the firing line for a kick, but Corris is far too much of a seasoned gentleman to do anything so inappropriate whilst Mrs B. is on his back.

As if this show of naughtiness was not enough, Havana's exuberance next caused him to think (or perhaps not think at all!) that it would be fun to nip Mrs B., as we moved forward and her thigh came level with his over-excited teeth.

ENOUGH!

Deciding that it was safer all round to get Havana out of everyone's way, I marched him smartly on, so we were leading.

At the end of the lane, with no hesitation, Havana turned right and strode purposefully on, up the lane to Gunstone.

Corris and Mrs B. rode some distance behind; Corris with a frosty, resigned expression, from which it was clear that – whilst respecting Mrs B.'s wish that he should accompany this idiot-baby in 'the outside world' – he was far from pleased to have been assigned the task.

We didn't go very far and, whilst idiot-baby grazed on the lush grass verge at the T-junction, protected by his naïve self-confidence, Corris stood like a sentry. He and Mrs B. kept a vigil in case a car should appear suddenly, from any of three possible directions, and surprise Havana.

After just enough grass to constitute a 'reward', Corris and Mrs B. delivered Havana and me safely back to the end of our familiar farm lane, along which we would make our own way home.

Corris's disdainfully high head carriage indicated his relief at being rid of his dreadful charge, so that he and Mrs B. could get on with the responsible business of going for a ride, unencumbered by an annoying juvenile.

Today, it was out of respect for Corris that Mrs B. and I decided we should not impose idiot-baby upon him again.

Havana walked brightly down the farm lane, anticipating yet another trip to 'the outside world' with his humans.

At the T-junction, for the first time he noticed the triangular red and white road sign with a picture of a horse and rider, warning drivers to 'beware of horses'.

The hawthorn has grown around the sign, so it appears to pop out of the top of the hedge; a curious sight for a horse. It startled Havana, but after he had watched it, with big round eyes, for a long time, he must have decided it was not a threat to horses. He was content to graze with his back to it, in the big, open gateway to the cornfield opposite.

The sound of shod hooves approaching diverted Havana's attention from the grass.

As the big, dapple grey horse, with his rider, came into view and halted at the junction opposite us, Havana was beside himself with panic and confusion.

In an instant, his vertical neck had thrust his head high, every vein on his face stood out and his nostrils and eyes were enormous with adrenaline overload: he was 'an Arab stallion'.

Havana's 'prepare for flight' elevation created a sense of his dynamic power making his body weigh nothing at all – so insignificant was the hold of gravity upon it. I felt that Havana could 'go' in any direction at any moment, and so, I'm certain, did he.

Havana was so completely overcome by the situation that his panic rendered him immobile; he really didn't know what to do so, thankfully, *he didn't do anything.*

Eventually – as the horse, calmly and obedient to his rider's wishes, turned down the lane towards Gunstone away from us – Havana moved his feet so he could look down the field in the direction of the disappearing hoof beats.

He watched … and watched … apparently confused that, by looking down the field in the direction of the sound, he could not actually *see* the horse (who was on the other side of a high hedge).

Havana finally tired of trying to work out where the horse had gone and the temptation of yet more grass overcame his curiosity.

On our way home, we were not far from our farm lane when Havana froze in alarm at the sight of a fluorescent cyclist, toiling up the steep hill towards us; a very curious monster indeed.

Seeing Havana's expression, the cyclist obligingly dismounted and, to be even more helpful, moved out of sight into the drive of a cottage.

This only increased Havana's alarm; a monster that you can see is bad enough, but one that you *can't* see is definitely hiding and just waiting to pounce on you.

Once I had called to the cyclist, he and his bike reappeared and he was kind enough to allow Havana to sniff the bike.

This desensitisation exercise had to end when the sniffing turned to gnawing; the bicycle looked expensive!

Havana's gaze showed that his attention had been diverted by a hen in the distance. The bicycle was obviously no threat at all and the cyclist was remarkably understanding about the horse-saliva on the saddle as he jumped onto it and rode off.

Again, Havana was psychologically exhausted by the time we arrived back to the safety of his stable, but I'm sure his third trip to 'the outside world' had been very interesting for him.

"… in 'the outside world'".

A BABY HORSE-TOOTH

Tuesday, 22 September 2009

*W*hat a miracle!

This morning, I received something that I had wished for twelve years ago – a baby horse-tooth.

When Cayman had started to shed his milk teeth, I had stood in front of him in the stable at Gunstone, wobbling one of his loose front teeth with my finger – he hadn't minded.

It had been very loose, but not loose enough to fall out, obligingly, into my hand. I could not have betrayed Cayman's trust by attempting to pull it out; that would have hurt him and he might never again have trusted a person to do anything with his mouth.

That tooth, and all of its companions, must have fallen out in the field; the chances of finding one were infinitesimal, so I never did get one of Cayman's baby teeth to keep.

This morning, as Havana devoured his breakfast from the green plastic manger, which hooks over the top of his stable door, I leaned against the doorpost outside the stable, watching him eat.

Whilst he ate, Havana characteristically pawed the air with an outstretched, horizontal front leg, demonstrating just how much he was enjoying his breakfast. Vigilant monitoring of this front leg is required, in case it becomes so over-enthusiastic that the flimsy stable door is demolished.

As I stood watching and monitoring the impact of Havana's enthusiasm on the door, my glance fell on the narrow concrete path immediately outside the stable, where a small triangular object caught my eye. It had one noticeably flat edge; I thought that was curious for a stone. Also, the gravel next to the path is grey whereas this object was a creamy colour.

Intrigued, I bent down to pick it up.

I could hardly believe what I was holding; joy burst out of my heart as I realised that between my thumb and finger ... was a baby horse-tooth!

Havana had finished his breakfast and didn't mind at all when I gently lifted his top lip to reveal an inch-wide gap, where one of his incisors used to be.

He looked so sweet, minus a tooth, that I had to laugh; but then I did explain to him that he needn't worry, he could still eat grass, and I could already see the 'grown-up' tooth which would fill the gap in no time.

Last week there were ladybirds everywhere. I noticed one on my leg in the car, and the sight of a shiny red and black ladybird, stoically climbing up Havana's equally shiny black forelock, was magical.

My book about the significance of such things told me that ladybirds mean:

'Your wish will be fulfilled soon.'

It certainly has been; I treasure my baby horse-tooth.

ROBIN'S PARTY

Sunday, 27 September 2009

*R*obin's birthday party, in Abergavenny, was an extravaganza!

The finest food, the finest wine, the finest company; a 'lunch' which extended way beyond 9 p.m., when I *just* managed to catch my train home.

The day of golden autumn sunshine had become a sharp, cold night. It was characteristically kind of Mr B. to turn out to collect me from the station at 11 p.m. last night, when I know he would have preferred to stay warm at home.

When I went to give Havana his breakfast this morning, I was 'the worse for wear'. Not quite hung over (Robin's wine was *far too fine* for that), but I definitely had not had enough sleep.

Getting Havana in from the field, which is never difficult at breakfast time, was executed on auto pilot. I don't really remember him eating his breakfast; what I was waiting for was the moment when his satiated belly told him it was the right time to buckle his knees and sink into the thick straw bed.

When Havana's knees did inevitably buckle, it was the most natural thing in the world for me to sink down with him.

I sat behind him with my legs folded under me, one arm was draped over his back, the other around his chest. My head rested on his shoulder and I could feel his warm, silky hair against my cheek.

For once, I was sleepier than Havana, but I *was* awake enough to realise that falling asleep directly behind a half-ton horse is not a very good idea.

I shuffled round on my bottom, so that I was by Havana's head. A forehead rub was my apology for disturbing him. I was sitting up with both legs sticking out in front of me, but it wasn't long before this was just too much effort.

"Sorry Boo – I've got to lie down." As I bent my supporting arms, so that I slowly lowered my back and head, to become completely horizontal, I was amazed to watch Havana roll his own weight down onto his shoulder – in perfect unison with my movement – so that *his* body was also lying flat on the straw. Only his neck remained raised, in what looked like quite an uncomfortable arch; as if he was trying, against all the odds, still to be a vigilant flight animal.

My arm, placed gently over his neck, easily coaxed him to give up his vigil. His neck extended and flattened, until the side of his face rested softly on my chest.

As he relaxed completely, his head quickly became far heavier than I had expected. His ears and mane tickled my face in a way that was not at all irritating. His eyes were closed.

I decided that it did not matter if the weight of his head on my ribcage broke all my bones! The experience was such an honour for a human, that I would do nothing to disturb this sleepy horse.

Havana's quiet 'dream whinnies' told me that he was sinking deeper into slumber. Had anyone looked over the door, we must have appeared like some sort of human-equine sacrifice to the Gods; both flat out and motionless – not a common sight in a stable – and the clearest demonstration of Havana's trust that I could ever wish for.

There was nowhere on earth I would rather have been and I certainly can't think of anywhere better to sleep off a party.

WELCOME HOME!
Monday, 26 October 2009

*I*t was only last night that Ricky got back from a very long stint, of several months, in Dubai.

As he was not naturally a horseman, I was pleasantly surprised when he announced this evening that he wanted to come to see 'Wormal', as he calls him.

The clocks had just gone back and it was unexpectedly dark as Ricky and I made our way down the field in search of the herd, chatting to each other as we walked.

About a third of the way down, we were met by a silent, dark ghost, elegantly gliding – horse-shaped – from the gloom.

I quickened my pace to meet Havana, thinking that I would put on his head collar so he could be re-introduced safely to Ricky, who is understandably apprehensive of unpredictable, half-ton creatures in the dark.

As I strode out to meet Havana head-on, I was nearly bowled-over as he continued his impulsive stride and passed within an inch of my body, then just kept going – making a beeline for Ricky. I should have known! I have seen him do this before.

Ricky was not at ease with Havana's confident approach, attempting to avoid it altogether by sidestepping out of the zealous little creature's path.

Havana was having none of it. Each time Ricky took an avoiding step in any direction, Havana effectively herded him back by deliberately bumping into him, albeit softly, with either his nose, shoulder or rump.

Ricky was going nowhere!

I sensed that he found being herded by a young horse alarming. His efforts to take control of the situation – by reprimanding: "*Havana!*" and taking longer, more assertive strides away from him – were met by more concerted herding, and less gentle bumps, from Havana.

"He wants you to stand still so you can greet each other properly", I explained to Ricky. "Stand in front of him and rub his forehead. Talk to him and let him sniff you."

Once Ricky observed proper etiquette, Havana settled and quietened.

Formal re-introductions over, Havana and Ricky walked off towards the gate, shoulder-to-shoulder, close together.

I lagged behind, unable to keep up with their pace and feeling a bit excluded by their fraternity. But I was also marvelling at Havana's confirmation of his contentment at Ricky's return, by making his *own* choice about who should accompany him up the field.

SHOOTING STAR
Tuesday, 27 October 2009

*T*he muted rumble of one set of distant, galloping little hooves was carried, dream-like, on the dense night air.

I stood, incredulously, at the top of the field; Havana's head collar and lead rope hanging loosely by my side.

The rumble – more distinct now – was a reality, not a dream. Sonic waves of physical thunder echoed through the ground.

Time stopped.

The vibration of the damp earth connected *my* feet to the flying feet of the magical creature who had jettisoned his herd and advanced, meteor-like, in my direction.

I stayed – rooted – for a long time.

With time equating to distance, the distance covered was great.

The furry, chocolate-brown, shooting star who flashed past me had no intention of slowing down for the pleasantry of a greeting, or for having his head collar put on.

It was feed-time.

The gate leads to the yard, which leads to his stable, and his feed; there was no reason even to slow down until he was at the gate.

Once there, his angelic manners returned and we walked calmly together to the stable.

Havana had evidently been right at the bottom of the eight acre field; I had not uttered a word. *How had he known I was there?*

ONE MORE GAME
Saturday, 21 November 2009

The horses' move to their winter field by the lane happened about three weeks ago.

Just as last year, Havana found the change of field very exciting. The main attraction was quite clearly the long, lush grass that had been left to grow after the haylage had been cut in August.

The horses gorged themselves and their bellies got big but, now that much of the grass's goodness has gone, thankfully no one got colic.

The field is square and flat.

It's good for galloping games; so good, that Havana would frequently still be galloping laps of the perimeter long after Rollo and Flower had tired. He was so engrossed in his 'race' that the fact he was the only one in it either didn't register or, if it did, then it simply didn't matter as he was having such fun.

Havana is getting used to what was originally the strange new routine at fetching-in time.

For him, approaching his stable by a different route (coming in past the *back* of the house rather than the familiar path along the front) was so strange that, to start with, he did it in uneasy staccato-steps, head high, eyes wide and nostrils flared, ears flicking continually to pick up any alarming sound in front or behind.

He might as well have moved to a field fifty *miles,* not fifty yards, away.

Tonight, in anticipation of his evening feed, Havana hovered a little way from the gate whilst Mrs B. put on Corris's head collar and led him out first, a protocol befitting Corris's senior status.

Once Corris was out of the way, Havana walked resolutely to the gate and stood quietly waiting for me to put on his head collar and lead him out.

Havana waited for precisely two seconds before, like a volcanic eruption, he tore across the field, catapulting himself into poor Rollo, who had innocently been grazing.

Rollo had no choice; he was in Havana's game.

The game was obviously catching because both Havana and Rollo then barged rudely into Prince, who had also been minding his own business, eating grass.

Havana's game was so infectious that, apparently, neither Rollo nor Prince had any choice but to career around the field at a frightening speed, led by a mad, baby racehorse.

There was more to this game; breakneck galloping clearly wasn't energetic enough.

How can a creature – who must by now weigh as much as a piano – launch himself into the sky ... and stay there ... for so long ... that he seems to be exempt from gravity?

How, whilst he is flying, can he do synchronised movements with his back legs that can only be described as 'ballet'? And how, when he finally does land, can he spring vertically back up into the air, like a springbok on a trampoline?

Why couldn't I see the theatrical harness by which he surely must have been suspended?

I watched in awe.

Havana's airborne display was made all the more impressive by Rollo's clumsy, and Prince's elephantine, attempts at flight.

Havana returned, politely, to the gate. His game was over, or so I thought, but evidently another game was wriggling about inside him.

As game number two exploded, Havana flew across the field as if his tail was on fire. More aerial ballet ensued. As I marvelled, I recalled my original plan to ride Havana in a head collar!

Seeing him so far off the ground, plunging and bucking in mid-air, my romantic notions were decisively dispelled. No, I will definitely have a bit in this little dynamo's mouth.

A brief return to the gate preceded game number three, evidently the fireworks had not finished.

This time, during the performance I had time to consider the science behind Havana's breath-taking athletic ability or, more precisely, the biology.

What was it that enabled him to perform such awe-inspiring physical feats?

In answering my own question the realisation that it was muscle, a huge quantity of very powerful muscle, was quite frightening.

I imagined myself actually on that fit, bay, little back – and my confidence as a rider quaked.

Moments later, Havana presented himself at the gate again, his steaming, luxuriant, winter-fur coat saturated with sweat and his big, bright eyes saying to me:

"Wow! That was a great game! I'm ready to go in for my feed now."

He didn't get his feed straight away; in fact he didn't get it until he had well and truly recovered from his exertions by cooling down and drying off, which took about an hour.

It occurred to me that, just like any other youngster, Havana had succeeded in squeezing in 'just *one more* game before bed-time' except, in his case, there were *three*.

STIRRUPS
Wednesday, 25 November 2009

*H*avana was so good at carrying a saddle for the first time a few weeks ago, that I decided the time had come to introduce him to the idea of stirrups dangling from the saddle on either side of him.

After breakfast this morning, whilst Mrs B. was grooming Corris ready for a ride, she didn't mind us borrowing his saddle.

I introduced Havana to the saddle again by holding it over my arm for him to sniff.

The trouble with Havana's investigation is that sniffing usually leads to biting, or in this case an attempt to gnaw at the leather of the seat with his big, new, adult front teeth.

I distracted him by encouraging him to sniff the webbing girth; he was less likely to do any permanent damage to that.

The messages relayed by the scent of the girth were evidently so fascinating that Havana was reluctant to allow me to remove the saddle from under his nose. As I gently withdrew it in the direction of his shoulder, his nose followed. I stroked his forehead, with its gleaming-white, off-centre half-star and lustrous black forelock. His big eyes, trusting and inquisitive, asked me:

"What are you doing?" I reassured him:

"It's alright baby – nothing to worry about." I placed the saddle, with its thin numnah, softly onto Havana's increasingly broad back. His ribcage seems to have expanded so much in the past couple of months and his body has lengthened.

It is easy to see his magnificent dark, Thoroughbred sire, Falconwood, when I look at Havana now.

So, 'saddle on back'. This was the first time that Havana had really felt a saddle.

Last time, I put Corris's saddle on top of the very thick quilted numnah, so its weight would have been more evenly distributed. This time, without as much cushioning, Havana would have been able to feel some of the saddle's weight just behind his shoulders and a little on his back, each side of his spine.

Quietly, I did up the girth around Havana's ribcage. Feeling the resulting slight increase in pressure behind his shoulders and on his back, as well as just behind his front legs, Havana nudged my left hip with his nose – a reciprocal gesture letting me know he could now feel the saddle, reminding me that he was tolerating the strange sensation ... and warning me not to take his compliance for granted.

'Girthing-up' over, I stroked Havana's neck and praised him for being such a "brave, grown-up horse".

I reminded him of the noises a saddle makes by first running my hand over it, then softly slapping the sides and seat.

Characteristically, Havana was not at all bothered by the various noises.

I decided to get on with the aim of the exercise, so – as gently and slowly as I could – I pulled the stirrup leather out of the stirrup iron and slipped the heavy, shiny iron down the loop of leather strap, from its storage to its riding position, so it dangled at Havana's side, level with his elbow. No reaction from Havana.

As I felt he really should investigate the strange phenomenon of stirrups, I encouraged him by holding the iron towards his muzzle.

That worked; a brief sniff – and Havana had the metal in his teeth. As it evidently neither tasted, nor felt, very interesting he released his grip, so gravity swung the iron back against his side, giving him a soft, dull, thump in the ribs.

No reaction.

I invited Havana to take the stirrup iron in his teeth a few more times and each time he dropped it, letting it bang against his furry side. I could see that stirrups were not an issue for this little horse!

For balance, I let down the stirrup iron on the other side, but Havana scarcely noticed. I wondered whether catching sight of the dangling, shiny things following him at a walk might alarm Havana, so invited him to walk forwards to the door and look out. Obligingly he did this, oblivious to the stirrups.

I stood and looked at him.

In a saddle, he really looked like an adult horse. I fleetingly remembered the crazy three-and-a-half-month-old ball of orange fluff who, in a summer meadow in North Wales, had been adamant that I should *not* ignore him.

I had shooed the little creature away when he repeatedly tried to get my attention in the only way he knew – by biting me!

"Go away, *you're too little*", I'd said to him.

He had disregarded my rebuff; he knew he had already made the impact upon me that he needed to make. He knew that his future was secure … *we had found each other.*

Fearing they would be down to Havana's knees, I had deliberately set the stirrups at my riding length.

Now, I could plainly see the bottom of the stirrup irons were level with Havana's elbow (the top of his front leg); a perfectly respectable place for them to be, especially at the age of only two years and nine months when he was still not fully-grown.

Looking at the magnificent horse in front of me, Havana's persistence was vindicated. Here was the proof … I could stop agonizing. *We'll be fine!*

To promote safety and good manners, I have taught Havana to walk a few steps backwards in his stable before going out of the door.

I was roused from my state of dream-like admiration by Havana, very purposefully striding backwards until he bumped his bottom on the back wall of the stable. As I watched incredulously, he executed a perfect ninety-degree turn so he was parallel with the back wall and then, as if to emphasise the point, continued walking backwards until his bottom met the side wall – and again, could go no further.

He stood alert, looking inquisitorially at me. I knew exactly what he meant:

"Which bit of walking backwards in my stable don't you understand? I've done all your 'saddle-stuff' – *now can I go out in the field and eat grass?*"

In a moment, I took off the saddle and rubbed Havana's back and chest. Corris got his saddle back and he and Mrs B. went off for a ride.

Havana didn't even want to join Rollo and Prince in their game of biting legs; after a long night in his stable he had some serious grazing to do.

CHRISTMAS CARD
Friday, 11 December 2009

*W*hen you're not quite three and you leave your familiar stable in the morning, to discover that the world outside is silent, the dense air has turned white and all of your friends – and even your field – have *vanished,* it makes you very apprehensive.

But then, when you discover that your field – and your friends – *are* still there, you feel so excited because of the mysterious white air, that you can't stop yourself galloping … round and round … as fast as you can go!

Havana Christmas Card 2009

CONTRABAND
Tuesday, 29 December 2009

*T*here was nothing unusual about the fact that, when Ricky and I arrived at the field this afternoon, a bit earlier than usual, Havana was galloping about excitedly.

What was unusual was that, for once, there did seem to be some purpose to his activity.

We watched as he galloped along the post and rails fence at the front of the field, did a big loop in the corner by the gate, galloped back along the fence and then vanished out of sight at the back of the barn, which now houses the stables for the rest of the herd.

It wasn't long before Havana re-emerged for a repeat performance, this time with Prince in pursuit.

We could see the other horses – all bays, with the exception of Faith, who is black – together close to the barn … but where was Corris?

If a white horse with a royal blue turn-out rug had been there he would have stood out. Corris was not there.

Anxiously, I got out of the car, climbed through the fence and walked in the direction of the milling bay herd and Faith. No Corris, and the other horses were *not quite* in the right place.

As I got nearer, I saw why. The electric fence was down and they were on the other side of it, in the (usually) prohibited area at the entrance to the barn.

I watched as a highly-excited Havana scrambled and stumbled over the muck heap before commencing another dash along the front fence.

With trepidation, I walked slowly towards the entrance to the barn.

Looking down the central passageway, I recognised the glistening white tail and the attractive royal blue rug.

As I got nearer, there was the royal blue neck cover but, as for Corris's head, it was completely submerged in a pale blue dustbin – containing horse feed.

Havana reappeared, steaming from his exertions, along with Rollo, who clumsily bumped into his rump as Havana stopped alongside Corris and took the opportunity to duck his muzzle into the feed bin as Corris came up for air.

In three days' time, on the first of January, Corris will technically be twenty-eight years old; old enough to know better than to steal food!

However, I couldn't help being impressed at how effectively he had commandeered all of the contraband for himself.

I thought it was so sweet that Havana, obviously aware of the cache of food, could only show his excitement by running around – actually getting very little of the booty – whilst Corris's vastly superior intellect and experience ensured he was able to gorge himself without interruption.

I felt mean, thwarting Corris by censuring him, replacing the lid on the dustbin and shutting the dustbin away in the nearest stable, out of anyone's reach.

A steaming Havana was led back in disgrace, to his own stable.

Next, Ricky retrieved Corris, whose indignant, shrill, stallion-like whinnying – at being removed from his herd – indicated he was not in the slightest bit penitent at the bad example he had set his impressionable stable-mate.

The reason Ricky and I had gone to the field early was to get Havana in, in good time for his three-monthly foot trim by Stuart, the farrier.

Instead of a quiet and composed youngster, with a gleaming, silky winter coat, Stuart was met by an agitated little horse, steaming and dripping with sweat, who wanted nothing more than to get back to his friends and continue his antics.

We decided the safest place for Havana to have his feet trimmed was in his stable.

This worked; the novelty of 'a visitor' distracted Havana enough for him to settle down to the demanding task (for a young horse) of standing on three legs whilst each hoof, in turn, is cut and then rasped to the farrier's satisfaction.

As Mrs B. had no way of knowing exactly how much stolen food Corris had eaten, she erred on the side of caution by giving him just a few bits of carrot for tea, so – much as he might have impressed Havana – Corris's misdemeanour didn't really pay off.

THE SNOWMAN
Saturday, 2 January 2010

*W*e have had the coldest weather for thirty years and snow on the ground for the past three weeks.

Havana's education would be incomplete if we didn't make a snowman!

I was very excited about the prospect as I went to bed last night and even more excited as I woke up this morning to a bright blue sky, with glitter-sprinkled snow twinkling in the sun.

As I turned him out into the field after breakfast, Havana relished the invigorating, crisp air, and being reunited with his herd in such a magical environment.

After three weeks, snow no longer necessitates immediate cavorting around the field with Rollo and Prince. Some preliminary investigation of the stuff on the ground satisfied Havana that it had not changed since yesterday … and was still not edible. The new haylage bale near the gate, a more certain and definitely less chilly source of nutrition, was magnetic.

With minimal disruption Havana quickly ensconced himself, by slipping into a position commensurate with his very junior position in the herd, alongside his friend Rollo. All eight horses, like individual segments of an orange evenly spaced around the solid, cylindrical bale, tore voraciously at the slightly sticky, tobacco-sweet forage.

With Havana settled, I went back to the stable to muck-out, change water and get his evening haylage from the barn.

When, eventually, my fingers had defrosted, I decided it was 'snowman time'.

The snowman needed to be in just the right place. I walked across the field, marvelling at the paw-print evidence that this was not just a horse field but part of the territory of a variety of creatures who had criss-crossed it resolutely since yesterday, but whose presence would usually go undetected.

About halfway across the field, I got to a place where the pristine snow was thick and inviting for a snowman maker. Squatting down, I industriously began scraping snow into a small mound.

I was facing the haylage bale and could see that, although he had his back to me, Havana was looking round to see what I was doing. He quickly became sufficiently curious to leave the fodder and walk intently, head low, across the field towards me. I continued scraping.

As Havana arrived at the site of my excavations his inquisitively round, bright eyes made me feel that an explanation was in order:

"Hello boy – look, we're going to make a snowman!" With a front hoof, deliberately and expertly, Havana proceeded to assist, by pawing away the snow at the edge of the patch that I had already cleared for my mound.

Poor Havana – much of what I do is unfathomable to him; he goes along with it, however, because of his extremely kind, polite and tolerant nature. His genetic make-up, inherited from at least four thousand years of ancestors who have co-existed with humans, probably also plays a part.

Anyway, today for once, as far as Havana was concerned, his human was engaged in an activity which he did understand the purpose of; she was helpfully scraping the cold, white stuff off the grass so he could eat it!

As I scraped, Havana's teeth instinctively mowed the limp, oxygen-starved shoots. No matter – they were grass!

Horses are designed to eat grass, and there was little enough of it about today. I sensed Havana was pleasantly surprised that his human was intelligent enough to realise this and was grateful for my assistance. From his perspective this was a good working-arrangement; I squatted down, clearing snow off the grass, just ahead of his automatically-snipping teeth.

Havana's interpretation of the situation was very sweet, but I really couldn't risk any more of his attempts to help me clear the snow as they involved his energetic front hoof pawing dangerously close to my head.

Anyway, *I* was trying to make a snowman and I had discovered this can't be done with powder snow, which simply will not stick to itself.

Havana looked disconcerted when I stopped scraping and stood up.

Why was I stopping, when our grass-excavation system was working so well?

"I'm sorry boy – I was trying to make a snowman, not clear snow for you to eat grass!"

I don't think my apologetic tone, the mane-scratching or the forehead-rubbing really made up for my unreliability as a snow-clearer.

As Havana, independently, made his way back to the haylage, his air of non-comprehension suggested he was concluding that humans are obviously not so intelligent after all.

"… still not edible."

RESPECT
Sunday, 3 January 2010

*I*t occurred to me a few weeks ago that, as he grows up, Havana might be getting a bit rebellious.

In his usual sabre-toothed dragon style, Corris had headed-off Havana's attempt to come to me in the gateway.

Havana did turn away submissively but, for the first time, he made a very brave stand against Corris's domination by turning his rump to his oppressor, bunching-up his back end and bucking. He bucked without extending his back legs at all, so what he actually achieved was an impotent 'bunny hop'.

It was significant though, because Havana had summoned up the courage to let Corris know: "*I could kick you!*"

This was a brave, defiant and, possibly, foolhardy stance for the most subordinate member of the herd to take. However, Havana's respect for Corris's status prevented him from actually kicking Corris.

Today, Havana was cavorting in the snow like a wild mustang.

He probably wanted me to join in his game but, as he bounded towards me, *too* close for comfort, often with his front feet off the ground, I decided this looked like a rough game he should play with Rollo – not with his human – and very decisively shooed him away.

Again, Havana turned his rump and 'bunny hopped', before careering off in the opposite direction.

As I stood in the snowy field watching the excited, furry creature – who was, by now, steaming – it became obvious that his exuberance warranted a very different sort of buck from his bucking repertoire; one so big that his back legs extend like a frog's when it plunges into a pond.

I felt gratified as it dawned on me that, by getting only a restrained 'bunny hop', I had just been accorded similar respect to that which Havana shows Corris.

An honour indeed! Perhaps I *am* doing a passable job of bringing up this youngster.

"… a wild mustang"

A TYING-UP PLACE
Sunday, 31 January 2010

*W*hy don't I follow my own advice?

I was looking for somewhere to tie Havana up and, casting my eye along the fence to the muddy paddock just outside the stable, thought about tying him to a fence post, but said to Ricky:

"If I tied him up there he'd get his foot caught in the sheep netting."

Straight after his breakfast, I had turned Havana out to play in the field for an hour or so whilst Ricky and I mucked-out his and Corris's stables.

I planned to do some sort of training with Havana but decided it was only fair to let him go out to play first. That way his passion for energetic games might not intrude too much into the training. He is not quite three after all and, for him, playing is a perfectly legitimate way of spending most of those waking hours which are not spent eating.

We had sat in the wood for a 'tepid chocolate' break; it should have been 'hot chocolate', but the new insulated mugs I bought yesterday evidently don't work!

Ricky then went off for a brisk walk down the lane and I went to get Havana in from the field.

I'm sure that Prince was relieved to see me. Havana was goading him with provocative nips to his chest, neck and legs. Poor Prince did not want to play. He had retreated until he couldn't retreat anymore and was pressed flat along the prickly hawthorn hedge – but still Havana continued provoking him relentlessly.

As I approached, it occurred to me that trying to put on Havana's head collar and lead him out of the field when he was in 'playfulness overdrive' might not be very safe. What if he wanted to involve me in a horse game? Horse games invariably involve teeth and, sometimes, hooves.

I need not have worried; as soon as Havana saw me deliberately striding towards him he was sufficiently distracted to leave Prince alone and to stand with his head high, watching me.

"Come on boy, we're going to do some training!" As I led Havana away from a relieved and long-suffering Prince, he walked eagerly by my shoulder. I got the distinct feeling he was glad that, although none of his horse friends wanted to play with him this morning, his person did.

I tied Havana to the muddy paddock fence post and, almost instantly, his inquisitive, pawing front hoof became entangled in the square mesh of the sheep netting. Havana – alarmed that something had 'grabbed his foot' – jumped back and, after a few persistent but not really frightened tugs, extracted himself. Why had I tied him up there? I had known exactly what he would do.

As I ran my hand down the back of his front leg and around his hoof, checking that the wire had not cut him, I was angry with myself. I had let Havana down by tying him there – I should have known better.

"I'm sorry Havana; let's find a really good tying-up place."

Decisively I led him in the direction of his field, not actually having a clue where to find "a really good tying-up place" – and there it was in front of us!

It was obvious; a stout five-foot post close to the gate, no sheep netting, just safe post and rails fencing. This was ideal. I got the bale string, that I had taken off the other post, out of my pocket and tied it round this one, ready to put Havana's rope through (in an emergency bale string breaks – stout posts do not!).

In readiness for tying Havana to the other post by the stable, I had hung the equipment we needed – numnah, surcingle, training head collar and my body protector – over the stable door. The bucket of grooming equipment was there too. Ricky was not yet back from his walk and I didn't want to leave Havana tied to our new post with no one to keep an eye on him. There was nothing else for it!

"We'll have to go back and get the stuff Havana."

We walked to the stable, where I collected armfuls of equipment.

Havana followed, walking obligingly behind me on a loose rope. With the first load delivered to the new tying-up place, I remembered that my riding hat was still in the feed shed. The feed shed is a place Havana frequently walks past, but knows he is not allowed in.

The feed is kept in rodent-proof bins; although I don't think Havana is able to smell it, he is curious about what goes on inside the shed.

What exemplary manners Havana had as he stood in the doorway whilst I darted in – to the length of his lead rope – and out again, having retrieved my hat.

With everything assembled in the correct place, I tied Havana to the post and began to groom him in readiness for a walk in 'the outside world'.

I am honoured that Havana regards grooming as a two-way process. As I scrubbed behind his left ear with the cactus mitten, he worked his proboscis-like top lip into my right shoulder, which always makes me laugh. Havana enjoys being groomed and I am certain he knows that *I* do too – the more I laugh, the more he grooms me!

Flower drifted to the haylage bale close to the gate and hovered there, absent-mindedly pulling at the haylage, whilst her attention was quite clearly on Havana and my antics. I suspect she felt she was missing something and was a bit jealous that Havana was receiving so much fuss.

Ricky reappeared from his walk and continued his exercise by doing slow motion stretches that involved him squatting on the ground close to the fence.

At his reduced height, and moving so unusually, he attracted the attention of Merle – the perpetually over-affectionate blue-eyed Collie. Merle sat down beside him as if to join in whatever it was that this curious human was doing.

Next came Mia, the tabby kitten – presumably attracted by the spectacle of the sinewy, stretching human and his canine chaperone. Mia settled herself just a few feet away from Ricky, calmly observing with her disproportionately huge kitten-eyes.

"Why are they watching me?" Ricky was unused to exercising in front of an audience of dogs, cats and horses but, really, I could not imagine a more harmonious scene.

As it was cold, and by now we had been at the farm for about four hours, Jan came out of the house with a steaming mug of tea for Ricky (she knows I don't like tea).

Inevitably, Havana thrust his muzzle towards the mug. He seemed fascinated by the warm steam rising into the chilly air.

"Go away!" Ricky didn't want a horse in his tea.

Havana's muzzle was once again aiming for the mug when I interceded:

"Let him feel the warmth of the mug – he's interested in it." Ricky held the now half-full mug of tea against the side of Havana's muzzle, in the indent above the corner of his mouth. Havana's pricked ears and bright eyes indicated that he enjoyed the sensation of warmth, but it was the smell of the tea that interested him most.

"Try him with some in your hand," I suggested to Ricky. Havana immediately got the idea and proceeded to lap up the rest of Ricky's tea, handful by handful.

Havana's relaxed contentment indicated he was very happy with his new tying-up place. I sensed he was gloating and I'm sure the fact that he was receiving so much attention from his humans – in full view of the other horses – was the cause.

"Grooming ... a two-way process"

LONG LINING
Wednesday, 10 February 2010

*A*s Havana will be three next week, I decided the time had come to introduce him to some more serious training, in the form of long lining.

I enlisted the help of Mrs B.

After grooming and tacking-up Havana in the old brown saddle and our training head collar, I clipped a twenty-foot lunge line to one side of the nose band, passed it through the dangling stirrup iron and looped the surplus line around the back of the saddle. I then repeated the procedure with a second lunge line on Havana's other side.

He stood, tied to the post by the gate, as if we did this every day.

The path, about twenty yards long, between the post and rails fence of Havana's field and the garden fence, which runs parallel, was ideal; it would help to give Havana a sense that he was being channelled along a route. At the far end by the barn, where the tractor is parked, there is a big turning circle for vehicles.

Taking a line in each hand, I positioned myself about a horse's length behind Havana's rump. Mrs B. was by his left shoulder, holding the independent lead rope attached to the back of Havana's nose band.

We agreed our strategy: Mrs B's job was to start Havana off and guide him in the right direction. I would give him verbal commands that we hoped Havana would associate with the movements Mrs B. was asking him to make.

"Havana – W-a-a-a-l-k ON!" My command was bellowed with military parade ground volume and authority that Havana had never heard from me before. As if fired from a cannon, he shot forward into a very active walk – I had frightened him. I resolved to turn down the volume next time.

We bowled along. I had never viewed Havana in motion from this angle before.

308

I was looking from the top of his cascading black tail, straight over his increasingly powerful rump and strong shoulders, along his arched neck with its silky, black and red mane to his fine, pricked ears – both pointing slightly backwards, listening to me.

I felt exhilarated. This was the neck I would look along and these were the ears I would look between when I rode Havana and it would not be long before that dream became reality.

As we were approaching the end of the path, I called out to Mrs B. to turn Havana to the left, so he could perform the easier turn – around her – rather than a tight, right turn.

"Havana – c-o-o-o-m-e round!" This time, whilst projecting my voice so Havana could hear it, I did try to make it sound gentle and cajoling, rather than frightening.

A perfect left turn. We went along the path again until we were level with Havana's field gate and did another – equally perfect – left turn, to reinforce the first.

On the straight, we did a couple of excellent "Halts" and "Walk-ons" – Havana already knows these commands from our walks. As we neared the end again, I called out to Mrs B.:

"This time we'll go right." With no difficulty Havana did exactly what was asked.

Halting again, midway along the path, I suggested to Mrs B.:

"On the next turn we'll go right, then I'll take over. You'll be there 'just in case' – but I'll steer!"

I felt like a learner driver with no dual controls, but I need not have worried as Havana seemed to know exactly what was expected of him and continued his happy, active walk along the path. At the top, and having first warned Mrs B. of my intention, we did another right turn.

On his way round, Havana did get very slightly distracted by the tiny henhouse at the side of the path, which is about at his nose-level, and stopped to sniff its roof before being reminded of what he was supposed to be doing.

"Havana – c-o-o-o-m-e round!" I shortened the right rein and around he came – but then, with Mrs B. no longer motivating him, he stood still. I felt impotent. My first insistent:

"Havana – w-a-a-a-l-k ON!" failed to produce any response, as did my second:

"Havana – W-A-A-A-L-K ON!" He was like a stalled vehicle, standing there perfectly happily – just not moving. I wanted to prod his rump. It was only then that I realised I should probably have brought my long lunging whip with me for just such an eventuality. Unsure of how Havana would react, I flapped the right rein against his flank, whilst insisting:

"HAVANA – WALK ON!" That did the trick. Havana woke up and obligingly resumed his lovely, willing walk. As I reassured him: "Good boy – walk on!" I quietly gave thanks for this sweet-natured little creature; some young horses would have kicked out at a flapping lunge line along their side.

When we were level with the field gate we made a left turn, which was effortless. We did some more "Halts" and "Walk-ons" before a final right turn, this time ignoring the henhouse, and ended our lesson by the tying-up post.

After quickly unclipping the lunge lines and whipping off the saddle, I gave Havana a robust back massage in circular movements with my fingertips, accompanied by probably more praise than is good for a horse.

"He was so good!" I enthused to Mrs B. "How much of the second part was you and how much was Havana?" I was not prepared for Mrs B.'s response though:

"It was a hundred per cent Havana!"

This little horse never ceases to amaze me. He does everything I ask him to do with such good grace, as if he has been doing it all his life. I sense that he is indulging me; that really this preparation for riding him is academic and I could actually just get on his back. He seems to know this.

RIDE and LEAD
Saturday, 13 February 2010

*I*t was too good an opportunity to miss!

Corris was tacked-up ready for a ride and I knew Mrs B. wouldn't mind lending him to me for half-an-hour. My riding hat was in the car and I had jodhpurs on under my ski pants – time for 'ride and lead'.

Watching over his half-door, Havana looked surprised when *his* person led Corris to the step opposite and proceeded to get on his back. Havana's incredulity rose as, instead of turning him out into the field as usual, I rode off – or so he thought – on Corris.

Moments later, Corris and I reappeared, having simply walked round the house in front of Havana's stable. His incredulity was turning to indignation. What was his person playing at? Why wasn't she attending to *him*? A shrill whinny voiced his protest.

Another lap of the house and, as we approached Havana's stable again, I could see from his quizzical expression that he was determinedly trying to work it all out.

"Can I have him now?" I called to Mrs B. who was on stand-by to attach the twelve-foot lead rope to Havana's head collar and lead him out of the stable. As Corris stood, rock-solid, on the yard in front of the house, I leaned down from his back to take Havana's rope from Mrs B.

The minute he was within striking distance Havana proceeded, ludicrously, to sink his teeth into Corris's neck. I know he was only trying to start a game but what on earth made Havana think this was acceptable behaviour? He wouldn't dream of attempting to bite Corris in the field, that would be more than his life was worth. Why then, did he think that because Corris was tacked-up and being ridden, he was fair game?

Corris's manners under saddle are impeccable and he didn't move a muscle. Havana released his grip, swung his rump out by ninety degrees so he was facing his target and, with a technique befitting a baby dragon, clamped another part of Corris's furry white neck between his sharp incisors. Again Corris remained immutable.

"Havana! No!" My protest was water off a dragon's scales. I jerked the lead rope, causing the nose band to tighten suddenly around Havana's nose, but there was no reaction. Baby dragon just wasn't listening.

In desperation, imagining what it might feel like to have my own neck bitten – and let down by my little monster's sudden and unprovoked attack – I took the law into my own hands and, with a decisive shove of Havana's dense jaw bone, managed to distract him sufficiently so he unclamped his jaw.

Rather than hang about for a repeat performance, I asked Corris to walk on along the path from the yard. With saintly patience he obliged, and Havana got the hang of walking alongside.

At our first attempt to halt, Havana carried on going and, when I pulled the rope to stop him, he crossed in front of Corris and ended up on the other side, facing the wrong way.

"Shall I come and get him?" Mrs B. called from the yard.

"No I'm OK!" I was not going to be beaten, even though the lead rope and the reins were as tangled-up as knitting wool and Havana was now grazing on the prohibited lawn.

What a good job Corris doesn't kick; he was amazing, standing perfectly square, neck arched. He knew he had a job to do that only an experienced elder-statesman of a horse could perform. His help was needed to educate this ridiculously incompetent, not to mention rude, youngster.

Eventually, I untangled Havana and reeled him in, then we set off again along the garden path. At the end, where the path meets the farm lane, we halted quite well. Next came the test: a wide one-hundred-and-eighty degree turn, so Corris made the tight turn and Havana made the more gentle turn by walking around him. Again, all went well and Havana was paying attention now.

Reaching the yard again involved another wide turn for Havana and Corris's neck-reining skills really came into their own; Mrs B. always rides him with the reins in one hand and Corris can 'turn on a sixpence' at the slightest request.

We walked along the garden path again and, when we reached the farm lane, I presented Havana with a challenge. This time I asked *him* to perform the tight turn and his obligingly-flexible body bent round effortlessly as Corris took the outside path around him.

Back in the yard, we did the same again.

Now for the big one! We went along the garden path, turned right into the farm lane and right again, along the front of Havana's field – where Prince, Rollo and Flower were lined-up by the fence with amazed expressions as they watched Havana's performance. Finally, another right turn brought us back to the yard, where we halted with military precision, Havana shoulder-to-shoulder with Corris.

I leapt off Corris and quickly handed him back to Mrs B. so he could get on with taking her for the ride they had planned. With my arms around Havana's neck, I stroked and praised him. In just twenty minutes he had gone from 'baby dragon' to 'quite competent horse'. I was very, very proud of him.

HAVANA'S THIRD BIRTHDAY

Wednesday, 17 February 2010

*T*his is the birthday we have been waiting for!

Being three means that Havana is officially old enough, because his body is mature enough, to be backed.

Of course, a party was in order to celebrate such a very important occasion however – Havana was *not* invited.

As he was so happy and settled eating grass with his friends in the front field, and for safety as he is rather full of himself at the moment, I decided he should stay where he was.

Havana did know something was going on though.

Methodically grazing out in the middle of the field, he monitored the distant arrivals. As cars parked by the barn and people got out of them, he looked up regularly but was not sufficiently bothered to leave the grass and walk to the fence to investigate further.

Sitting on straw bales and appropriately wrapped-up against the damp and chilly weather, Havana's human friends enjoyed chocolate cake, sparkling wine and very welcome hot drinks in the rustic shelter of the barn. All being 'horsey people', they were perfectly at home in our down-to-earth venue.

Along with a display of his mouth-watering fruit and vegetable birthday presents, there was an exhibition of Havana's 'family photographs', including:

a compulsory 'baby picture' of Havana aged just fourteen weeks, radiating more determination to be noticed than any foal so young should be capable of;

an idyllic picture of Havana's mother (dam) Bonnie and his father (sire) Falconwood grazing contentedly side-by-side on their North Wales farm, with his 'aunts' and 'cousins' also grazing in the background;

a grainy black and white image taken in 1915 of a racehorse named Gainsborough, who was just one of Havana's illustrious ancestors through his paternal bloodline. He had caught my eye when I researched the Weatherbys website archive. In this truly beautiful stallion I had seen something unmistakable: Havana's poise, fine head and exquisite expression – Havana's essence;

then, there was Crumpwell Red Adair, Havana's magnificent red-chestnut maternal grandfather (damsire). He was a rock-solid chunk of Welsh Section D stallion; with the muscular arched neck of a legendary warhorse, sturdy legs – the stronger for their conservative length, the dense chest and shoulders of a bull, a billowing forelock down to his flared nostrils and tail cascading to the ground. He was definitely a horse to be noticed and very likely the source of Havana's precocious presence!

For a few hours, we all enjoyed a lovely relaxed afternoon – eating, drinking and chatting. New friendships were made and established friends caught up with each other's equine and other news.

When Gill's husband, Tim, asked whether he could take their little boy, Mackenzie, who was nearly two, across the field to see Havana, I had no hesitation in agreeing. Tim is a farmer and experienced with horses.

As Tim and Mackenzie approached Havana in the middle of the field however, I was alarmed at how rude and rough Havana was. Having spent all afternoon grazing, he was obviously very excited by the diversion of one big and one tiny visitor – two new playmates! 'Why waste time, why not start a game now?'

Havana frantically nipped at Tim's legs, first one then the other, and

– to make sure of a reaction – barged into him with his shoulder, goading him to reciprocate.

Tim's very sensible reaction was to scoop Mackenzie into his arms, turn his back on Havana and stride determinedly away.

Baffled that his new visitors seemed not to understand how to play, Havana persisted; gambolling around Tim and Mackenzie at an impetuous trot, as if trying to corral them, and making their retreat both difficult and dangerous.

I shot through the post and rails fence to capture my embarrassingly delinquent little horse.

Havana was so intent on making his visitors play that I don't think he even noticed me marching up to him from the side, like an irate headmistress. In a moment my right hand had grabbed a hank of mane, just behind his ears, and my left arm had locked itself firmly around the front of his nose, whilst I wedged my right hip into his chest.

Havana was stalled. My 'horse-wrestling hold' stymied any further attempt by him to pursue his visitors across the field.

Both Tim and Mackenzie escaped safely, although Mackenzie's delighted laughter at suddenly being whisked across the field by his father showed that he, at least, enjoyed the 'game' of fleeing from hooligan Havana.

I was ashamed, but felt reassured that my apparently mean decision, *not* to invite Havana to his own third birthday party, was well and truly vindicated.

CAYMAN'S SADDLE
Saturday, 20 February 2010

*A*s usual I had turned Havana out to graze for an hour or so before we started our training.

When I went to get him after I had finished the stable, he wasn't sure whether he wanted to leave the field. He was resolutely grazing and had not yet had time to get bored and start doing something else, such as nibbling twigs from the hedge or looking for someone to play with.

He didn't understand why, having so recently turned him out, I was now back, had put on his head collar and was asking him to walk across the field to the gate. But, with his characteristically accommodating good manners, he walked with me.

As he approached the gate Havana's attention was drawn to the fence opposite, on which I had hung an array of equipment: the usual things such as my body protector, numnahs and head collar. But unusually, there were *two* saddles.

The first was the little brown one, which we had used for training before; the second was a very special saddle, and I had had to steel myself to bring it today. It was Cayman's black saddle – on which, over our nine years together, Cayman had carried me for ten thousand miles.

Havana did some intensive sniffing of both saddles before I tied him to our new tying-up post. As usual our grooming session quickly descended into a mêlée of mutual grooming and, on my part, whoops of laughter as Havana's teeth worked insistently on the various strong plastic fittings around the waist of my padded ski pants. Yes, I know I am making a rod for my own back here. In summer, I shall not be wearing ski pants and my thin summer jodhpurs will mean that Havana's teeth will then be in contact with my skin and bones! Oh well, I'll cross that bridge when I come to it.

For now, we were having fun, so much fun that our antics attracted Flower. She stood on the other side of the post and rails fence as if hoping to join in whatever it was that Havana was up to. It wasn't long before the cactus cloth grooming mitten had been stolen from our side of the fence; Flower stood with it provocatively between her teeth, determined to be noticed and included in our activities.

Having brushed-off Havana's visible mud and restored his thick and ripply Welsh tail to some sort of glory, by pulling out pieces of straw and crushing solid lumps of earth to dust between my thumb and finger, I could procrastinate no longer. The time had come.

Cayman's saddle is a big general-purpose saddle made especially for him when I first had him. He was three then and already well on his way to his eventual 17hh.

Havana was three last Wednesday and, although his ribcage is so big and his back has become so wide, I hardly dared try on the saddle in case it engulfed him. Was I mad to think that Cayman's saddle might possibly fit him? But I had to know.

In case the black saddle felt cold on Havana's back, I first put on the thin blue numnah which always went under it, then, with trepidation, the saddle.

It was bound to be huge on this fine little youngster who, although he is Cayman's half-brother, has inherited far more of their racehorse father's physical characteristics. Also, his mother is a compact Section D Welsh Cob, not a 16.2hh Irish Draught horse, as Cayman's mother was.

No, the saddle couldn't possibly fit – how could I ever imagine that it would?

Incredulous joy welled inside me as I placed the saddle gently in position, eased it slightly backwards then slightly forwards, not daring to settle it in the right place, and realised *it fitted!*

Unable to believe what was in front of me, I then lifted the saddle and pulled out the numnah before replacing the saddle directly on Havana.

I stepped back, looking at it from each side and every angle. Standing at Havana's shoulder the saddle made him look so grown-up – and so tall!

Havana was not remotely bothered by the big, possibly chilly, thing on him – but the unusual way in which I was peering, disbelievingly, at his back did seem to make him slightly uneasy. He was looking at me with a 'What are you doing?' expression; the one where his head is turned towards me with a fixed, enquiring gaze.

By way of explanation, I moved to his head and rubbed his forehead with the flat of my hand.

"I can't believe it fits you Havana! That's incredible!" I carefully lifted the saddle off Havana's back and returned it, reverently, to the fence, before giving him a thorough back massage all over his luxuriously furry winter coat.

Maybe the saddle had felt chilly, because Havana languidly stretched out a long back leg behind himself, giving his back muscles a relieving stretch.

By this time Flower had got bored and gone off to join the others who were grazing in the middle of the field.

For today's training I had planned to do 'riding from the ground'.

I attached reins to the rings on either side of the nose band of Havana's head collar then, standing by his left shoulder and holding a rein in each hand as if I was riding, I commanded him smartly:

"Walk on!" Of course he did.

Similarly, when I requested: "Havana – Halt!" he did as I asked, and as I shortened the left rein and asked: "Havana – Come round", he performed a perfect turn to the left. Then again, I shortened the right rein, and he did a perfect turn to the right.

We 'rode' along the path, right round the farmhouse and back to where we started at our tying-up post by Havana's field gate.

Our circumnavigation of the house was only interrupted by Havana halting of his own accord by the lawn overlooking his summer field. I urged him:

"Havana – Walk on!" But no, he was looking – his gaze in the far distance – way down the familiar field. Evidently he had noticed something that I hadn't. "Havana – Walk ON!" I was insistent. No reaction – he hadn't finished looking.

Finally, satisfied by his observation, Havana's attention reverted to our immediate environment and he graciously resumed his perambulation, performing one more perfect circuit around the farmhouse. My right shoulder ached from holding my arm over Havana's withers and I decided that he was actually too tall for us to do 'riding from the ground'.

As we approached our tying-up post again, I felt that Havana, although perfectly willing to do what I asked of him, did not understand why we were doing it. I had a strong sense that he was thinking:

"Why are you messing around; why don't you just get on my back and ride me?"

Well … it was very tempting but, although he was now three years old, part- Thoroughbred foals such as Havana, who are not intended to become racehorses, are usually born in early summer when the weather is warmer, not in February!

I have decided that, as he was such an early foal, I'll wait until he's had some spring grass and sunshine to build up his muscles and skeleton before I ride him.

Although I believe we already trust each other enough for me to get on Havana's back today if I wanted to, there's no rush. We have a long life together ahead of us … we'll take our time.

VERY FUNNY
Thursday, 11 March 2010

*T*his evening, as I pulled up my car and parked it alongside the tractor, I could see Havana waiting patiently to be brought in for his feed.

Rather than looking over the gate or the post and rails fence, he was standing about ten yards into the field and was separated from both the gate and the fence by a wide strip of drying mud running right across the front of the field.

Alert and looking in my direction, he obviously recognised the car.

"Back in a minute Boo!" I called to him, as I got out and walked briskly away to get his head collar.

A minute later, I ducked through the fence by the tractor, head collar in hand.

Very sweetly, with his head low and eyes soft, Havana came to me – carefully picking his way over the rutted earth – even though this meant walking away from the gateway that is the route to his feed.

This reminded me of an entirely different episode about ten days ago, when Havana was standing in the same place waiting to come in for his feed.

I had thought that, as he particularly disliked walking through what was then deep, sticky mud, it would reassure him if we walked through it together.

However, as I was approaching him and was only midway across the muddy strip, Havana strode purposefully away from me through the mud – which he hates – towards the gate.

I couldn't stay literally 'stuck in the mud', so I ploughed on to the other side and the safety of the grassy field, where Havana had been standing. The result was that, after I had crossed ten yards of semi-set clay to help him with his apparent fear of mud, the ungrateful little monster arrived safely at the gate without my assistance.

To get to Havana so I could lead him in for his feed, I still had to wade, in very ungainly fashion, through the quagmire opposite the gate.

As I did so, Havana watched me wide-eyed, with a bemused 'What is my human doing?' expression.

I strongly suspect the sight of me trudging stoically through the heavy mud towards him – on only *two* unstable and inadequate legs – was something Havana found very funny!

MORE LONG LINING
Saturday, 27 March 2010

The week before last, I couldn't wait until the next Saturday, when I would have time to try long lining Havana by myself for the first time. It had been kind of both Mrs B. and Ricky to help us to get started, by first leading Havana and then – as he learned what was required of him – walking by his shoulder to boost his confidence.

The week before last, we did have a bit of an altercation; not Havana and I, but Ricky and I – with Havana caught in the middle. It upset me that Havana should experience human discord; it must be difficult enough for him to work out the strange antics of humans when they are behaving themselves, let alone when they're having a 'domestic'.

I must say it was nothing serious really but, as it affected Havana, then – to me – it was very serious. I am protective of my young horse – for which I make no apology.

I had explained to Ricky that Havana turning a circle to the right, in a confined space – with me behind him, connected to the long lines – was like an articulated lorry going round a roundabout in the road. Havana needed to start by moving out a little to his *left*, so he would have enough space to make a gradual three-hundred-and-sixty-degree turn, to face the direction from which we had come.

As I slightly shortened Havana's left line, from behind, to start the gentle turn, Ricky – walking by his head – attempted to move him in an abrupt right angle in the opposite direction. Havana's compliant movement to the left, which I had asked for, was immediately thwarted by Ricky pushing him over to the right. His ears, one back, listening to me, the other straight up, told me that he was confused by the contradictory requests of his humans.

"No! Go left!" I shouted at Ricky.

"You said *right*!" was his defensive reply. "You obviously don't know your left from your right!" Ricky was sure of his ground.

"The horse got it right – you're just muddling him up!" I shrieked. I was livid; irrationally imagining that Havana's progress towards becoming a psychologically balanced, adult riding horse had just been irreparably damaged by impossible instructions and exposure to a marital spat. I had to take urgent steps to protect Havana. We walked forward a few strides and halted nicely.

"That's it – we're not doing any more long lining today," I decreed. Ricky seemed surprised; we'd only just started.

"Next time I'll do it by myself; that way Havana won't get confused."

Last Saturday could not come soon enough; anxious to repair any damage done, I was eager to try long lining Havana alone.

After giving him his breakfast, I turned Havana out in the field whilst I mucked-out his stable, filled his haylage net and changed his water. Then I brought him out of the field, tied him by the gate and spent forty minutes or so grooming him and tacking him up in his training head collar and saddle.

Finally, I attached the long lines, carefully securing their coiled surplus length. We were ready to go. I thought it would be best if I reminded Havana where I wanted him to walk, by first leading him, before asking him to walk on ahead of me on the long lines.

We had walked only ten yards when all the horses in the field stopped grazing and stood, heads up – for a split-second – before flying excitedly to the top corner of the field. They all stood there, motionless, looking in the same direction; eyes wide, ears pricked.

In an instant innate reaction, Havana's mind was with them; he had no choice as he is a herd animal. He also turned to face the source of the excitement and stood transfixed, with his head erect and his ears and eyes locked onto the shrill sounds and energetic movement which had captivated the herd.

In the distance on the next-door farm, four or five children were running playfully in the field. Their infectious shrieks and laughter, carried on the air, showed how much fun they were having and, had there not been a very high, dense hedge between them, they might very well have had eight additional *equine* playmates.

There was no hope of reeling in Havana's mind, so he would concentrate on long lining. In his imagination, he was playing with those children on the next-door farm.

I whipped off his tack.

The speed with which Havana shot across the field to join the herd, all poised by the hedge, was proof that lessons would have to wait another week … after all, there was no rush.

Finally, today, I got to long line Havana by myself. He was ever so sweet and helpful. This time I tacked him up in the stable and took him for a short walk along our proposed long lining route, between the front of the house and the lawn.

As I attached the long lines, Havana stood stock still on the yard and 'assisted' by catching hold of the lines in his mouth as I clipped them each side of his noseband; an endearingly babyish characteristic which reminds me, if ever I needed reminding, that he is still so young.

I took up my position behind Havana's rump and very firmly commanded him to

"WALK-on!" Havana meandered slowly in the direction of what, to him, must have looked like a buffet but was actually an assortment of garden urns – each containing a plant. When he reached them, he proceeded to nip the tops off several of the plants (which would surely die), before my remote steering – with its built-in time lapse – succeeded in over-correcting him in the opposite direction. As a result, he now thought that it was alright to walk on the showpiece lawn.

At the end of the lawn we turned round and, if Havana was a horse who kicked, I might not be here to tell the story; our turn was only completed because I pushed his bottom for the last half.

Once straight, he got the hang of a fairly direct walk back to our starting point on the yard.

More assertive commands and a wobbly circle later, we were passing the urns again when it occurred to me that I couldn't see Havana's ears. In fact, not only could I not see his ears, I couldn't see any of his neck either.

From where I was standing, directly behind his tail, I could see nothing of Havana beyond his withers! Stepping to the side slightly, I saw why.

Havana was walking with his muzzle a hair's breadth off the tarmac path – a posture of total submission.

Poor Havana wasn't enjoying it one bit and, actually, neither was I – *it wasn't fun*. I remembered my good friend Jennifer's words on successful horse training:

"You've got to ask yourself, 'What's in it for him?'" I knew the answer: 'Nothing!' We turned and went fairly straight, back to the yard, where the long lines were speedily removed. They remained stashed in a loopy pile under the bench in front of the cottage that used to be stables, whilst Havana and I escaped along the farm lane on an adventure to 'the outside world'.

Havana's soft eyes and impulsive stride, propelled by his increasingly powerful haunches, confirmed that now he *was* enjoying himself.

At the end of the farm lane Havana grazed in the wide, safe, field gateway – definitely an activity he appreciates.

On the way back to the yard we played a new game. With a few encouraging tongue clicks and some over-emphasised jogging on the spot on my part, Havana quickly got the hang of trotting along by my side when I 'trotted', walking when I walked and halting when I did.

His shiny eyes and pricked ears told me that trotting a sharp right angle with me, around the corner of the house, was fun – but when I walked, he was happy to slow down and then to halt by my side.

When I recounted today's exploits to Ricky, who has recovered from our long lining debacle, he said:

"Sounds like a bit of a disaster!"

No, it wasn't a disaster, but I did need reminding that Havana's confidence is fragile. Long lining without someone by his shoulder is daunting and confusing for him. We'll try it again, with the helper receding gradually, but for now – games work!

MY FIRST EVER DREAM ABOUT HAVANA
Thursday, 8 April 2010

*H*avana and I were in the barn at the farm; it was dark.

I felt encouraged by Havana to get on his back for the first time. He didn't have a saddle on. I sat quietly on Havana's back; he was completely relaxed and peaceful – standing still.

It was then Havana's idea that we should go out into the field. I was unsure, as I had only just backed him, but next thing I knew, we were cantering effortlessly in circles in the enveloping velvety-darkness of the field.

I felt completely safe and happy; I trusted Havana. It was as if we had merged into one but had retained our own identities.

I was also aware that Cayman and Havana were one and that, for the first time, they were together in Havana's golden-brown body. Previously, I had been aware of Cayman in his huge, dapple grey body.

I also felt that my first horse, Jah, was there too; Havana had his proportions and Jah was combined with Cayman and Havana.

I felt very calm and reassured; this feeling stayed with me as I woke and lasted all day.

I also felt elated at the prospect of riding Havana soon – when a new channel for experiencing the bond between us will open up.

FAT BOY
Wednesday, 14 April 2010

*H*avana's quizzical expression indicated he hadn't a clue why I was back in his field so soon after turning him out to graze for the whole day, or so he thought.

"Have you forgotten Boo? I told you Sue is coming to give you your injection today. Come on!" Somewhat bewildered, Havana followed me unenthusiastically.

As we came up the bank at the top of the field, I could see Sue's car already on the yard and, at the same time, my mobile phone rang. I couldn't deal with a disruptive phone and a potentially disruptive little horse all at once, so I ignored the phone.

"I bet that was Sue! Come on Boo, we need to hurry." Obligingly, Havana trotted by my side to the gate – which we opened and closed like 'handy horse' competition veterans – and then continued trotting with me along the path to the yard.

This approach gave Sue a head-on view of what I hoped she would think was a magnificent three-year-old, with an active, floating stride.

I was mortified at Sue's greeting:

"He's fat!" I had attended one of her salutary lectures on the perils of overweight horses.

Once inside the stable Sue asked:

"Is he four this time?" When I replied that Havana was just three, Sue said he was "quite mature".

I wanted to be sure that, by starting to put some weight on his back,

I would not do Havana any harm. Having seen him grow from a scrappy little foal to a half-ton horse, and every stage in-between, I wanted Sue's confirmation that he had grown enough for me to ride.

I was intrigued by Sue's explanation that 'smaller horses' mature faster than big ones, so a Shire will continue growing for many more years than a Shetland. Havana is somewhere in the middle. Sue did concede that, as Havana's rump was still an inch or so higher than his withers, he would even-up; that will make him at least 15.2hh – a useful height.

Anyway, he doesn't know he's a 'small horse'. He's such a dynamo of a little creature and his energy is huge!

I showed Sue the feed scoop I use, and was decisively told to halve the amount of "Mare and Young Stock" mix Havana was getting. I made a mental note to cancel the further sacks of 'mix' I had just ordered.

In mitigation, I did explain to Sue that the horses had only moved onto their summer field last Thursday and the fresh spring grass had caused Havana's belly to swell visibly.

For my next trick, I wanted to demonstrate to Sue how Cayman's saddle now fitted Havana. Settling it on Havana's back, the channel of daylight visible through the front of the saddle as it perched, too high, on Havana's back plainly indicated the saddle was now, in fact, too small for 'Fat Boy' Havana.

As Sue and I talked, Havana stood with us in the stable but, for a young horse, inactivity quickly becomes boring. Havana's provocative nip to the top of Sue's arm was his attempt to 'liven things up'. I was disgraced:

"Havana! You don't bite your vet!" An expert horsewoman, Sue's reflex action flick under Havana's muzzle was instant chastisement. Surprised, Havana stood and considered the situation for a while as we continued to talk. His expression did not indicate that he was in any way chastened; it was more one of puzzlement, as if he was trying to work something out. Whatever his thought process, the outcome was a second nip, this time to Sue's lower arm.

"Havana - NO!" He knows my 'angry voice' and when he has pushed his luck too far.

Being now totally ignored by both Sue and me for being so rude, Havana backed himself to the rear of the stable and stood looking expectant – his way of saying:

"Well, if you're not going to play, will you just let me out please?"

Eventually, Sue and I finished our discussion. As she drove away, I led Havana back out to the field … but what were all those white things on the grass?

Closer inspection revealed about a dozen large slices of white bread strewn by the top fence. The rest of the herd were out of sight at the bottom of the field so Havana had no competition – this was manna from Heaven.

I attempted to frighten Havana away from the bread by transforming myself into an angry monster: lethal claws (my splayed fingers) curved and menacing, extended arms held just above shoulder height and squared shoulders, created the illusion of a huge, scary body. I fixed my eyes ferociously on his and my expression was angry.

My monster impression had no effect whatsoever – Havana continued snatching and devouring the glutinous slices of unnecessary carbohydrate.

I roared and took a few impulsive strides in his direction. Mildly inconvenienced, Havana cantered around the perimeter of the picnic, so we were on opposite sides, and continued gorging.

As I again lunged towards him, Havana became annoyed at my interference and let me know he had had enough by turning his rump towards me and bucking – not just a 'bunny hop', but a semi-serious 'back legs slightly extended' type of buck. He was telling me, in no uncertain terms, that he was prepared to fight me for the bread.

I had a brainwave. Why was I trying to shoo Havana away? Why didn't I just pick up the stupid slices of bread?

As quickly as I could, I collected Havana's picnic, slice by slice. Poor

Havana was dismayed at my act of sabotage. He looked uncomprehendingly as I placed the offending bread in a stack on the lawn, on the other side of the fence.

Havana was cross with me for stealing his bread. Why was his person, who always fed him, depriving him of food?

Thwarted, he cantered off down the field in disgust at my illogical behaviour; I sensed that we were not very good friends.

This evening when I went to get Havana in, he moved away rather than coming to greet me as usual. His manner confirmed my suspicion that he wasn't sure he wanted anything at all to do with me. Fortunately, I was able to catch him and, after he'd had his feed and some fuss, Havana's sweet nature meant he was incapable of staying grumpy and we were friends again.

Actually, he didn't seem too bothered that his evening feed was only half the size of his breakfast – vet's orders!

MONSTER
Wednesday, 21 April 2010

*T*his week Havana turned into a monster!

The three-phase transformation began on Sunday evening. When I tried to bring him in from the field, Havana sidled off in the opposite direction. He has an uncannily reptilian way of slithering out of reach and, with his ears back and his neck outstretched, he looked like a serpent. However, it was not difficult for me to ambush him and, in the same no-nonsense way a mother encases her protesting toddler in his clothing, I was able to get Havana into his head collar.

Once caught, he quickly forgot his objection and walked with me, as obligingly as ever, to the stable for his evening feed.

By Monday evening, the monster-transformation had resumed – only worse.

To start with, Havana followed me very sweetly up the field; at the top, he drifted off to the water trough. Fair enough, he was thirsty – but I wasn't prepared for what came next.

With an explosive volley of flatulence, he turned on his haunches and galloped, riotously, back to the bottom of the field.

Dutifully I trudged after him. As I approached, Havana deliberately turned his hip towards me – in an explicit act of defiance – before trotting away in a gentle curve, head low, ready to be reunited quickly with the grass once he had dealt with my unwelcome intrusion.

I knew what to do … the jangling keys trick works every time!

I produced a set of car keys from my jacket pocket and dangled them so they chimed together. The jangling metallic sound, coupled with their silvery dancing in the dwindling light, caught Havana's attention and intrigued him sufficiently that he chose to stride over to me for a closer investigation.

In no time the monster had subsided, his head collar was on and my keys were safely back in my pocket. The forehead rub that I gave Havana did seem to compensate him for the fact that he had been tricked.

Last night, Havana's transformation into 'more monster than horse' was complete.

When I arrived in the field, he was senselessly careering about; wrapped in his own over-excited world and oblivious to the fact that the other seven horses were grazing peacefully.

The extent of Havana's delirium became evident when he turned his rump towards me and appeared to bounce on the spot, before catapulting himself away and repeating the same hyperactive manifestation of whatever was going on in his head. The trouble was, this time he was well within the 'personal space' of the matriarch, Beauty.

There is something regal about the black mare's sombre, round, matronliness and her distinct intolerance of insubordinate youngsters.

Beauty *had* been grazing quietly in the corner of the field.

Havana's enthusiastic athleticism was a bad breech of protocol. He had inadvertently corralled himself; with the electric fence in front of him, the hedge on his right and an equine 'Queen Victoria' – who most definitely was *not amused* – on his left.

Momentarily he did seem chastened and I felt heartened that his rudeness towards me could not have been meant, because he had just been equally rude to Beauty – something it would be more than his life is worth to do intentionally.

I knew it was the almost narcotic effect of abundant spring grass that had produced such inappropriate behaviour in this adolescent horse.

He really could not help himself.

In a second, Havana's volatility was reignited, as he extricated himself from his predicament with a couple of backward steps, before turning to canter off down the hedge line.

I stalked Havana for a while, but each time I got close he lifted his head from the grass and moseyed away. I was not having that! I have never failed to catch Havana and I was not going to fail now.

I decided upon a tactic. Whenever Havana stopped to graze, rather than approaching gently to try to catch him, I would shoo him away so he wouldn't get the grass he wanted. I hoped he would eventually decide for himself to come to me, as continually being sent away was not achieving anything.

I set about shooing Havana away. When he stopped, I marched assertively towards him – my eyes locked onto his, my shoulders square – and flicked the long lead rope at him.

Each time, Havana threw up his head and cantered off in an arc, before settling, only to be sent away again.

My tactic was working in that I was unsettling Havana, who I hoped would eventually ask me to cease by approaching me to negotiate a truce. The trouble was, this would all take time which I did not have, as it was after 9 p.m. and rapidly becoming dark. Also, as the other seven horses were grazing, randomly spread over the field, it was unfair that they were being continually disturbed by Havana cantering amongst them.

No, although frost was forecast, I would leave Havana out for the night. The rest of the herd have been out overnight since they moved from their winter field a couple of weeks ago. Now Havana had made it plain that he wanted to be with his herd and I couldn't blame him for that.

Frost was forecast each night until the end of the week; after that he could stay out overnight for the next six months. But I was certain that, by the following evening, Havana would be ready to come into his cosy stable.

Tonight, just as I anticipated, he didn't think twice about following me out of the field. Thankfully, monster-horse seems to have vanished overnight; I'm glad, as I didn't like him. He was so ill-mannered – not at all like Havana!

FAT CAMP
Saturday, 24 April 2010

*F*at Boy has gone to 'Fat Camp'!

This morning, I decided to move Havana to the 'starvation paddock' – where the two ponies, Toffee and Freddy, lead lean and healthy lives.

The 'starvation paddock' isn't nearly as grim as it sounds. It comprises two areas: 'the muddy paddock' – which at this time of year is bone-dry and covered with dock leaves – and the top corner of the field that Havana's herd is in. This has plenty of *short* grass, compared with the long, lush grass in the rest of the field on the other side of the electric fence.

Havana galloped excitedly back and forth in the grassy part, which was made all the more exciting for him by the fact that the land falls and goes round a corner, so his down-hill gallops had a centrifugal force all of their own.

Toffee and Freddy were too busy grazing to take any notice of Havana.

When he had finished galloping, Havana set about exploring his new environment.

First, he went to the top of the grass field, where there is a low, galvanized hen house. In summer its roof becomes burning hot. The edges of the roof have metal channels which, over the autumn and winter, have caught twigs falling from the overhanging branches of one of the old oak trees in the muddy paddock.

Havana systematically devoured every single sun-baked twig – for him, truly a delicacy. He had no intention of moving until the last one was finished.

When he did move, it was to go through the open gate into the muddy paddock and straight into the big, open barn. Thankfully, he seems to have forgotten that this is where he was castrated two years ago.

In the middle of the barn were the remains of a large hay bale; Havana pulled a few mouthfuls before walking to look over the gate separating the paddock from the yard.

The gate is no more than ten yards from his and Corris's stables and the farmhouse; for a sociable horse like Havana, an ideal vantage point from which to observe people's comings and goings – something Havana seems to find endlessly fascinating. In this case it was Mrs B., sweeping-up outside Corris's stable, who had caught Havana's attention – but there was more to explore, so he couldn't stay too long by the gate.

Surprisingly, to a human, the massive yellow JCB digger parked outside the barn didn't merit investigation at all.

Next, Havana investigated the 'secret passage' along the back of the barn which, when he was younger, was his and Flower's 'den'. The passage is narrow and secluded, with the barn wall on one side and the wood on the other, enabling Havana to 'pop out' right next to his own stable – a more covert place from which to observe the yard.

After this, Havana was off, walking purposefully along the winding path between the oak trees and the hedge. For him, the hawthorn hedge was very alluring. He spent a long time browsing; delicately and precisely snipping-off the tender new hawthorn shoots, one at a time, with his front teeth.

Spring is the time for one of Havana's greatest afflictions, 'tickly tail'.

It was his overwhelming need to scratch the top of his tail that finally prised Havana away from the hedge. The mature oak trees seemed to have been designed for the purpose!

In no time, Havana found just the right tree – with just the right area of abrasive bark at just the right height – to accommodate his rump.

Horses' ecstatic expressions – with large, glazed eyes; elongated and pointed top lip; arched neck; ears angled back and head slightly turned towards their rump – indicate total concentration on the tops of their tails. The sheer bliss they derive from either scratching their tickly tails, or having them scratched, is incalculable and Havana is no exception.

I stayed with Havana for a couple of hours to make sure he was completely settled.

For him, I don't think 'Fat Camp' is going to be any hardship. He can still talk with his friends, Rollo, Flower and Prince, over the electric fence and – in addition to excellent tail scratching and yard observation facilities – he now has an airy barn to retreat to, out of the rain and away from the evening midges.

In fact, I suspect Havana thinks he has been *up-graded* to 'First Class Grazing'.

FIRST BACKING
Sunday, 25 April 2010

Wow! Today I sat on Havana's back for the first time! What a wonderful feeling – I wanted to stay there forever.

My original idea was just to lie across the saddle so Havana could feel some weight on his back.

To make myself high enough to do this, I thought I could stand on a bale of straw. I imagined this introductory exercise taking place in the safe confines of the barn, where the straw bales are stacked. However, the barn is a bit congested at the moment with a vehicle, a trampoline, big round bales of hay and a stack of breeze blocks, in addition to the straw.

Thinking about bales of straw gave me the inspiration for an activity.

Ricky obligingly moved eight bales from the barn to the front field, which the horses had come off for the summer, and we positioned them – four on each side – to make a channel through which I would walk Havana.

Havana was excited to be led into his 'winter field'. He had only left it a few weeks ago to move to the summer one, but that's horses for you; they get excited by anything new, and old familiar things – such as winter fields – quickly become 'new' once they leave them.

As the field is quite big, I attempted to give Havana the impression that our 'activity area' was confined, by positioning the channel of bales in a corner, only about twelve feet away from the post and rails fence. Also, as a precaution against total insurrection, I closed the field gate behind us; even though that still allowed Havana eight acres of freedom, in the unlikely event that he would find anything so objectionable that he needed to run away from it.

Wearing his head collar and carrying the old brown saddle, Havana hardly noticed me leading him through the bale channel. To get him thinking, I asked him to halt halfway along and then reverse out.

Havana obviously had a different, far more familiar activity in mind. His reaction, when I prodded his chest with my finger to ask him to walk backwards, was to drop his muzzle and give my shin a soft, reciprocal nip. He thought I was starting a game.

"Havana, NO!" An abrupt jerk of the lead rope brought his head up and my assertive tone told him this was not a game; I was asking him to do something.

The penny dropped and he obligingly took a step backwards. Repelled by my squared shoulders, my stare focused on his back end and my command to go "b-a-a-a-c-k!", Havana willingly walked backwards a couple more strides out of the channel.

Then I asked him to halt – for a split-second – before almost instantly walking him actively forwards; I don't want him thinking that walking backwards indefinitely is an option as it could cause untold difficulties in his future career as a riding horse!

We halted again and he got a forehead rub, with lots of reassurance about what a "good boy" he was.

We had another go at this exercise, which he performed perfectly, and then – to make it trickier and more interesting – Ricky and I, with Havana's help, moved some of the bales so the channel became an 'L shape'. Havana didn't think twice about backing round the right-angle bend. The first time, his back legs crashed into the last bale but, by his second attempt, only the corner of the bale brushed his leg as he walked through.

His bright eyes and pricked ears told me that Havana was certainly enjoying our activities. This inspired me to try something else; deconstructing the 'L shape' so the bales had random gaps in between them, also proved a hit.

We played 'follow my leader', with Havana following me eagerly on a loose rope, as I weaved in, out and round the bales.

Finally, a real challenge: as I took a big stride right over the top of a bale, I called to Havana: "Come on boy!" Without hesitating, he lifted his legs one-by-one and strode over the bale. In fact, it was such fun that we picked another bale and repeated the game.

"I'm going to try leaning over his back." I told Ricky.

I halted Havana alongside a bale and he began eating the one in front of him; he loves the clean, soft, barley straw which I use for bedding in his stable. I passed the lead rope to Ricky, who stood on Havana's other side by his head.

First, I just put my arm over the saddle and slapped the leather gently with the palm of my hand. Havana seemed not to notice. Next, I tried to lift my ribcage over the saddle, but I was too low.

I quietly added a second storey to my straw mounting block. Standing on the second bale gave me all the extra height I needed to lean forward so that, from my hips up, I was across the saddle and my feet were off the bale.

For the first time ever, Havana had weight on his back. In long, calm sweeps, I stroked his neck with my right hand. Havana kept munching the straw. If he *had* noticed that he now had a nine stone human across his back, he didn't show it.

"Put your leg over the saddle!" Ricky's encouragement was well meant, but it didn't fit in with my mental plan. I had intended to do no more today than lean over Havana's back, maybe a couple of times – but why not? He was so unconcerned by what I had already done and so calm and happy eating straw, why not?

Very slowly, I swivelled my hips round, so I could lift my right leg clear of the back of the saddle and – sitting astride – face forwards. I kept my head down and my back and neck flat; I was clamped like a baby monkey onto Havana's back.

As I calmly stroked Havana's neck again, I could hardly believe he still seemed not to have noticed what was going on.

I'm sure it helped to have Ricky standing by his head. Havana likes 'big people' and he is always keen to stand by Ricky's side. My explanation is that horses innately seek a 'herd leader' to protect them and 'do the thinking'. So, for Havana, the fact that he now had a monkey clambering on his back didn't really matter as he had a 'big person' to guard him.

"Sit up!" Ricky was on a roll. But actually there didn't seem to be any reason for me not to sit up. With every atom in my body radiating a volatile mixture of anticipation and apprehension, I gradually lifted my head and slowly unfolded, so I was now seeing the world from Havana's back – a new world beckoning us to ride into it.

Riding into it started sooner than I expected! As Havana walked forwards, I instinctively grabbed a hank of silky black mane, holding it firmly by the root in my clenched fist so I was anchored to him. He was actually just investigating the next bale to see how tasty it was but, seizing the impetus, I put both feet into the dangling stirrups and, in a calm low voice, asked Ricky to:

"Walk him on." Havana walked like a lamb alongside his 'big person', in a circle around the scattered bales.

"Walk him the other way." Ricky led Havana in a circle in the opposite direction.

"Stop him by that bale on the left." My intention was to slide off and that would be the end of our first-ever ride.

Havana had other ideas: he did stop by the bale on the left, but then turned to face it and proceeded to climb over it!

I sat very still, fearful of disrupting his balance by breathing and aware that, if I intended to use bales as barriers, it had been pretty stupid of me to encourage Havana to walk over them in the first place.

I needn't have worried, Havana was fine. Ricky led him round to another convenient bale and I quietly slipped off his back.

The little creature was then submerged in torrents of praise and effusive neck and face rubbing. I ran-up the stirrups and slackened the girth. As Ricky went to get the camera from the car, I sat on a bale. Standing by me, Havana dropped his head and stood with his forehead resting gently against my chest.

We were both tired. First backing can be traumatic for a horse (and rider), but Havana had taken it all in his stride – in fact he hardly seemed to notice. In just ten minutes this generous little horse had accepted my weight on his back, taken me for our first-ever ride and coped with the strange new sensation he would have felt as he attempted to balance himself when he clambered over the bale.

As I sat, with Havana's forehead still against my chest, the atmosphere was more than calm – it was tranquil. What more could I ask for?

What a little star!

"What more could I ask for? What a little star!"

HAVANA'S LONGEST WALK
Monday, 3 May 2010

*W*ell, things are moving on!

Today, ably assisted by Mrs B., Corris and Ricky, Havana went for his longest walk by far in 'the outside world' and I'm sure he really enjoyed it.

In a protective bubble between Corris and Mrs B. at the head of the entourage, and Ricky at the rear, we walked – with appropriate grazing breaks – all the way to Gunstone.

Once there, Corris and Havana banqueted for half-an-hour on the mixed salad of the enormous grass verge on the lane that leads up the hill behind the stables.

Whilst Corris and Havana were feasting, Ricky walked to the nearby stable yard at Gunstone Hall (which had been Cayman's yard), to announce Havana's arrival to his many well-wishers there. However, Ricky found the yard deserted; today is Badminton Horse Trials, one of the most popular equestrian events in Europe, so many of the Gunstone horse-owners would have been there.

Not to worry! We had a chat with our friend Jess, who lives at the farm at the top of the hill; Jess loves Havana already, having first met him as a young foal.

Anyway, perhaps it was better not to make our triumphant return to Gunstone Hall while Havana was wearing two coats at the same time: his fluffy, chocolate-brown winter coat – which was now looking slightly tatty – and his sleek, almost chestnut, summer coat – which was emerging in patches. No, we'll wait until he has moulted fully and become immaculate, which won't be long.

Havana was docile as we walked back home – actually I think he was rather tired.

I walked by his shoulder, my right hand resting over his neck and the lead rope draped across my body into my left hand. We were both relaxed.

Following Corris's silver-white swaying rump, with his shimmering rippled tail, and with Ricky behind us, I could tell that Havana felt safe – and so did I.

Havana's increasing confidence in his new environment was evident in the cheeky way he attempted to start a game with Corris, as they walked, by nipping at the tendons above his hocks. I don't think an apprehensive horse's mind would have turned to games!

Just before we turned left on the final stretch of our return journey, Havana chose to stop for a chat with a neighbour; he seemed fascinated by the loud music from the radio in her stable yard. I told her his age and how he had taken her two cavorting miniature Shetland ponies – one black, the other chestnut – in his stride as we had passed by on the way to Gunstone.

Back in his stable, I carefully checked Havana's feet and legs. Apart from a slightly frayed offside front hoof there was nothing untoward, although that did cause me to question my hope that I might save a fortune by not shoeing him.

When I turned Havana out into the paddock, he walked straight to the far end and stood by the fence; as the crow flies, the nearest point to his grazing companions, Toffee and Freddy. He must have wanted to graze with them, but all he did was stand as if in a trance, looking at them. I honestly believe he was so psychologically exhausted by his excursion into 'the outside world' that he had forgotten he needed to go through the open gate into the rest of the paddock, where Toffee and Freddy were.

Hearing me calling his name and clapping my hands broke his trance, then he walked back towards me and followed me through the gateway.

My comical exaggerated jogging, with flailing arms, encouraged him into a canter and, once round the corner of the field, he dropped his head to graze with his companions.

He was pooped – and so was I!

SADDLES, TEETH, SADDLES
Saturday, 8 May 2010

*W*e've had a busy week.

Last Sunday, John – a master saddler – came to assess Cayman's saddle, which now seems far too small for Havana. It perches high on his shoulders and looking through the gullet from front to back is like looking through the Channel Tunnel.

When I had called in to see John at "Horse and Country" the previous day, he had said that he remembered putting in some extra flocking to raise the front of the saddle on Cayman.

Now, he needed to assess whether taking flocking out might make the saddle fit Havana. He hadn't been hopeful, but I'd asked him to try this anyway as it would be less expensive than a new saddle. He understood my rationale and was willing to try.

I hadn't given John very clear directions about exactly which, of three neighbouring farm lanes, was the one he should take.

Whilst we were waiting for him to arrive, I tied Havana to the gatepost in 'the muddy paddock' and set about sprucing him up.

Havana didn't bother that I was grooming him more diligently than usual; Ricky was standing by his head, giving him so much fuss and attention that I'm sure he really couldn't have cared less what I was doing!

When John arrived, he had sensibly brought with him an eighteen-month-old, second-hand saddle.

He very quickly got down to the business of measuring Havana's back, with what looked like a pair of mariner's compasses – but I'm sure they weren't. The prodding instrument must have felt strange to Havana, but he didn't flinch.

Next, Cayman's saddle was positioned on his back in a very 'no nonsense' way. It probably felt cold; Havana is used to the cushioned feeling of a padded numnah under his saddle.

Here was a master craftsman at work, eliciting every relevant detail of saddle and horse. Dutifully, 'horse' stood as solid as a rock. I was proud of him.

Remembering our vet Sue's appraisal of Havana twelve days ago as "fat", I asked John with trepidation:

"How much 'too fat' is he?"

"He's not fat!" was John's immediate reply. I could have kissed him. Phew! – 'Fat Camp' had obviously worked.

I had seen a difference in Havana in the week that he had been on the starvation paddock. He was far less bloated and there was a definite dividing line between the end of his neck and his shoulder. This area had previously been one, blurred, length of fat.

Pointing at Havana's chest, John went on:

"Once you get him walking on the road these muscles will develop, and his shoulders." He pointed to the fat behind Havana's withers: "And this'll go."

Inexplicably, a wave of sadness rolled over me.

The last few grains of sand were just about to slip inevitably through the egg timer. I couldn't stop the hour-hand sweeping to twelve o'clock. My foal would never be a foal again.

Havana is very nearly an adult horse.

I was snapped out of my melancholy as John placed the second-hand saddle on Havana's back, its fit was perfect. What a skilful man, he had never seen Havana before. All I had said the previous day was:

"Although he's Cayman's half-brother, he's not as big as Cayman. He's 15.1hh, but his rump is 15.2hh and he's got a huge 'barrel' of a ribcage."

The sight of Havana, apparently kitted-out and ready to go – in a saddle which enveloped his back rather than perching on top of it – made me so excited about all the riding we were going to do, that I quickly forgot my ridiculous sadness that my boy had grown up. *Of course* he had, that was why I had bought him – *to ride!*

I am glad, though, that all of the things Havana and I have done together so far have been so enjoyable that I had almost forgotten the main purpose of having a horse.

John took away Cayman's saddle, and left the second-hand one for us to try.

Wednesday was 'teeth' and, as last year, Havana was a brave little star.

Geraint is so kind and understands horses very well. He greeted Havana with a long forehead rub before starting work on his mouth.

Unlike last time, when I'd stayed outside, Geraint wanted me to be with Havana as he stood in the back of his stable.

I'm glad I was. With the gag in, so he couldn't close his mouth and had difficulty swallowing, Havana's eyes were enormous spheres of fear as Geraint drilled away the rough edges of his teeth with a succession of different-sized drill bits.

Standing by Havana's shoulder, I stroked along the top of his neck in firm regular sweeps. I encouraged him and praised his bravery.

After about five minutes, the mechanical drilling ceased and Geraint finished off with a manual rasp. Havana's eyes, although still frightened, reverted to their normal shape. Obviously the screaming drill had terrified him.

Havana's only overt protest at any of this was right at the end, when he pawed the ground three times with his nearside front hoof; a huge action, right from his shoulder – expressing frustration at being unable to close his mouth and confusion at the whole process. It was an emphatic demonstration that he was very nearly at his wits' end – and asking for help.

Help came quickly: the gag was out, and Geraint was once again making friends with his young patient, whose forehead was now low and pressed into Geraint's hand as more soothing, forehead-rubbing was administered.

I led Havana out to the field for a feast of carrots – and out of earshot of the drill.

Corris was next. Mrs B. told me that:

"As usual, Corris put up a token fight but, once he knew he was beaten, he settled-down."

I am very, very proud of Havana. To be so calm, in such a frightening situation, shows that he is kind through-and-through; but I do already know that kindness is in his genes.

What was it that his sire's owner had said about her stallion?

"Falconwood: the kindest stallion on earth." How true that was.

Today was saddles again.

John brought back Cayman's saddle, with some of its flocking removed. It looked a lot better on Havana, but nothing like as good as the other saddle, so we're going to try both.

OUR SECOND WALK TO GUNSTONE
Sunday, 9 May 2010

*T*oday we decided to walk to Gunstone again, so that's exactly what we did.

In our usual safe formation – Mrs B. and Corris leading, Havana and I in the middle and Ricky bringing up the rear – we marched, non-stop, for the entire mile.

No grazing breaks for Havana; there was no need as he was so keen to repeat last week's expedition into 'the outside world' that he powered himself along with effortless, floating strides.

"Nearly there Boo – you'll soon be grazing at the bottom of the hill behind the stables." I probably didn't need to remind him of the feast which lay ahead.

Once through the narrow gate at the side of the wide, five-barred gate across the lane, Havana was given his head to select the best grazing. As if he had a lead weight in his muzzle, his head disappeared – up to his eyes – in the succulent and varied herbage. It was a very well-earned reward for such remarkably good in-hand walking.

I hoped we would meet up with some of our friends from Gunstone and, sure enough, after only fifteen minutes, there was Liz on the other side of the wide gate.

"Hello! Is this Havana?"

I was glad to see Liz, an experienced horsewoman, and to show off my youngster. The trouble was that Havana had totally signed-off from any activity other than devouring grass. It's difficult to show off a horse when he is up to his eyes in grass and dandelion leaves. Fortunately, Liz knows enough about horses to evaluate one in a less than ideal environment, and she did seem to think that Havana made the grade.

"How big will he be?" she asked. I gave my stock reply:

"Well, his withers are 15.1hh and his rump is 15.2hh, so he'll be at least 15.2hh – I hope!"

I think it's a safe bet that I will not have a slanting horse; their bottoms and shoulders usually do even-up, eventually.

When Liz had had Rupert and I had had Cayman, at Gunstone, we used to debate which horse was taller. Liz had been sure about Cayman: "He's taller than Rupert," just as I had been sure about Rupert: "No, Rupert's taller than Cayman."

The truth is they were both 17hh but, as Rupert was bay and Cayman grey, some sort of optical illusion must have been going on.

Very sadly, Rupert died last year from a twisted gut, just as Cayman had three years before.

When Liz asked me about Havana's height, I cautioned her:

"Because Havana is Cayman's half-brother people expect him to be big, but his mother is Welsh Section D, not Irish Draught like Cayman's mother. I don't want him to grow-up hearing everyone saying he's little! Just as Cayman didn't know he was big, Havana doesn't know that he *isn't* and, anyway, his presence is huge." Liz agreed, and warned me that Havana, at just three, probably still had some growing to do. She told me her new horse, who was aged five when she bought him last year, continued to grow and is now about 18hh.

Given that Havana had only just come off the 'starvation paddock', I decided that half-an-hour's feasting was enough, so we got into formation and started our return journey. After only about half-a-mile, we saw our friend Sarah in her farmyard. Havana and I stood in the gateway for another half-hour's social visit, while Ricky sat on a large stone by the road-side and Corris dozed, resting a back leg, as Mrs B. sat quietly on his back.

Havana, however, had no intention of resting; he was intrigued by Sarah's two Rottweiler guard dogs: Dax and Bruce, who were prowling menacingly around the yard. He was not in the least bit frightened of them and proved this by sticking his head dangerously far over the gate into their territory.

In the field behind Sarah's house, Havana could see her retired mare, Rhapsody, grazing. He watched her intently.

Eventually, as Sarah gently rubbed his forehead and gazed into his huge, enquiring eyes, Havana's attention came back to the gateway. Realising that Ricky and Mrs B. might just want to get home this evening, Havana and I said goodbye to Sarah and we all set off again.

Once back at the stables, we had another task; I needed to sit on the saddle that John had left for us to try.

Havana had carried this all afternoon; it looked comfortable for him and he had certainly walked-out beautifully in it, but I needed to find out whether it would be comfortable for Havana with me sitting on it and whether it would be comfortable for me.

Ricky and I decided that the barn in the 'muddy paddock' would be a safe, semi-enclosed area in which I would get on Havana's back, for only the second time.

Ricky went off with the wheelbarrow to get two straw bales to use as a mounting block.

As Havana was already quite tired, both physically and psychologically, from our expedition to Gunstone, I only intended to sit on his back for a moment, but I did feel that I should tell John, as soon as possible, whether I wanted to buy his saddle.

When the straw bales were in place – one on top of the other – in the barn, I led Havana in and handed the lead rope to Ricky, so he would be in control of him whilst I got onto his back.

As soon as Havana got close to the bales he started pulling at the delicious straw. It took some doing for Ricky to position him alongside the edible mounting block, so I could lean over the saddle.

As Havana was plainly not going anywhere, I put my right leg over the saddle and sat up – within only a few seconds. No reaction from Havana.

So that I could get a feel of the saddle, I asked Ricky to lead Havana around the bales.

Havana was cross. He wanted to eat, not walk; he'd already done enough of that this afternoon.

I could feel him swishing his tail in annoyance like an angry cat and, as Ricky propelled him in a circle, Havana communicated his displeasure by nipping belligerently at Ricky's shins.

The saddle felt slightly more cushioned than Cayman's saddle but, despite this, my seat bones were painful. Then I remembered; yesterday, for the first time since last October, I had ridden with Alison for about two hours. I had a bruised bottom, which was useless for trying saddles.

I jumped from Havana's back.

It didn't take much empathetic head-rubbing to reassure him that I knew he'd had enough for one day and to restore his usual sweet-natured equilibrium.

Saddle assessing could wait and, anyway, my bottom needed at least a week to recover!

A RIDING MORNING
Saturday, 15 May 2010

*T*his was the most inviting 'riding morning' imaginable.

At 8 a.m. it was starting to be sunny and far warmer than the past couple of unseasonably icy weeks. A promise of summer was carried on the light air and the prospect of rides with Havana beckoned.

When I arrived at the stables, Mrs B. was just starting to groom Corris ready for a ride. I went to fetch Havana in from the field for his, now miniscule, feed.

Miraculously, as I appeared in the gateway, Havana and Prince appeared, at a fast canter and perfectly side-by-side, over the top of the bank.

Illuminated by subtle morning sunlight, they were dream-like.

My good fortune didn't last; the pair stopped momentarily at the top of the field, Havana just an arm's length from me, before turning in unison and galloping thunderously, right back down to the bottom.

Enjoying the beauty of the morning and glad to be in the field, not in an office, I ambled halfway down the bank. The herd was spread out, all facing the same direction, and grazing contentedly near to the bog, which has been fenced-off with smart posts and rails.

As usual I fixed my gaze on Havana's back end and slowly counted to ten, before turning and walking steadily back up the field away from him. After half-a-dozen paces, I cast a surreptitious glance over my shoulder. Good boy! He was meandering up the field after me.

Whilst Havana ate his feed, Mrs B. got onto Corris's back by using the step opposite Havana's stable door as a mounting block.

As they rode away to the right and disappeared out of sight, around the corner of the house that used to be stables, Havana leaned out over his door, craning his neck as far as he could to the right to see where Corris and Mrs B. had gone. He maintained this observational position for some time; his big, dark eyes vigilant, hoping to catch a glimpse of them.

I do think that Havana wanted to go with Corris and Mrs B., he seemed disappointed at having been left behind this morning.

After a twenty-minute snooze in the cool gloom of the stable, Havana's tall, 'sea horse' stretch told me he had woken-up.

I really wanted to take him into 'the outside world' for an adventure – it was just that sort of morning. But, as Ricky is away in Dubai for a week, we have temporarily lost our 'rear guard'. I don't think it's fair to expect Havana to cope with a fast car or a noisy motor bike coming up behind him unexpectedly.

He thinks that he has already conquered 'the outside world' and I want him to carry on believing this, rather than have his confidence shattered. So, until Ricky is back to walk twenty yards behind us on the narrow lanes, it is definitely safer not to go exploring.

In the 'muddy paddock', which is now dry, I placated Havana with some grooming.

Actually, there was very little real grooming. Through his endearing habit of pressing whichever bit of himself he wants rubbing into the brush, which was quickly dispensed-with in favour of my scratchy fingers, Havana managed to get me to rub: first his left cheek, then his forehead, then behind his left ear.

The ecstatic effect of this resulted in him stretching his neck and head down, so his muzzle was almost on the ground, and tilting his head to the left to increase the pressure as I rubbed his ear.

I thought it was unfair to leave out his right ear so, squatting down in front of him, I worked with both hands on both ears simultaneously.

The way Havana thrust his nose still further forward, while the skin under his eyes appeared to wrinkle, indicated I was on target.

Next, he got a good scratch of his mane and the top of his head, and so it went on.

After about half-an-hour, we finished off with some conventional grooming with a brush … but only for a couple of minutes!

"Sorry boy – you've got to go back into your field now." I felt that I was letting Havana down, because we were not going on any sort of adventure today.

"Let's go round the back of the house!" It wasn't much of an adventure, but I thought it would be less boring for him than our usual route to the field past the front of the house.

When we reached the path to the field gate, to our left, Havana very purposefully turned right – along the farm lane which leads to 'the outside world'. He had made up his mind what he wanted to do.

He was so confident and relaxed as he strode down the lane that I felt completely comfortable walking along by his nearside flank, with my right hand resting gently on the top of his rump.

Havana was taking me for a walk … and it was lovely.

At the end of the farm lane we stopped and he quickly submerged his muzzle in a large patch of fresh clover leaves.

He showed no sign of wanting to turn right, up the lane where we had walked with Ricky, and Corris and Mrs B.. He was quite content here but, after a week in the field, he had obviously felt the urge to go somewhere.

"It won't be long boy, we'll soon go for rides – just a couple more weeks, you'll see."

Havana was quite happy to walk back down the farm lane to his field; he had satisfied his need to respond to the lure of this beautiful morning.

* * *

I don't think it was a coincidence that, when I got home and lifted the garage door to go through to the back of the house, I saw that Cayman's bridle had mysteriously 'jumped off' its hook under the saddle rack and deposited itself, in a heap of straps, on the floor. How could I not notice it there?

I am getting used to such things now!

WHICH SADDLE?
Sunday, 16 May 2010

On Friday I was sure the girth I had bought would fit Havana.

I had carefully measured Cayman's girth which, when buckled-up on the last holes, held the new saddle on Havana's back, but not tightly enough to be safe for riding.

I calculated how much shorter a new girth needed to be, so it could be buckled-up on the middle holes of the saddle's straps. This would allow for adjustment in the highly-likely event that the circumference of Havana's belly would increase or, less likely, decrease.

Confident in my calculation, I had bought a forty-six-inch girth.

Yesterday, when I tried the new girth on Havana, it was obviously about four inches too short; it just about reached the first holes of the saddle's straps.

How did that happen? I had been so sure of the maths. However, logic now dictated that what I needed was a fifty-inch girth.

I rang "Diamond Saddlery", 'Auntie Alison's' business; they had a forty-eight-inch black girth of the type I wanted, but a fifty-inch one would have to be ordered and would be in for Tuesday or Wednesday.

I was disappointed, but asked Alison to order the girth. I would have to wait to try both the new saddle and Cayman's saddle, with its newly-reduced flocking, and then decide which was the best fit for Havana.

This morning was bright and sunny like yesterday, so I badly wanted to get Havana's saddles sorted out. I wanted to get on with riding him and a saddle was a prerequisite!

I was still confused about why my girth calculations were not right.

Then it occurred to me … why not measure the girth I had just bought to find out exactly what forty-six-inches meant?

I was glad that I did, because I found out that girth manufacturers and I evidently don't have the same idea of what should be measured.

My calculation had been based, rather literally, on the length of the strap around the horse's belly: 'the girth' – whereas the manufacturer's measurement included the buckles, which in this case accounted for two inches at each end of that strap.

That was where I had gone wrong! But, as the peg of the buckle is only halfway up it, that meant the remainder of the buckle didn't actually contribute any additional length. Maybe what I needed was a forty-eight-inch girth? This was getting complicated.

Determined, I gathered up the new saddle, Cayman's girth and the reject girth, and sped off to "Diamond Saddlery". I would sort this out. I *would* sit on Havana's back today – and try-out both saddles.

With the new saddle on Alison's 'saddle horse', and Cayman's girth on the last holes, it was as good as having Havana in the shop.

It didn't take long to find the right girth, which was more easily done by sight than by mathematical calculations, although it did turn out to be the forty-eight-inch one.

The saddlery was so well stocked that, as usual, I found something else I didn't know I needed until I saw it; a brown numnah with a shaped seat, which fitted perfectly under our new saddle. I was ninety-nine per cent sure we would be keeping that saddle!

I couldn't wait to try it all – saddle, numnah, and girth – on Havana. As soon as I got home I rang Mrs B., and 3 p.m. became the appointed hour.

At 3 p.m. I turned down Jan's offer of some metal caravan steps in lieu of a mounting block, in case Havana banged his legs on them.

Instead, I transported four bales of straw from the barn and, against my better judgement, constructed two separate, edible mounting blocks in the same corner of the winter field where I had first got on Havana's back two weeks ago.

I hoped the continuity of location and mounting blocks would quell any apprehension Havana might have about me sitting on him again.

Having put the two saddles and their respective numnahs on the top rail of the fence and made sure I had everything I needed in the bucket of grooming equipment, I brought Havana out of the front field where he had been grazing.

Seeing how the recently-fertilized grass in his winter field had sprung-up, Havana walked enthusiastically into the field with me. He seemed slightly surprised when, instead of leading him out into the lush pasture, I marched him alongside the fence to where I had set up camp. However, once I had tied him up and commenced some serious tickly-tail combing and rump scratching, he soon rested the back foot nearest to me – rolling his hip lower on that side, so I could massage his rump more effectively. His closed eyes told me that Havana was thoroughly relaxed.

It seemed a shame to wake him up to put on the new saddle, but I did want him to have an opportunity to sniff not only the saddle, but also the new brown numnah. As I held this under his muzzle he was curious about the 'new cotton' smell.

To investigate properly it had to go into his mouth, but I drew the line at his attempt to chew it, and gently removed the soggy, grassy part before it was ripped.

With no reaction from Havana at all, the numnah was in position and the saddle on. I buckled up the new girth so the saddle was firm, then checked that there was no pinched skin by pulling each of Havana's forelegs out in front of him at chest height, stretching the skin behind his elbow where the girth lies.

Next, I tightened the girth more; this was the tightest Havana had ever felt anything around his chest. I had to make sure that, when I was mounted, the saddle would not slip; not only could I be injured, but also a slipping saddle would frighten Havana.

Again, he didn't react.

To get him used to the feel of his new saddle, I put the stirrup irons down and led him around the field. I'm sure he thought the purpose of this was to locate a good place to begin grazing – that's what he was doing.

After enough walking to be sure the saddle was comfortable for Havana, I led him to the straw bales and, with Mrs B. holding the lead rope, prepared quietly to lean over the saddle.

To distract Havana, I thought it would be a good idea for him to pull at the straw, but this seemed to cause him problems. Each time he tore at the straw he evidently had pain in his mouth, because he violently threw up his head. He kept on trying to eat the straw, but with the same result every time. He was getting quite frustrated and distressed.

Poor Havana; when Geraint, the dentist, had examined him last week, he had noted on Havana's dental record that he still had molars which might, by his age, have been shed for adult replacements.

No wonder he was in some discomfort; he was trying to chew tough straw with one or more wobbly baby teeth, which were obviously shooting painful twinges through his jaw.

To save Havana from further self-inflicted torture, we needed to get him away from the bales. But how was I going to get on his back? What was I going to use as a mounting block?

With a mature horse, I would have no hesitation in climbing a fence, whilst the horse stood parallel to it, then reaching my right leg out and easing myself, very gently, onto the saddle; but this would only be the third time in his life that Havana had had a person on his back.

Never mind, I trusted him and actually had little doubt that we could do it this way.

I led Havana out of the field and along the fence, so we were standing looking into our base camp, rather than out from it. Sitting on the top rail, I was able to lean forward over the saddle when Mrs B. positioned Havana alongside.

Havana didn't really notice his person, once again, dangling over him; he had his head down, grazing the long grass at the base of the fence posts.

Almost immediately, I put my leg over the saddle and unfolded my body, so I was sitting up. There seemed no reason not to.

My seat bones had recovered. The saddle was comfortable – quite luxurious in fact. I liked it.

Looking down at its fit across Havana's shoulders, it looked right.

To get a better idea I needed Havana to walk on. Mrs B. gave a slight pull on the lead rope and Havana brought his head up from the grass.

Led by Mrs B., he walked obligingly along the path by the fence, although the sharp stones on its surface could not have been comfortable for his feet, and onto the softer grass of the field.

He seemed perfectly happy, both with the saddle and with me on it.

Next, we needed to try Cayman's saddle, to see how this compared with the new one.

Back at our mounting place by the fence I switched saddles, whilst Havana grazed, and prepared to get on for the second time. Havana, still with his head down, grazing – and not quite parallel with the fence – had created a wedge-shaped gap, narrowest at his head and widening towards his rump. This meant I needed to launch myself from the top rail of the fence with more velocity than before.

Once again, despite his human catapulting herself across his back and almost instantly sitting up and putting both feet in the stirrups, Havana continued to munch away at a particularly tasty tuft of grass.

This time, when I wanted him to bring his head up and walk a little way, I asked him by giving a pull on the lead rope and pressing both of my legs against his sides. This was a sensation he had never felt before and one which could quite easily, in a young horse, produce a buck, varying from 'token bunny-hop' to 'head between the knees bronco'.

Not Havana ... he simply walked forward as I had asked!

It felt lovely to be sitting in Cayman's saddle again after four years. It felt so familiar. But, looking down at its fit over Havana's shoulders, there was no doubt that the new one was the better fit, for now anyway. Havana's shape will change as he develops and we may eventually need Cayman's saddle.

It was good that we had got Havana's saddle sorted out; we were now very close to going for rides.

"… the purpose of this was to locate a good place to begin grazing."

FIRST BIT

Monday, 17 May 2010

*A*t last – we've got a bit!

I would not have believed how difficult it was; first, to work out what size bit Havana needed and, second, actually to get one.

The process started three weeks ago. I needed something with which to measure the diameter of Havana's mouth and was pleased with myself for coming up with the ingenious idea that a wooden spoon might work. After all, its handle is rigid and about the same thickness as a bit, also I hoped it would feel natural to Havana, who does regularly eat twigs.

Armed with the long-handled wooden spoon that we use for mixing Christmas cakes, a pencil and the retractable steel ruler, I was ready.

After Havana had finished his feed and settled-down for a 'standing-up snooze', before going back out into the field, I produced my spoon and tried to insert it into the corner of his mouth.

Havana's glazed eyes told me that he was in a deep slumber. Try as I might, there was no way I could persuade the spoon handle to slide into the corner of his mouth, across his tongue and out the other side.

I could see the route was totally obstructed by Havana's tongue, which seemed to fill his mouth so completely that its sides bulged-out over his gums in the space between his molars and his incisors; there was certainly no room for a spoon handle.

I decided I would just have to wait for him to wake-up, so that I might persuade him to open his mouth.

Eventually Havana did wake up and had no problem at all in allowing me to stick the spoon handle into his mouth.

The sound of wood fibres being crushed alerted me to the fact that I had not quite put the handle in at the right angle. I adjusted the angle, so the end of the handle just protruded from the opposite corner of

Havana's mouth, and made an accurate pencil mark on the wood at the corner of his mouth on my side.

The steel ruler indicated the diameter of Havana's mouth was three-and-a-half inches, which is ludicrously tiny! He does have a petite head … but three-and-a-half inches? Add on the requisite quarter-of-an-inch clearance each side and it was still only four inches; that's what my spoon told me.

In honour of this milestone in Havana's development, our Christmas cake mixer will forever have commemorative horse tooth marks and a pencil line on its handle!

I wasn't happy with that three-and-a-half inches; it couldn't be right. I looked-up 'biting' in a text book and learned that one method for measuring a horse's mouth is to use *string*. How logical! Why hadn't I thought of it?

Again, Havana had no objection when I threaded a length of bale string into one corner of his mouth, across his tongue and out the other side. In fact, he dozed through my second measuring session, which produced a different result from the first; four-and-a-half inches plus half-an-inch, making five inches! I was losing confidence in the validity of my findings. How could the width of Havana's mouth have grown an inch in a day?

I resolved to decide the issue finally, so the next time, during a 'post-feed snooze', I gently inserted a twelve-inch, wooden school ruler into Havana's mouth. There was no reaction whatsoever from the trusting, sleepy little horse, but there was *another* result.

According to the ruler, it was five inches, plus half-an-inch, which would give a bit size of five-and-a-half inches. I was getting nowhere.

My measurements told me we needed a bit between four and five-and-a-half inches. Bits are sized in increments of a quarter-of-an-inch, so that gave us a choice of *seven* bits and was really no help at all.

I was despairing of ever being able to ride Havana in a conventional bridle.

What made my exasperation worse was that I had already identified a beautifully-designed, gentle, starter-bit, which I felt would be ideal for Havana. It fitted my requirements exactly, being made from metals which warm-up quickly in a horse's mouth and taste sweet. What more could I ask for? I was determined that Havana's first experience of a bit was going to be as good as it could possibly be.

I don't know why, but when I was driving home from work this afternoon, an idea came into my head: "Get a five-inch bit". I made a slight detour and bought the only five-inch bit, of the make I had identified, in stock. I took it on the understanding that if it did not fit I could return it and have my money back.

I couldn't wait to try the new bit. For a second opinion, I arranged with Mrs B. that she would feed Corris slightly later than usual, at the same time as I was feeding Havana.

After Havana had eaten his feed, I stood at the left side of his head, with the top of my old bridle in my right hand and the bit resting on my flat left palm. Very gently, I placed my palm under Havana's muzzle with the command: "Open!" He walked backwards until his rump met the back wall of the stable with a soft thud.

Unable to retreat any further, Havana duly un-clenched his front teeth and I was able to slide the bit past them, into his mouth. At the same time, with my right hand, I guided the top of the bridle over his ears, which produced an unexpected effect. Havana loves having his ears rubbed and, when he felt the slight pressure on both ears as I slid the top of the bridle over them, he must have thought it was a very effective 'simultaneous ear-rubbing device'. He instantly lowered his head in an accepting way, just as he does when he wants his ears rubbed. Havana did get his ears rubbed, although his mouth was my priority, not his ears.

He just couldn't fathom what was in his mouth! His tongue was working hard trying to move the thing – which he could neither chew nor swallow.

It was time for some distraction; I'm certain it reassured Havana to learn that he could still eat chopped apple, even with this strange object in his mouth.

Then for my piéce de résistance ... treacle! Using the handle of the hoof pick, I dolloped a handle-full of the sweet, sticky stuff into Havana's feed bucket.

Havana doesn't usually lick feed buckets, as horses tend to bite at even small amounts of food rather than licking-up the last remnants, as a dog does. However, for Havana treacle is the exception. The saliva produced as he licked treacle from his bucket caused brown foam to froth out from each corner of his lips. He was in raptures at the sweetness which filled his mouth. I sensed he was thinking:

"You can put whatever you like in my mouth ... *just give me more of that lovely sticky food!*"

Mrs B. and I spent a while checking and double-checking the fit of the bit, by carefully slipping our thumb-ends in between the corner of Havana's lips and the bit rings, to make sure it was neither too long nor too short.

Although this was an inexact science, we reassured each other that five inches was the right size. Even so, by not removing the two dangling labels, I had the peace of mind that if I had got it all wrong – and if by tomorrow Havana's mouth was a different size – the bit could be exchanged.

Havana – tired of our deliberations, and doubtless concluding he had had his treacle ration for the day – drifted to the back of the stable where he stood dozing, eyes glazed and head low, obviously not at all bothered by his new bit.

LEAD-REIN PONY
Sunday, 23 May 2010

*N*ew saddle, new bit; we were equipped to begin some proper riding.

To be safe, this would start in the confines of Toffee's and Freddy's paddock. Our plan was that, with me mounted, Ricky would lead Havana and, very gradually, I would 'take-over the steering' by gently guiding Havana's direction with the reins, whilst keeping him going forward with my legs. Ricky would continue to walk with Havana, keeping hold of the lead-rope … just in case.

Havana was quite happy to be tied up to the gatepost to have his saddle put on. He didn't react at all to the girth being tightened, little by little, to riding tightness, so it would hold the saddle safely in place in the event of any aerial acrobatics.

Again, as a precaution against pinching folds of skin behind his front legs in the girth, I asked Havana to let me pull each of his front legs forward in turn. He so enjoys having his legs stretched like this that he volunteers them; lifting the second knee the instant the first leg has been stretched and that hoof is back on the ground.

A command of: "Open!" was all that was needed for Havana's new bit to slide into position in his mouth. The throat lash was buckled-up and Havana was ready – wearing his bridle over the head collar, to which Ricky attached the rope.

I got onto Havana's back from the fence and he stood happily whilst I checked the girth and put both feet into the stirrups.

It was then that I discovered I had put the stirrups onto the saddle the wrong way round! Our safety-stirrup irons go one way, but I had put the left one onto the right stirrup leather, and vice versa. Not wanting to unsettle Havana by getting off him to sort the stirrups out, I sat a bit further back in the saddle and managed to ease each leather from the metal bar it hangs on – not easy when the saddle is on a horse – swap them over, then wriggle the leather back onto the bar on the correct side.

What all of this fiddling about must have felt like to Havana, goodness knows! Although however it felt, he was perfectly content to doze whilst I sorted myself out.

The downside of attempting to do anything with a horse in a field in which he has grazed is that the horse is unsure whether he is expected to work, or whether he can play.

As Havana's default mode – other than 'eat' or 'doze' – is 'play', it was unsurprising that, as Ricky led him down a slight peaty incline in the middle of the field, Havana skipped into a trot, whilst attempting to catch Ricky's arm in his teeth.

It was warm and Ricky was wearing a T-shirt, so his bare arm was a novelty that Havana could not ignore. His second attempt to get Ricky's arm was successful.

"STOP IT HAVANA!" Ricky jerked the lead rope and Havana got the message that Ricky did not want to play 'biting' and what was required of him was work.

We halted in front of the hedge at the end of the paddock. Havana seemed surprised that, on the other side of the hedge down the field, he could see his herd: Rollo, Prince … everyone.

He stood transfixed, unable to believe his eyes. He'd still be standing there now if Ricky hadn't urged him to turn towards the gate and I hadn't encouraged him, with a gentle squeeze from my legs and a command to "W-a-a-a-l-k-on!"

Relying on Ricky for guidance, Havana successfully crossed the paddock back to the gate, while I sat as still and quietly as I could (apart from reassuring him that he was a "good boy") so he could find his own balance on the uneven ground.

Once back at the gate, Havana must have assumed 'that was it' for the day and he could now relax, by dropping his head and resting a back leg. Poor Havana – if only learning to be a ridden horse was so easy!

Our lesson continued with Ricky leading us in some very big circles, whilst I accustomed Havana to stopping and starting.

My number one priority for feeling safe on a horse's back is that I know 'how the brakes work'. Walking side-by-side with Havana, our 'brakes' had become virtually telepathic, but from on top, for now anyway, I'd be relying on reins and a bit, so it was important that Havana understood this new language.

As usual, he got it in no time.

We ended the lesson by riding across the paddock and halting at the gate by ourselves, without – for us both – the physical and psychological support of Ricky.

We were already 'off the lead-rein', which is often a rite of passage for a novice rider. Today, it was a rite of passage for a novice horse, although unsurprisingly rapid for one as bright as Havana.

DRESS REHEARSAL
Thursday, 27 May 2010

*H*avana has been so good about carrying me, and his new saddle, that we are planning his first proper ride in 'the outside world', with Corris and Mrs B., and Ricky. It will be next Sunday lunch time, when the lane to Gunstone should be quiet.

To bridge the gap between being ridden in the safety of Toffee's and Freddy's paddock and being ridden in 'the outside world', Mrs B. and I decided that Havana would benefit from a short ride to the end of the farm lane with Corris.

We could not go any further today, as Ricky was not available to act as 'rear traffic marshal', protecting Havana and me from cars. Drivers sometimes forget that around any bend in a country lane there might be a young horse on his first ever trip into 'the outside world'.

To enhance Havana's experience of becoming a riding horse, we decided to tack-up both horses in their stables, so Havana gets used to this routine which, over the years, will become as familiar to him as eating grass.

As Havana is easily able to see over the partition that divides their stables, he has actually had the opportunity to see Corris being tacked-up on many occasions – but has rarely been particularly interested. Now, I hoped he would have a sense of doing what Corris was doing, 'like a big boy', as I often say to him.

I even envisaged that, possibly, Havana might be inclined to emulate the behaviour of his accomplished stable companion.

Both horses ate their token 'breakfast': Havana's handful of chaff being simply a carrier for his vitamin and mineral supplement, and Corris's a carrier for his joint-easing glucosamine and his dried nettles, which sooth indigestion. (He has asked two separate animal communicators for this remedy!). Then, they were groomed in readiness for their tack.

"Are you ready to put Havana's saddle on?" Mrs B. called from Corris's stable.

"Yes, I'm just finishing his tail – he's about ready." I don't need to tie Havana up when I groom him in his stable because he so enjoys the relaxing massage, which can scarcely be called 'grooming'! It usually involves firmly brushing whichever bit Havana indicates is most tickly, so the rest of him only gets a cursory flick-over with the brush.

Having made him look presentable, I was just about to leave the stable to collect his saddle from the fence where I had put it ready, when I noticed Havana's knees buckling. I watched as he gently … lowered himself … into the straw of his bed.

For a mature horse like Corris, the familiar pre-ride grooming routine would cause his adrenalin level to rise in eager anticipation of an exciting ride. Not so for Havana; for this youngster the 'breakfast-grooming routine' is a prelude to feeling very sleepy.

"He's having a snooze!" I called to Mrs B. "We'll have to wait for about fifteen minutes."

I sensed Mrs B.'s slight annoyance at this interruption to her own and Corris's well-established routine, but there was nothing else for it; Havana was snoozing and that was that.

Mrs B. and I chatted quietly so we didn't disturb the sleeping little horse sitting in splendour in the centre of his fluffy, straw bed.

Sure enough, after about fifteen minutes, Havana blinked and stretched his neck so it was vertical, with his head high. Then he seemed to re-discover some food in his mouth and started chewing. As he gazed calmly out over the stable door, he looked more like a resting camel than a horse.

Havana did eventually decide to get up and – with youthful bravado manifesting itself in long, light, strides – we led Corris and Mrs B. on a ride down the farm lane and back.

Although Corris's detached demeanour indicated he was rather unimpressed by the entire escapade, Havana was not at all bothered about today's ride being short. He was evidently very happy to be going for a ride in the morning sunshine.

FIRST RIDE
Sunday, 30 May 2010

Wow! Wow! Wow!

We've just been on our first ride in 'the outside world' and, guess what? Havana was a little star.

Corris and Mrs B. led the way, whilst Ricky brought up the rear. In the midday sunshine Havana just bowled along. In no time he had got the idea of walking on the left side of the road and, when I asked him to, he walked on the grass verge.

As we approached Gunstone, he saw the mares grazing in their field on the hill.

High up on our left a vertical grass bank, about three-feet-six-inches high, separates the mares' field from the lane.

There was no time between Havana turning his head to look at the mares and finding myself sitting on his back on top of the bank!

I haven't a clue how it happened.

We were in a perilous position, perched on a narrow ledge next to a barbed-wire fence, with a sheer drop onto the lane below. It didn't take me a second to make the decision to slide off Havana.

Once on my feet, I looked down at the lane. No! There was no way we were taking the direct route.

Looking along the grassy ridge I could see that, if we could manage to stay on it along the fence line, we would gradually descend to the level of the lane.

Urgently I shouted back to Ricky:

"Stop any traffic!" Fortunately, there had been none, except a couple of bicycles, on our trip – but we couldn't risk falling off the bank onto anything, or anyone.

Without a second thought Havana followed me through the knee-high grass, staying close to the fence. He was obviously concentrating on the task in hand and had forgotten about the mares.

What a relief it was to feel the surface of the lane under my feet again.

"Can you give me a leg-up?" I called to Ricky. It wasn't really a request, it was a question. For the first time in his life, Ricky gave me a leg-up onto Havana's back and, for the first time, Havana was the recipient of a 'legged-up' rider. Both passed their test with flying colours.

Just as when we had walked to Gunstone, I had promised Havana a picnic on the enormous grass verge at the bottom of the hill.

To help him to relax after our outward journey, I had put his head collar under his bridle and Ricky carried the twelve-foot rope, so I would be able to take off Havana's bridle and his grazing break would not be hampered by his bit.

Whilst Havana and Corris grazed – as if they had never been fed in their lives – I had an opportunity to reflect on Havana's ludicrously bold athleticism in scaling the bank. It seemed as if, for him, there is no time-lapse between thinking of something and doing it. I cautioned myself that I must be ready for this.

Riding Havana is not like riding his half-brother Cayman. Cayman's ideas became actions in exactly the same time it took me to realise what was happening, so I was rarely caught out. However, this little fellow is an entirely different physical prospect.

If he stays as he is – fearless and frighteningly athletic – he could make a wonderful eventer.

After about twenty minutes' grazing, during which Havana and Corris were admired by several walkers, I put Havana's bridle back on and, receiving an expert leg-up from Ricky, was once again on Havana's back – for the photograph I have waited so long to have taken.

This was the first photograph of Havana and me on a ride 'in the outside world'; the picture I will send to Havana's breeder and to all the other people who have helped us both so much.

As we were almost opposite, we took the opportunity to wander into the stable yard at Gunstone. Apart from a couple of dogs who grudgingly roused from their slumber as we approached, it was unsurprisingly deserted; it was Sunday lunchtime after all.

We stood on the yard for a while.

What was Havana feeling? I don't know … but he was not at all like a horse in unfamiliar surroundings. He was completely peaceful there.

Our homeward journey was tranquil. Havana was so relaxed that he felt safe enough to stand on the roadside motionless, back legs splayed, for a very long 'call of nature' – not something a worried or frightened horse would risk doing. No, Havana was totally at ease.

Back in his stable, even more sliced carrots than usual confirmed to him that he had been very, very good.

This evening, something hit me … I exclaimed to Ricky:

"You know, I've just realised that where you photographed me and Havana today – on the grass verge at the bottom of the hill, behind the stables – is exactly the same place where Cayman and I had our first photograph taken together, when he was three."

I am certain that Havana enjoyed our first ride today and I am full of joy and gratitude to this remarkable horse – to whom I already owe so much – that we have a lifetime of rides together to look forward to.

First ride – Sunday 30 May 2010

POSTSCRIPT

The magic that has always surrounded Havana goes on.

Through numerous dreams and unexplained events, both Cayman and Falconwood continue to let us know they are there.

In the following pages are just a few examples.

UNEXPLAINED EVENTS (1)
Saturday, 5 March 2011

*O*ur longest ride yet! 'Short Hattons', with Corris and Mrs B..

When we rode over the canal bridge for the first time ever, a shiny red barge chugged underneath.

As it approached the bridge I thought I caught sight of its name but … in disbelief … I waited until it emerged from the other side to confirm that it was called 'Falcon'!

UNEXPLAINED EVENTS (2)
Saturday, 12 March 2011

*E*arly this morning Havana achieved another milestone – our first ever unchaperoned ride. No Corris and Mrs B., no Ricky, no support team at all, just Havana and me. He was a complete little star!

For me a dream come true – the achievement, after the five years since Cayman's death in 2006, of my greatest desire – the freedom to tack-up my horse and go for a ride, just the two of us together.

When I got home, there was a package for me – my first from Dubai; it had five identical stamps, each a picture of a falcon.

UNEXPLAINED EVENTS (3)
Easter Sunday, 23 April 2011

*T*oday we were having a lunch for my family and some friends.

My good friend Judy was recounting her 'Cayman Dream' from 2006, about bathing a foal with a sponge, and I reminded her that a few days afterwards, when she had visited us, I had been shocked to find Cayman's sponge in the middle of our garage floor.

When we were tidying-up after everyone had left this afternoon, Ricky went to put the wine bottles in the recycling bin in the garage but came straight out again, exclaiming that I should: "Come and look!"

There, on the garage floor, was Cayman's white numnah – which had been stowed very securely, on a high shelf, for years.

UNEXPLAINED EVENTS (4)
Tuesday, 22 June 2011

*O*n Sunday, for the first time after being ridden, Havana had a girth mark so, as I didn't have a sponge, I had borrowed one of Corris's sponges from Mrs B., to wipe away the sweat from behind Havana's front legs.

Also, on Sunday evening, I'd put Cayman's old saddle soap and a new cloth in the back of my car to take to the stables, so that in future I could clean Havana's tack after our rides.

Yesterday I was annoyed to find a carrier bag, with the handles tied in a knot, dumped by the boot rack in the garage, obstructing my way.

I was annoyed because I assumed the bag contained shredded paper and it had been left there carelessly by Ricky, who had either forgotten its contents should go in the paper recycling sack or, more likely, been distracted en route by the phone.

Determined that if Ricky left the bag in such an inconsiderate place, he should be the one to remove it, I had simply stepped over it.

Today, seeing the bag still sitting there in exactly the same position, and getting more annoyed, I decided to check what was in it.

I was shocked to discover the bag contained one of Cayman's sponges and his old tack cleaning cloths.

For four years, these have been stored on the highest shelf above the boot rack. I had forgotten all about them. As the shelf is way above my head height I had no idea that they were even there.

CAYMAN DREAM

Tuesday, 23 August 2011

I was in a large garden next to a lawn, on my right was more land and a path.

I was told that my first horse, Jah, was in the stables down the path. I walked down the path and looked into a large, high, airy loosebox. It felt as if it was in a row of similar looseboxes, although I didn't see these.

Cayman was sitting, dozing, at the back of the loosebox – in a straw bed, with deep straw banks. He looked just as he did when he was twelve; 17hh, and white.

The expression on his face when he saw me looking at him was elated surprise. I sensed that he could not believe his eyes that I was really there – and that he had thought he would never see me again. He let out an involuntary whinny of pure delight.

Cayman stood up and I hugged him tightly with both arms up around his neck; we stayed like that. I was aware there were damp patches on his neck from the straw, but I didn't mind.

I felt love gushing from Cayman straight into the base of my throat between my collar-bones – it was all-consuming.

I sensed that Cayman felt left out now that I'm riding Havana more and our rides are getting more exciting.

He wanted me to be having fun with him, Cayman, in his 17hh

white, twelve-year-old body, not with him in his 15.2hh, four-and-a-half-year-old Havana body.

I reminded Cayman that he is Havana.

He let me know that I should not forget him as a 17hh twelve-year-old white horse and should not let cheeky young Havana supersede him.

I told him that I would make a greater effort to acknowledge him more equally.

I felt that I was being prompted not to forget the miracle that had happened to us, whereby Cayman continues to be in Havana.

I sensed that my failure to acknowledge this resulted in the two fragmenting – and that Cayman was telling me he felt I was letting go of him and this made him sad.

He was also telling me that he really wants to hold onto me, but can only do so if I acknowledge and hold onto him; the energy has to come from me.

When I woke up I was crying.

I was sad that Cayman felt left out, and overcome by the power of Cayman's vast and endless love which had poured straight into me – as if he was so relieved to be able to give it.

So much emotion had been stirred that its force caused Ricky to wake up too.

HAVANA DREAM
Sunday, 5 August 2012

This was a very faint dream, so faint that whilst I was having it, I was wondering whether I was actually having the dream, or remembering it from the previous night.

In this dream, Havana was practising kissing me. He was juvenile with a tiny little velvety muzzle, as it was when he was about a year old.

He was trying very hard; repeatedly depositing a single kiss squarely in the middle of my lips, conscientiously trying to get the right 'mwah' kissing sound.

With each kiss the sound became louder and more perfect.

Yesterday morning when I was schooling Havana, he had slipped and gone down onto both knees. Shocked, he stayed on his knees for a while – immobile. I sat quietly, still on his back, until he regained sufficient composure to get onto all four feet again.

Once standing, it was clear that the wind had completely been taken out of his sails; he stood – petrified. I stroked and comforted him, but he didn't want to move at all. When I asked him to move forwards, he was adamant that he couldn't; his confidence had dissolved.

When I insisted, in the hope of proving that really, he was perfectly alright, he simply walked backwards – obviously very upset.

I sensed that Havana was embarrassed about slipping over whilst I was on his back and that, in this dream, he was trying to make amends by proving that, even if he is not yet fully competent at being ridden, he is good at kisses!

CAYMAN DREAM
Saturday, 2 November 2013

*I*t had been a long time since I had a Cayman Dream, and this was an 'ordinary strength' dream.

Ricky and I lived in a house in the centre of Brewood village. It had walls and a roof, but no glass in the windows and no doors – just gaps in the walls where doors would usually be. Cayman lived in the house too, so it was easy for him to come and go.

Cayman had got out of the house and I saw him a short distance down the road in front of me, at the 'T' junction which leads onto Bargate Street.

He was standing, alert, at the junction, big and strong, and dapple grey. He was being led in a halter by an experienced horseman who, thinking he had strayed, was going to put him in a safe place.

I tried to call Cayman; it took a great effort to make my voice come out.

Using all of my strength I managed to call out, but only in a very quiet voice, which I thought Cayman might not be able to hear.

I intended to call: "Cayman!" However, what came out was: "Havana!"

Immediately I called out, Cayman raised his head very high – as horses do when there's a noise directly behind them from a source they can't see.

He very obviously recognised his name, and that it was me who was calling him. There was an instant connection between us.

I am aware that, recently, I have been so preoccupied by Havana's enormous character, that I have – consciously and subconsciously – been 'letting go' of Cayman, feeling it was right to allow him to move on.

This dream showed me clearly that they are still one-and-the-same soul and united.

Although at present it's Havana's all-encompassing juvenile energy which is to the fore, they are truly merged.

From Havana's visitors' book:

From a ball of ginger fluff - determined to be noticed ...
to the beautiful little horse you are ...
and the beautiful big horse you will be.

Havana - welcome!

Mr & Mrs B.
12 September 2007

Hi Havana,
I can see you watching with interest as I approach your stable door.
Hello little man, so quickly you let me look in your big brown eyes - and further.
How brave you are, so sure of yourself, for such a little one (your mum's nattering away all excited).
I can hear you say "I'm here."
You certainly are, and will be spoilt rotten!
I feel a bit rude holding two conversations - your mum has to win. We'll speak soon.
Hope you have a lovely time together.

Sarah
(Harrison's person)
13 September 2007

What a wonderful partnership already!
Enjoy your time together.

Sue and Alfie
19 September 2007

What a personality! He's gorgeous!
On one hand, I don't want him to grow up …
but on the other, I'm desperate to ride him.

Have fun together.

Edward
xxx
23 September 2007

A beautiful pink sunset unfolded as I walked across the fields with Liz, to be introduced to you.

I'd seen you tearing about wildly, a few evenings before, and was so nervous about meeting you that I put my foot in a hole, and twisted my ankle.

But you seemed to know that this friend of Liz is useless with horses and grazed calmly, assuringly. How considerate of you to put me at my ease.

I gazed admiringly at your poise and beautiful form.

It was clear to see you and Liz are a match made in Heaven.

Judy
30 September 2007

To Havana,
I didn't really need to see you, as I knew you
already.

After all your mum's proud pictures and tales, I
knew you would be lovely.

Was I the first person to tap your nose when you
tried to eat my hair?

The next few years will be great fun and I will
come to see you again if you are good.

To Liz,
Havana is a joy. But the biggest joy is seeing
your love for him.

Love ('Cayman's Auntie') Alison
16 June 2008

HAVANA'S GROWTH

	Withers	Rump
17 November 2007 (9 months)	13.2hh	13.3hh
19 February 2008 (12 months)	14hh	
25 June 2008	14.1½hh	
23 August 2008	14.2hh	
18 November 2008	14.2hh	
23 March 2009 (2 years)	14.2½hh	
21 April 2009	14.2½hh	15.1hh
11 July 2009	14.3hh	15.1hh
20 September 2009	14.3½hh	15.1hh
11 December 2009	15hh	15.1½hh
17 February 2010 (3 years)	15.1hh	15.1½hh
24 July 2010	15.2hh	15.2hh

In tribute

to

Corris

1982 - 19 March 2017
with
respect and gratitude

An accomplished horse who put duty and service first - and was "very fond" of Mrs B.

"I know more than you'll ever know!"
[Corris to equine shiatsu practitioner Sarah Dakin in 2016]

"An accomplished horse ..."

With love